D0939265

BRARY
5814
10/2021

THE

Magnolia Jungle

THE LIFE,
TIMES AND
EDUCATION OF
A SOUTHERN EDITOR

by P. D. East

Editor, The Petal Paper

SIMON AND SCHUSTER

NEW YORK · 1960

ALL RIGHTS RESERVED
INCLUDING THE RIGHT OF REPRODUCTION
IN WHOLE OR IN PART IN ANY FORM
COPYRIGHT © 1960 BY P. D. EAST
PUBLISHED BY SIMON AND SCHUSTER, INC.
ROCKEFELLER CENTER, 630 FIFTH AVENUE
NEW YORK 20, N.Y.

FIRST PRINTING

LIBRARY OF CONGRESS CATALOG CARD NUMBER: 60–10973
MANUFACTURED IN THE UNITED STATES OF AMERICA
BY GEORGE McKIBBIN & SON, NEW YORK

To My
Dear Friends

EASTON KING and IRVING JAY FAIN

Without whose confidence, encouragement and
help this book would not have been written

and to

DR. W. W. STOUT

By far the best teacher
I've ever known

My way of joking is to tell the truth.
It's the funniest joke in the world.

—BERNARD SHAW
John Bull's Other Island

Foreword

P. D. East is an enigma to everybody who knows him, most of all, I suspect, to himself. I have seen him once for a couple of hours, corresponded with him, and have twice read the galley proofs of his book. And, as a distinguished mayor of Louisville once said in a public statement commenting upon an issue he hadn't resolved in his own mind, "I am confused."

Here is a man who calls himself a coward and refutes it in every action and every word. Here is a man who derides formal religion and yet somewhere along the line was so obviously snake-bitten by a shouting evangelist that he has become one himself. Here is a man who says, "Hell, integration isn't possible here" but who, by his sarcasm and ridicule of those who defy the Supreme Court school decision of 1954, has driven away from his paper all the local subscribers and almost all the advertisers. Here, in short, is a man. And here is the only newspaper editor in the United States who can boast that he doesn't have a paid subscriber in his home town.

How did he do it? Hodding Carter, who wears as a badge of his courage in the same fight a denunciation from the Mississippi legislature, has said, "P. D. East's *Petal Paper* represents the damnedest combination of uninhibited personal journalism, stream-of-consciousness writing and a lemminglike urge to self-destruction I've ever run across, to say nothing of the guy's guts."

East left the financial security of the editorship of two union papers in Hattiesburg and community acceptance as a member of the Kiwanis Club to take over a little weekly in the town of Petal, across the Pearl River from Hattiesburg. That was in

ix

1953. He did well with it, got it up to almost 2,000 circulation. A year later he still felt so good toward the world, and particularly toward his subscribers, that he considered having a Coco-Cola party to celebrate the anniversary. But in that year came the "Warren Court" decision. It made little impact upon East until Mississippi politicians began to rush around frantically to defeat the decision by tightening voting laws and, if necessary, by abolishing the public schools. A great admirer of Tom Paine, East broke with his "respectable" friends, with the chance of security as a country editor, and blasted away in an editorial; "Us—and Them Other Crawfish." When it appeared Hodding Carter wrote him, "I hope you leave a forwarding address."

East says that what brought forth all the anger and indignation of his soul, cloaked as it was in satire, was not segregation or desegregation but the conviction, as he told Albert Vorspan of *The Reporter* magazine three years ago, "that the state has no right to operate by guaranteeing constitutional freedoms on a 'For White Only' basis."

In the state that spawned the White Citizens Councils and supports 300 of those "uptown Ku Klux Klans," he laughed one chapter out of existence in a fake ad—an ad that has been reproduced in 37 states and three foreign countries. Senator james o. eastland (as East refers to him), the great statesman who bottles up in his Senate Judiciary Committee any civil-rights bill that he can, has been a particular target.

The East vs. Eastland battle pits two antagonists who come from different economic poles in Mississippi. The senator has 5,000 acres of good Delta land and East is the product of the raw, brutal life in the turpentine and lumber camps of one of the roughest sections of Mississippi—from a county adjoining one that seceded from the Confederacy rather than fight the fight of the slave-owners from Eastland's domain.

Eastland has become the symbol of his class antagonism, but it goes deeper than that with East. He is a born rebel against authority—a high-tempered, brawling youth always ready with his fists, now matured to the point that he was able to say to a man who recently invited him out of his car "so's I can mop up the street with you": "Sorry, pal, that ain't inducement enough." East remembers all the injustices of the past, all the discrimination against Negroes and whites who were different, all the exploitation by piney woods bosses of their peons, all the bitterness of the condescension of those who knew before he did that he was the son of a mother who gave her child away rather than take it home. And it all pours out, even though he cloaks it with humor.

It takes a long time in this book to get to the story of *The Petal Paper,* but all that goes before is pertinent to what East did with the paper and what has happened to him, which is best summed up by the novelist John H. Griffin: "There [in Mississippi] when men persuade themselves that the most scabrous injustice is both holy and patriotic, the one who speaks for justice invites personal disaster."

Personal disaster as the world measures it has indeed come to P. D. East. His paper is a hobby now rather than a business. How he lives nobody knows except himself and perhaps his wife. The story is, as Mr. Griffin said, "like a novel by Dostoevsky." But it's not a disaster to East. Six Negroes out of 12,000 were eligible to vote in Forrest County, Mississippi, when the hulking lug opened up his editorial guns, but because of him— and others who say with him, "I can't look the other way when the most important issue of my life hits me smack in the face"— we may still achieve justice and constitutional government in this country.

MARK ETHRIDGE

Part One

Chapter 1

New York City, the first week of February 1957, was not only cold, but it was wet. The chill penetrated, and as I returned to my hotel that Thursday, I shivered. Under the door to my room I found a note asking that I call a person at a national weekly news magazine. I called. I was told that the magazine was interested in doing a story on my paper and would like to interview me. It was then that I shuddered.

The better part of the afternoon was devoted to the interview. The researchers probed, backed up, and probed more. I stood still for it, wondering then, as I still wonder, exactly what they were looking for. No one had said, but I suspect they were looking for material that would lend itself to an upbeat profile of a dedicated, liberal Southern editor doing battle against the forces of ignorance and evil, an editor of the Hollywood version, clean-cut, fearless, and an idealist dedicated to his convictions, come hell or high water.

To mislead a research team into thinking that I was what they were looking for was something I had no intention of doing. I had the feeling they left my room that day shaking their heads and wondering if they'd not had a ride to the moon, or some place in outer space.

Whatever their motives, and mine, the story did not see print, but I don't think it was for the want of material. Over a year after the interview, copies of the reporters' and researchers' dispatches fell into my hands; I was interested to see that these men, all of them well trained in the business of reporting, seemed to be as baffled about who and what I really am as I have always been.

Here are edited excerpts from some of the dispatches to their home office. The first of these was from the magazine's stringer in Mississippi.

I FILED WITH YOU A WORD BY WORD DESCRIPTION OF PETAL PAPER EDITOR P. D. EAST'S FULL PAGE AD ON "YES, YOU TOO CAN BE SUPERIOR" IN WHICH EAST PANNED THE CITIZENS COUNCILS AS A SUGGESTION FOR PRESS. ALTHOUGH I GOT NO NOD FROM YOU, OUT OF CURIOSITY I BEGAN RESEARCH ON THE CHARACTER RESPONSIBLE FOR THIS FUNNY IF HIGHLY FOOLHARDY (BUSINESS-WISE) BUFFOONERY.

HERE IS WHAT I COULD DIG UP FROM THE MORE REPUTABLE AND LESS RABID NEWSMEN WHO KNOW OR KNOW OF EAST:

HE BEGAN AS A RAILROAD CLERK IN HATTIESBURG, WHERE HE GOT THE WRITING BUG AND STARTED MAILING OUT FICTION AND ARTICLES TO VARIOUS PUBLICATIONS. HE FINALLY GOT ONE PUBLISHED IN THE NEW ORLEANS "DIXIE ROTO" MAGAZINE AND CARRIES A COPY OF IT AROUND WITH HIM STILL TO SHOW ACQUAINTANCES WHO SEEM TO DOUBT HE IS A WRITER. HE GOT HIS FIRST CHANCE IN JOURNALISM WHEN HE QUIT HIS RAILROAD JOB TO ASSIST IN THE PUBLICATION OF THE "HERCULES POWDER PLANT," A UNION HOUSE ORGAN. HE TRIED TO GET JOBS ON SEVERAL PAPERS OF GENERAL CIRCULATION BUT MET WITH FAILURE. THEN HE TOOK OVER "THE PETAL PAPER," WHICH IS PUBLISHED IN A SMALL TOWN SEPARATED FROM LARGER HATTIESBURG BY ONLY THE RIVER. THE PEOPLE OF PETAL READ THE HATTIESBURG PAPER EXCEPT FOR THOSE CURIOUS ABOUT WHAT UNEXPECTED THING P.D. WILL SAY NEXT. PETAL MERCHANTS HAVE ALWAYS ADVERTISED IN THE HATTIESBURG "AMERICAN" AND "THE PETAL PAPER" WAS NEVER ANY ROARING FINANCIAL SUCCESS EVEN BEFORE EAST TOOK OVER.

PEOPLE IN HATTIESBURG HAVE ALWAYS CONSIDERED HIM SOMETHING OF A SCREWBALL AND AT BEST HE HAS BEEN A PROFESSIONAL NONCONFORMIST.

LITTLE OVER A YEAR AGO, WHEN THE "STATE TIMES" WAS FIRST EDGING INTO THE JACKSON SCENE, EAST WAS FREQUENTLY QUOTED IN THE JACKSON "CLARION LEDGER" AND THE JACKSON "DAILY NEWS" BECAUSE HE HEAPED PRAISE ON FRED SULLENS AND ON THE HEDERMANS (WHO OWN THE JACKSON PUBLISHING

4

COMPANY WHICH PUBLISHES THE AFORESAID NEWSPAPERS) AND
BECAUSE HE RIDICULED EFFORTS OF THE "STATE TIMES" AND
HAD ALMOST AS MUCH EDITORIAL FUN WITH CALLING ITS EDI-
TOR NORMAN BRADLEY A "LIBRUL" AS HE IS NOW HAVING CALLING
THE CITIZENS COUNCILS "SUPER SUPERIOR." JUST WHEN FOLKS
WERE BEGINNING TO WONDER WHY HE TOOK SO MUCH INTEREST
IN THE JACKSON NEWSPAPER SQUABBLE, HE SHOWED UP AT THE
HEDERMANS' OFFICES ON A JOB HUNTING VISIT, IT BEING RU-
MORED THAT SULLENS WAS NOT LONG FOR THIS WORLD AND
NEEDED AN "ASSISTANT EDITOR." THEY SAID NO.

NO ONE KNOWS HOW EAST KEEPS GOING FINANCIALLY, BUT NO
ONE CAN ESCAPE KNOWING WHERE HE WANTS TO GO, AT ANY
GIVEN TIME, THAT IS.

HE HOPPED ON THE ANTI-CITIZENS COUNCILS BANDWAGON
AFTER MY EDITOR HAD STUCK OUT HIS NECK ON SEVERAL OC-
CASIONS AND AFTER OTHER EDITORS AND REPORTERS WITH A
GREAT DEAL MORE TO LOSE THAN HAS EAST MADE BRAVE IF
COMPARATIVELY QUIET STANDS IN MISSISSIPPI ON THE SIDE OF
JUSTICE. THE COUNCILS HAD BEEN NO GREAT ISSUE IN FORREST
COUNTY BECAUSE OF A LIGHT NEGRO POPULATION AND LACK OF
RESPONSIBLE COUNCIL-MINDED LEADERSHIP BUT WHEN EAST
BEGAN TILTING THE WINDMILL IT WAS TRANSPOSED. WITH HIS
MEAT CLEAVER TACTICS OF SEPARATING THE FAT FROM THE
LEAN, TO SHIFT A METAPHOR, PEOPLE BEGAN JOINING RATHER
THAN STAY ON HIS SIDE OF THE BLOCK. ONE FORMER STATE REP-
RESENTATIVE SAYS, "IF P.D. KEEPS ON, HE'S GOING TO DRIVE US
ALL INTO THE COUNCIL TO KEEP FROM BEING ASSOCIATED WITH
HIM."

THAT'S A DEFENSE AGAINST HIS KISS OF DEATH THAT MY EDI-
TOR UNFORTUNATELY CAN'T USE, HAVING BURNED HIS BRIDGES
IN THAT DIRECTION. (INCIDENTALLY HE BADE ME BE "AS KIND
AS POSSIBLE" TO EAST IN MY REPORT, BUT NOT TO LEAVE THE IM-
PRESSION THAT HE IS IN ANY WAY A PROTEGE OF HIS NOR, AS I
SEE IT, ANY MORE OF A MARTYR THAN ONE WHO SLASHES HIS
WRISTS AND BLEEDS IN THE PUBLIC STREETS.)

IT MIGHT BE PREDICTED THAT IN FAILING TO GET EITHER A
PULITZER OR A NIEMAN, EAST WILL TURN UP WITH SOME NEW
CAMPAIGN, MAYBE ANTI-VIVISECTIONISM, WHICH HE WILL WAGE
AS FURIOUSLY AS THIS. HE SEEMS DESPERATELY TRYING TO DE-
STROY WHAT LITTLE IS LEFT OF THE PETAL PAPER SO HE CAN

5

STEP ON ITS CARCASS TOWARD A BETTER JOB. SO FAR HE HAS NO TAKERS.

I HAVE NEVER MET NOR TALKED TO EAST, AND PERHAPS WE ALL MISJUDGE HIM. IF YOU STILL CARE TO DO SOMETHING ON HIM I WILL BE GLAD TO INTERVIEW HIM.

BEFORE YOUR SECOND WIRE ON EDITOR P. D. EAST ARRIVED HAD TALKED WITH HIS WIFE, BILLIE, 32, WHO SAID HE HAD RUSHED OFF TO NEW YORK AFTER ASKING HER TO BLEACH OUT HIS UNDERWEAR BECAUSE IT LOOKED KIND OF GRAY (BUT DIDN'T SAY WHY HE WAS GOING TO NEW YORK—APPARENTLY SHE'S USED TO NOT ASKING QUESTIONS ABOUT THE STRANGE AND ERRATIC COMINGS AND GOINGS OF EAST). SHE SAID HE ESTABLISHED "THE PETAL PAPER" AFTER THE "FORREST COUNTY NEWS" FOLDED. THE PAPER IS EDITED AT EAST'S HOME IN HATTIESBURG, A MODEST LITTLE THREE BEDROOM HOUSE WITH ASBESTOS SIDING AND A SCREENED PORCH, WORLD WAR TWO VINTAGE, AND IS PRINTED ON CONTRACT IN PASCAGOULA. ITS CIRCULATION SHE THOUGHT WAS BETWEEN FIFTEEN AND TWENTY THOUSAND OR WAS ABOUT SIX MONTHS AGO. NOW IT IS MORE THAN THAT WITH BOTH DELIVERY AND MAIL OUT SUBSCRIPTIONS, INCLUDING OUT OF STATE. THEY DON'T LIVE IN PETAL . . . AND DON'T HAVE MANY SUBSCRIPTIONS THERE NOR MANY ADS FROM THERE. THEY OPERATE MOSTLY ON NATIONAL ADS, SOME LEGALS AND SHE SAYS A SURPRISING NUMBER OF LOCAL ADS THOUGH THE LATTER HAVE FALLEN OFF.

REACTION TO EAST'S LIBERAL EDITORIAL VIEWS ON RACE, WHILE THEY HAVE OUTRAGED A NUMBER OF HUMORLESS PEOPLE, HAS NOT BEEN AS BAD AS THEY EXPECTED. "WE HAVEN'T HAD ANY CROSSES BURNED ON OUR LAWN YET," SHE SAYS, "THOUGH THERE HAVE BEEN THREATS, ANONYMOUS AND OVER THE TELEPHONE."

THEY DON'T BOTHER WITH NEWS, SOCIETY OR SPORTS IN THEIR PAPER, WHICH IS MORE A VEHICLE FOR EAST'S EDITORIAL VIEWS THAN ANYTHING ELSE. "WHY PRINT NEWS? THE HATTIESBURG 'AMERICAN' HAS NEWS EVERY DAY," SAYS MRS. EAST. SHE HELPS TO SELL ADS AND COLLECTS, "GENERAL FLUNKEY" SHE SAYS. BESIDES THE RACE ISSUE, WHICH IS CONSTANTLY ON THE PAGES, EAST DISCUSSES LOCAL ISSUES, CITY GOVERNMENT, THEY TOOK UP FOR A LOCAL PROMINENT FAMILY WHOSE LAND WAS SOUGHT BY THE GULF REFINING COMPANY AND MADE IT SO HOT FOR GULF

6

THAT GULF CANCELLED ALL THEIR ADS, THEY PUT OUT SIX PAGES USUALLY WITH ABOUT TWO PAGES DEVOTED TO TELEVISION SCHEDULES. THIS HELPS TO SELL THE PAPER BECAUSE IT IS CONVENIENT FOR VIEWERS AND MRS. EAST SAYS THEY HAVE PROBABLY SOLD MOST OF THEIR LOCAL SUBSCRIPTIONS ON THE STRENGTH OF THE SCHEDULES.

EAST IS ONLY 35 BUT LOOKS OLDER, SHE SAYS, SORT OF LIKE RAYMOND MASSEY. HE'S SIX FEET THREE AND WEIGHS BETWEEN 230 AND 245 POUNDS. DID HE EVER PLAY FOOTBALL? "HEAVENS NO, HE CAN'T EVEN PLAY PING PONG," SHE SAYS.

HE WENT TO SCHOOL AT MISSISSIPPI SOUTHERN AFTER GETTING OUT OF THE ARMY AFTER WORLD WAR TWO. (HE WAS STATIONED IN WASHINGTON) HE STUDIED JOURNALISM COURSES AS A PASSING FANCY AND PUT OUT THREE ISSUES OF A COLLEGE HUMOR MAGAZINE (WHICH SOME OF "THE PETAL PAPERS" STRONGLY REMIND ME OF—ON THE ORDER OF HARVARD'S "LAMPOON" MAYBE). MRS. EAST SAYS SHE DOUBTS HE FINISHED ANY OF HIS COURSES, HE JUST TOOK WHAT HE LIKED AND THEN LEFT SCHOOL.

A PAMPHLETEER MAYBE? "YES," SHE SAID, "HE IS A GREAT ADMIRER OF TOM PAINE." SHE ATTENDED MISSISSIPPI SOUTHERN TOO. BOTH ARE NATIVE MISSISSIPPIANS.

SHE SAID SHE'D HAVE HIM CALL ME. "I'LL MAKE A NOTE OF IT. I HAVE ONE NOTE ALREADY. THE BANK CALLED. THEY WANT THEIR MONEY."

HOW DOES HE TALK? DOES HE DRAWL? "WELL," SHE SAID, "HE TALKS DIFFERENTLY WITH DIFFERENT PEOPLE. HE SORT OF ADAPTS HIS ACCENT TO THEIRS. I SAID THAT MAY BE A QUICK WAY TO GET SOMEONE'S CONFIDENCE: SHE SAID SHE DIDN'T KNOW. YOU MIGHT LOSE YOUR INDIVIDUALITY THAT WAY.

SHE DOESN'T KNOW MUCH HOW RACIAL TENSIONS ARE THERE. PEOPLE DON'T TALK TO HER ABOUT THAT IF THEY TALK TO HER AT ALL. THEY HAVE A NUMBER OF CLOSE FRIENDS BUT THEY RARELY DISCUSS SUCH THINGS.

DO THEY HAVE ANY CHILDREN? "I HAVE TWO CHILDREN, ONE IS FOUR AND THE OTHER IS THIRTY-FIVE." THEY HAVE A DAUGHTER, KAREN, WHO IS FOUR. . . .

A BIT OF NEEDLING HERE AND THERE THAT INFURIATES THE MOST ARDENT [CITIZENS] COUNCILERS. ONE STOOD UP AT THE FIRST ORGANIZATION MEETING OF THE COUNCIL IN HATTIESBURG AFTER THE JACKASS AD APPEARED AND WAVED IT IN THE AIR BEFORE THE ASSEMBLY, SHOUTING, "I CANCELED MY SUB-

SCRIPTION AS OF TODAY." IT TURNED OUT THAT HE HAD NOT PAID HIS SUBSCRIPTION FOR A MONTH OR SO AND WASN'T EVEN TAKING THE PAPER ANY MORE.

TO QUOTE SEVERAL PEOPLE: [HODDING CARTER] THE EDITOR OF THE DELTA "DEMOCRAT TIMES": "P. D. EAST'S 'PETAL PAPER' REPRESENTS THE DAMNEDEST COMBINATION OF UNINHIBITED PERSONAL JOURNALISM, STREAM OF CONSCIOUSNESS WRITING AND A LEMMINGLIKE URGE TO SELF DESTRUCTION I'VE EVER RUN ACROSS TO SAY NOTHING OF THE GUY'S GUTS."

INTERESTING NOTE: SHORTLY AFTER HE STARTED THE "PETAL PAPER," EAST REPRINTED AN EDITORIAL FROM THE JACKSON "DAILY NEWS," HEAVILY PANNED THE NEWLY ORGANIZED "STATE TIMES" AND DUMAS MILNER, ONE OF THE BIGGEST STOCKHOLD-ERS IN THAT NEW JACKSON PAPER AND SENT A HUNDRED COPIES TO THE "NEWS" AT THEIR REQUEST. HE WAS INVITED TO A TESTIMONIAL DINNER FOR JACKSON "NEWS" EDITOR IRASCIBLE MAJOR FREDERICK SULLENS AND APPROACHED THE ASSISTANT TO THE PUBLISHER FOR A JOB. HE WAS ABOUT LINED UP FOR "ASSISTANT TO THE EDITOR" WHEN THE PAPER'S TOP BRASS DID SOME INVESTIGATION, SO THE FORMER ASSISTANT TO THE EDITOR TELLS ME. HE DID NOT SAY WHAT DECIDED THEM BUT THEY DID NOT HIRE HIM. HE HAS SINCE ATTACKED SULLENS TIME AND AGAIN. I DON'T KNOW WHAT HE WANTS BUT IT APPARENTLY IS NOT TO STAY WITH "THE PETAL PAPER."

ROBERT "TUT" PATERSON, EXECUTIVE SECRETARY OF THE MISSISSIPPI CITIZENS COUNCILS OF GREENWOOD, SAID "I DON'T KNOW EAST. I HAVE NO OPINION. I'VE SEEN HIM QUOTED IN THE 'DAILY WORKER' AND THE 'PEOPLE'S WORLD.' THEY PRAISED HIM HIGHLY. HE GETS A LOT MORE NOTICE OUTSIDE MISSISSIPPI THAN HE DOES HERE IN THE STATE."

MAYOR D. GARY SUTHERLAND, WHO IS A YOUNG (ABOUT 30) LAW-YER AT HATTIESBURG, SAYS THAT HE DOES "NOT KNOW EAST PERSONALLY BUT HE LIVES IN A NICE NEIGHBORHOOD AND HAS A NUMBER OF FRIENDS. MOST PEOPLE THERE TOLERATE HIM THOUGH THERE ARE SOME WHO TAKE A STRONGER VIEW. BUT I'VE NEVER HEARD OF ANY REPRISALS OR ANYTHING OF THAT SORT. HE HAS A GOOD LITTLE BIT OF BUSINESS FOR A PAPER HIS SIZE. HE GETS LEGAL WORK AND LOCAL ADS. THE FIRST NATIONAL BANK HAD AN AD IN THE LAST PAPER. WE THINK HE IS ENTITLED TO SAY WHAT HE WANTS TO. IT'S HIS NEWSPAPER. HE'S A LONG WAY FROM STARVING. I'D SAY HE'S COMFORTABLY FIXED. HE'D

PROBABLY LIKE TO LET YOU BELIEVE HE'S GOT A CROSS TO
BEAR BUT WE'RE NOT GIVING HIM TOO MUCH OPPORTUNITY FOR
THAT. HE TAKES AN INTEREST IN POLITICS. HE GIVES HIS VIEWS
ON CANDIDATES. THAT'S A GOOD THING." ASKED ABOUT THE JACK-
ASS AD, HE SAID "OH THAT! HE REPRINTS THAT ABOUT EVERY
OTHER ISSUE, I THINK."

THE MAYOR SAYS THE TOWN IS ONLY ABOUT 30 PER CENT
NEGRO, WHICH IS MUCH LESS THAN IN OTHER PARTS OF THE
STATE. THE AREA IS GROWING AND PROSPERING. . . .

WHAT MAKES P. D. EAST TICK AND HOW DOES HE SURVIVE WITH
HIS HUMOROUS LAMPOONING OF RACIAL BIGOTRY? THE BEST AN-
SWERS SO FAR COME FROM EASTON KING, EDITOR AND PUB-
LISHER OF ONE OF THE BEST (AND BIGGEST) WEEKLIES IN
MISSISSIPPI, THE "CHRONICLE-STAR AND ADVERTISER" OF PAS-
CAGOULA, MISS.

KING, WHO IS VERY WELL TOLERATED IN HIS AREA WHERE
ONLY FIFTEEN PER CENT OF THE POPULATION IS NEGRO, IS NOTED
FOR HIS OWN LIBERAL VIEWPOINTS AND HAS BEEN A FRIEND OF
EAST FOR A NUMBER OF YEARS. HIS OWN "ADVERTISER" PUBLISH-
ING COMPANY IS CONTRACTED TO PRINT "THE PETAL PAPER"
EACH WEEK.

"P.D. IS AN AMAZING GUY," SAYS KING. "HE'S HAD A PRETTY
HARD TIME OF IT AND I DON'T SEE HOW HE'S SURVIVED MYSELF.
HE LIVES A HAND TO MOUTH EXISTENCE AND BARELY MAKES A
LIVING. HE'S REALLY A CONSERVATIVE TAFT REPUBLICAN ON
FISCAL VIEWS (AND ON THAT WE DISAGREE VIGOROUSLY) BUT
HE HAS FIRM AND DEEP CONVICTIONS ON THE RELATION OF MAN
TO MAN. HE FEELS INTOLERANCE AND BIGOTRY IN RELATION TO
THE NEGRO IS INTOLERANCE AND BIGOTRY THAT COULD BE AP-
PLIED TO ANY MAN, THAT COULD BE APPLIED TO HIM (EAST).
THOUGH HE DENIES ANY CHURCH RELATIONSHIP I BELIEVE THAT
HE IS A REAL CHRISTIAN. HE RECOGNIZES THAT RIDICULE IS THE
MOST EFFECTIVE WEAPON AND SO HE USES IT. HIS COUNTY IS
RATHER TYPICAL OF MISSISSIPPI, AN AGRARIAN ECONOMY, WITH
ITS COUNTY SEAT OF HATTIESBURG COMING OUT OF THE GLOOM
(THAT HIT WHEN CAMP SHELBY CLOSED) WITH NEW INDUSTRIES.
IT'S GROWING. THE NEGRO POPULATION OF HATTIESBURG IS NOT
AS HIGH A PERCENTAGE AS UP IN THE DELTA BUT OUT IN THE
COUNTY PROPER IT IS ABOUT FIFTY FIFTY I THINK.

9

"P.D. IS IN AN INTOLERABLE COMPETITIVE SITUATION WITH THE HATTIESBURG 'AMERICAN' JUST ACROSS THE RIVER. HE HAS A SMALL WEEKLY WITH A SMALL CIRCULATION AND COMPETES WITH A LARGE DAILY WITH A LARGE CIRCULATION. HE HAD AN OFFICE IN PETAL BUT CLOSED IT RECENTLY FOR ECONOMIC REASONS I UNDERSTAND. THE ONLY PHONE LISTED NOW IS AT HIS HOME IN HATTIESBURG.

"BUT HERE IS A MAN IN PETAL MISSISSIPPI WHO SPEAKS HIS MIND WHETHER PEOPLE AGREE OR DISAGREE AND HE SURVIVES. THAT HEARTENS PEOPLE IN THIS STATE WHO WANT TO COMBAT THE HYSTERIA, THE PUNITIVE MEASURES AND THE ECONOMIC PRESSURES ENGENDERED BY THE RACE SITUATION. (WITH HUMOR HE HELPS CLEAR THE AIR OF ANGRY NONSENSE BY MAKING IT MORE NONSENSICAL, I SUGGESTED. HE AGREED.) WHAT WE NEED IS TO SIT AROUND A CONFERENCE TABLE WITH THE NEGROES— AND THERE ARE PLENTY OF GOOD LEADERS AMONG THEM—AND WORK OUT OUR PROBLEMS OVER A PERIOD OF YEARS (AND NOT PUT A WALL BETWEEN THE TWO RACES AS THE CITIZENS COUNCILS HAVE DONE, I ADDED).

"HOW DOES P.D. LIVE? WELL, HE IS A FRUGAL MAN. HE DOESN'T DRINK. HE LIVES SIMPLY. HE HAS MODERATE HABITS. HE IS DEEPLY SINCERE, WITH A MARVELOUS SENSE OF HUMOR. . . .

WHAT KIND OF DENT IS EAST MAKING ON THE ENEMIES HE TRIES TO "LAUGH TO DEATH"? WELL, DUDLEY CONNER, ATTORNEY AND HEAD OF THE HATTIESBURG CITIZENS COUNCIL, SAYS: "WHEN WE FIRST ORGANIZED THE CITIZENS COUNCIL, EAST PUBLISHED SOME RATHER AWKWARD STATEMENTS ABOUT THEM. IT WAS MY ADVICE TO THE COUNCIL, AND IT STILL IS, TO IGNORE IT. WE REFUSED TO REPLY AND WE STILL DO NOT. WE NEVER REFER TO THE MAN. WE JUST IGNORE HIM, AND GRADUALLY THE PEOPLE HAVE DROPPED SUBSCRIPTIONS TO THE PAPER IN THE AREA—NOT DUE TO ANY CITIZENS COUNCIL ACTION, BUT THAT THE GENERAL PUBLIC JUST IGNORES HIM." WHAT ABOUT HIS ADVERTISERS? WELL, ONE OF THEM IS THE FIRST NATIONAL BANK OF HATTIESBURG. ITS PRESIDENT, LAWRENCE FOOTE, SAYS THAT FINANCIALLY "EAST IS DOING OK SO FAR AS I KNOW. HE HAS HIS OWN VIEWS AND HE HAS A RIGHT TO EXPRESS THEM. I RARELY READ THE PAPER. I RARELY HEAR ANYONE DISCUSS IT. HE SEEMS A GOOD FELLOW PERSONALLY, THOUGH I DON'T SUBSCRIBE TO HIS IDEAS. THIS COUNTRY'S NOT READY TO ACCEPT SOME OF HIS VIEWS. BUT NO ONE HAS DONE HIM ANY VIOLENCE. HE HAS

10

PRINTED SOME PRETTY GOOD STUFF IN 'THE PETAL PAPER' BUT
HE GOES OFF ON A TANGENT ONCE IN A WHILE. . . ."

ONLY OTHER COMMENT I GOT WAS FROM A JACKSON NEWSMAN
WHO WOULD NOT BE QUOTED BY NAME BUT WHO SAID "HE SEEMS
TO HAVE THE IDEA HE IS GOD OR SOMETHING." EAST MAY BE
CAUSING MORE COMMENT OUT OF MISSISSIPPI THAN INSIDE BUT
HIS "PETAL PAPERS" ARE PASSED AROUND QUITE A BIT AND SOME
OF THEM ARE RARE COLLECTORS ITEMS WHICH CAUSE QUIET
TITTERS IN MANY MISSISSIPPI HOMES AMONG THOSE RESIDENTS
WHO DO NOT BOW IN EITHER REVERENCE OR FEAR TO THE CITI-
ZENS COUNCILS.

ONE CORRECTION PLEASE, MRS. EAST SAID THE CIRCULATION
WAS BETWEEN FIFTEEN HUNDRED AND TWO THOUSAND SIX
MONTHS AGO (NOT FIFTEEN THOUSAND AS SENT IN PREVIOUS
WIRE).

FAULKNER STILL UNREACHABLE FOR *COMMENT ON EDITOR P. D.
EAST* BUT HERE ARE COMMENTS FROM HIS GOOD FRIEND AND
SOMETIME ADVISOR-CRITIC RABBI CHARLES MANTINBAND OF THE
B'NAI ISRAEL CONGREGATION:

"HE'S A GOOD FRIEND OF MINE, I ADMIRE HIM. HE HAS A SMALL
PAPER AND I DON'T KNOW HOW MUCH INFLUENCE IT HAS BUT IT'S
CLEVER AND COURAGEOUS. I READ IT WITH RELISH, BUT FEAR
IN LARGE IT DOES NOT REPRESENT THE SENTIMENT HERE. HE
USES THE WONDERFUL WEAPONS OF SATIRE AND RIDICULE. IN
THE CLIMATE OF OPINION HERE ON THE RACE ISSUE ONE CAN'T
ARGUE THE QUESTION LOGICALLY SO THOSE ARE THE MOST EF-
FECTIVE WEAPONS. HE IS REGARDED HERE IN DIFFERENT WAYS.
THOSE OF LIBERAL THOUGHT THINK HE'S A GOOD MAN. WE DON'T
KNOW HOW LONG HE'LL LAST. HE'S NOT SUBSIDIZED IN ANY WAY.
HE STRUGGLES HARD. OTHERS THINK HE'S A CRANK, A PINK AND
SO FORTH AND DON'T HAVE MUCH CONFIDENCE IN HIM. HE IS
PROBABLY LIKE THE PROPHET WHO IS NOT WITHOUT HONOR SAVE
IN HIS OWN COUNTRY."

CONCERNING P. D. EAST. . . .

HIS HEIGHT IS SIX FOOT TWO AND HIS WEIGHT TWO TWENTY
FIVE.

I ASKED IF HE HAD EVER WORKED FOR ANY OTHER PAPERS. HE
HADN'T. HAD HE EVER SOUGHT A JOB WITH ANY, LIKE THE JACK-
SON "DAILY NEWS" FOR EXAMPLE? "I DON'T THINK SO," HE SAID.

11

THIS DIRECTLY CONTRADICTS WHAT TWO JACKSON PEOPLE TOLD ME ABOUT HIS ASKING FOR A JOB ON THE "DAILY NEWS." ONE WAS WARREN DENNISTON . . . WHO WAS THEN ASSISTANT TO THE PUBLISHER OF THE JACKSON "DAILY NEWS." HE SAID EAST APPLIED FOR AND WAS SLATED TO GET A JOB AS "ASSISTANT TO THE EDITOR," A POSITION LATER ACCEPTED BY TOM KARSELL. DENNISTON SAYS THAT EAST "PROMOTED" THE JOB FOR SEVERAL WEEKS INCLUDING REPRINTING "DAILY NEWS" EDITORIALS AND POKING FUN AT NORMAN BRADLEY, THE EDITOR OF THE NEWCOMER "STATE TIMES" AS A "LIBRUL." HE SAID THAT EAST WAS REFUSED THE POSITION AFTER SOME CHECKING AT HATTIESBURG INDICATED HE WAS NOT SUITABLE FOR THE JOB.

HOW DOES HE MAKE ENOUGH TO LIVE ON? HE SAID THAT THINGS HAD NOT BEEN "ALL THAT TOUGH" BECAUSE HE HAD A "LITTLE SAVINGS" BUT THAT STARTING IN THE FALL HIS FINANCES BEGAN TO "TIGHTEN UP" BUT THAT NOW THINGS WERE GETTING "PRETTY TOUGH." HE DOESN'T DO ANY FREE-LANCE WORK BECAUSE HE HAS NO TIME THOUGH HE HAS HAD "OFFERS." HE HAS NO SOURCE OF INCOME BESIDES "THE PETAL PAPER." HIS FRIENDS, THOSE WHO KNOW HIM BEST AND ARE IN THE BEST POSITION TO KNOW, AGREE THAT HE IS "HAVING IT TOUGH FINANCIALLY." ALL WEEKLY PAPERS IN FORREST COUNTY HAVE EVENTUALLY FOLDED BECAUSE OF FINANCIAL DIFFICULTIES. ONE NEWSMAN SAID THAT EVEN HAD EAST NOT GONE OFF ON HIS LAMPOONING TANGENT AGAINST THE CITIZENS COUNCILS HE WOULD BE IN BAD SHAPE FINANCIALLY, AND THAT HIS EDITORIAL STAND, OFFENDING THE SENSIBILITIES OF THE MAJORITY OF PEOPLE IN THE AREA, HAS ONLY MADE MATTERS WORSE. . . .

EAST HAS BEEN A CURIOSITY TO A NUMBER OF MISSISSIPPI NEWSMEN, ALL OF WHOM HAVE IDEAS OF THEIR OWN ABOUT HIM. EXCEPTING EASTON KING, MOST OF THEM SEEM TO AGREE HE MUST BE USING "THE PETAL PAPER" AS A STEPPING STONE. WHETHER HE IS OR NOT I AM IN NO POSITION TO JUDGE. IF DEPRIVING HIMSELF AND HIS FAMILY IN ORDER TO CONTINUE MAKING FUN OF RACE PREJUDICE IS HIS PRIME GOAL IN LIFE HE MUST BE A LITTLE CRAZY. IF IT IS A MEANS TO A MORE PROFITABLE END HE IS MORE SLY THAN HE PRESENTS HIMSELF BUT AT LEAST MORE UNDERSTANDABLE. I DONT KNOW WHAT DENT IF ANY HE IS MAKING IN THE ARMOR OF THE TRADITIONAL SOUTH, BUT HE IS PROVIDING SOME WONDERMENT AND OCCASIONAL CHUCKLES AMONG A SELECT FEW.

12

FOR PRESS STORY P. D. EAST, FORREST COUNTY IN 1950 HAD A POPULATION OF 45,055, OF WHICH 32,090 WERE WHITE AND 12,965 WERE NEGRO, OR LITTLE OVER 28 PER CENT NEGRO, WHICH COMPARES TO NEARLY 50 PER CENT NEGRO POPULATION IN THE STATE AT LARGE AND 70 AND 80 PER CENT IN SOME COUNTIES. THE NEGRO POPULATION THERE NOW WOULD BE, IF ANYTHING, EVEN LESS NOW BECAUSE OF THE AGRICULTURAL MIGRATIONS SINCE 1950. THE MAJORITY OF THESE NEGROES LIVE OUT IN THE RURAL AREAS, SO THE POPULATIONS OF HATTIESBURG AND PETAL WOULD PROBABLY BE NEARER 20 PER CENT NEGRO, THOUGH I HAVE NO FIGURES ON THAT.

FORREST COUNTY'S AVERAGE INCOME IS HIGHER THAN THE REST OF THE STATE ACCORDING TO 1954 FIGURES, WHEN THE PER CAPITA BUYING INCOME IN FORREST COUNTY WAS $1,087 AND THE PER CAPITA BUYING INCOME IN THE STATE AT LARGE WAS ONLY $817. THIS COMPARES FURTHER WITH WASHINGTON COUNTY IN THE "RICH MISSISSIPPI DELTA" WHICH HAD AN AVERAGE PER CAPITA BUYING INCOME THAT YEAR OF $881 AND METROPOLITAN (JACKSON) HINDS COUNTY WHICH HAD A PER CAPITA INCOME OF $1,396. THE SOUTH WIDE PER CAPITA BUYING INCOME THAT YEAR WAS $1,220 AND FOR THE NATION, $1,545.

IT MIGHT ALSO BE MENTIONED THAT HATTIESBURG IS A "COL-LEGE TOWN" (MISSISSIPPI SOUTHERN) WHICH USUALLY LENDS SOMETHING TO A MORE LIBERAL ATMOSPHERE. A NUMBER OF LIBERAL EDUCATORS AND RELIGIOUS LEADERS HAVE SPOKEN THERE WITHOUT INCIDENT. . . .

OF MISSISSIPPI EDITOR P. D. EAST, NOVELIST WILLIAM FAULK-NER SAYS: "I KNOW MR. EAST. HE HAS CALLED TO SEE ME. IN MY OPINION, BASED ON THESE MEETINGS, HE IS SINCERE IN WHAT HE IS DOING. WE ARE INTERESTED IN THE SAME CONDITIONS IN OUR STATE."

AS TO BEING A FORCE FOR HELPING THE NEGRO, FAULKNER SAID IT WAS "DIFFICULT TO SAY. HE WANTS TO HELP. WHETHER WHAT WE'RE DOING CAN HELP, I DON'T KNOW. IF WHAT WE DO DOESN'T HELP, THEN NOT MANY PEOPLE IN MISSISSIPPI ARE MAKING AN EFFORT."

FAULKNER'S COMMENT ON OUR QUESTIONS TO HIM ON EAST: "THESE QUESTIONS ARE SLANTED." FAULKNER IS AT UNIVERSITY OF VIRGINIA AS FIRST "WRITER-IN-RESIDENCE" UNDER A NEW PROGRAM. . . .

13

A CORRESPONDENT FROM THE ATLANTA STAFF SALLIED INTO MISSISSIPPI AND ALABAMA THIS WEEK, PICKING THE BRAINS OF A COUPLE OF UNUSUAL SOUTHERN EDITORS, AND THIS IS HIS REPORT:

P. D. EAST IS A STRAPPING (6-2, 220), GREYING, HAM-HANDED MISSISSIPPIAN WHO LIVES IN HATTIESBURG AND MAKES A "DAMNED POOR LIVING" AS A COUNTRY EDITOR. EAST'S WEEKLY PRODUCT, "THE PETAL PAPER," IS NOT BIG (CIRC. 1,800). IT IS NOT PARTICULARLY WELL-WRITTEN. BUT IT IS NONETHELESS AN IMPORTANT FACTOR IN MISSISSIPPI, IF FOR NO OTHER REASON THAT IT IS THE ONLY PAPER TO SPEAK UP WITH PLEAS FOR A FAIR SHAKE FOR MISSISSIPPI'S BIG NEGRO POPULATION.

"THE PETAL PAPER" CARRIES THE HOME-TOWN SLUG OF THE HATTIESBURG SUBURB OF PETAL, MISS., WHOSE POPULATION RANGES FROM 2,100 (RAND-McNALLY VERSION) TO 5,000 OR MORE (ESTIMATE OF PROUD PETALIANS). YET IT IS NOT REALLY PETAL'S PAPER . . . IT IS WRITTEN SOLELY BY EAST IN HIS MODEST ONE-STORY WHITE FRAME HOUSE IN HATTIESBURG, AND IS PRINTED IN PASCAGOULA, MISS. . . .

IN A STATE WHERE THE PATTERN OF SEGREGATION REMAINS FIRMEST OF ANYWHERE IN DIXIE, EAST HAS DEVISED A NEW APPROACH. NO RANTER OR RAVER, HE LAUGHS AT THE STATE'S RACISTS, POKING A HUMOROUS NEEDLE AT SUCH INSTITUTIONS AS SEN. JAMES OLIVER EASTLAND AND THE WHITE CITIZENS COUNCILS AND KU KLUX KLAN. EAST, BY HIS OWN ADMISSION, IS NOT AN INTEGRATIONIST.

"HELL," HE BOOMS IN HIS DEEP BASS VOICE, "INTEGRATION ISN'T POSSIBLE HERE. I SIMPLY TRY TO BE MISSISSIPPI'S CONSCIENCE, AND I LIKE TO THINK I'M GETTING THE IDEA ACROSS THAT THE STATE HAS NO RIGHT TO OPERATE BY GUARANTEEING CONSTITUTIONAL FREEDOM ON A 'FOR WHITES' ONLY BASIS."

EAST FEELS THAT THE JOKING TECHNIQUE HE USES IS FAR MORE EFFECTIVE THAN THE "OUTRAGED BLAST" APPROACH. EAST'S FAVORITE TARGET IS EASTLAND, WHOSE NAME HE ALWAYS PRINTS IN LOWER CASE. EASTLAND IS REFERRED TO AS "OUR GEM" IN "THE PETAL PAPER," WHICH DETAILS "GLORIOUS EXPLOITS OF OUR EXALTED LEADER" IN WONDERFULLY SARCASTIC STYLE. TROUBLE IS, EAST SAYS RUEFULLY, THAT THE SARCASM RIDES OVER THE HEADS OF MANY OF HIS MISSISSIPPI READERS. ("WHY, THE OTHER DAY, AFTER I BLASTED HELL OUT OF THE CITIZENS

14

COUNCIL, ONE OF THE LEADERS CALLED ME TO SAY WHAT A GOOD JOB HE THOUGHT I WAS DOING FOR THE CAUSE.") . . .

PAGE ONE IS HIS RACIAL SOUNDING BOARD. HIS DOUBLE COLUMN IS THE CATCHALL FOR P D.'S OBSERVATIONS ON MISSISSIPPI. THE DOUBLE-COLUMN ON THE RIGHT SIDE IS USUALLY DEVOTED TO FURTHER LAMPOONING OF MISSISSIPPI, LIKE THE CURRENT ISSUE'S DIXIECRAT VERSION OF THE KING JAMES BIBLE. SAMPLE: "'FOR GOD SO LOVED THE WORLD THAT HE GAVE HIS ONLY BEGOTTEN SON—JOHN 3:16.' CLEARLY THIS SHOULD READ 'FOR GOD SO LOVED MISSISSIPPI THAT HE GAVE IT OUR GEM—DIXIECRAT JOHN 3:16.' "

EAST USES FAKE ADS TO GOOD ADVANTAGE IN HIS LAMPOONING. HIS MOST FAMOUS IS A FULL-PAGE AD INVITING SUBSCRIBERS TO JOIN "THE GLORIOUS CITIZENS CLAN," PICTURING A JACKASS IN THE MARGIN. "YOU TOO CAN BE SUPERIOR," THE AD PROCLAIMED. "JOIN THE CITIZENS CLAN AND BE SAFE FROM SOCIAL WORRIES. FREEDOM TO YELL 'NIGGER' AS MUCH AS YOU PLEASE WITHOUT YOUR CONSCIENCE BOTHERING YOU," ETC.

ANOTHER AD IN THIS WEEK'S ISSUE ADVERTISES "PRE-SOAKED KEROSENE DOUSED, TWO-BY-FOURS, IDEAL FOR CROSS BURNINGS." . . .

BECAUSE EAST TAKES THE JOKING APPROACH TO RACIAL PROBLEMS, HE HAS NOT BEEN SET UPON VIOLENTLY AS YET.

"ONE DAY," HE SAYS, "I PULLED UP TO A TRAFFIC LIGHT AND A FELLOW INVITED ME OUT OF THE CAR SO HE COULD WIPE UP THE STREET WITH ME. DISLIKING THIS KIND OF INVITATION AND BEING A COWARD AT HEART, I DROVE OFF IN GREAT HASTE." . . .

EAST STARTED "THE PETAL PAPER" TO "MAKE MONEY," SOON GAVE UP THE PROFIT MOTIVE, CONTENT TO KEEP HIS HEAD ABOVE WATER. INJUSTICES DONE MISSISSIPPI NEGROES STUNG HIM. THE PAPER BEGAN POKING FUN AT MISSISSIPPI. HIS SUBSCRIPTIONS DROPPED, HAVE NOW RECOVERED BECAUSE OF OUT-OF-STATE SUBSCRIBERS (MORE THAN HALF THE CIRCULATION IS OUTSIDE MISSISSIPPI).

EAST, WHO HAS TERRIBLE SINUS AND A PERFORATED ULCER, SAYS HE DOESN'T THINK ABOUT THE FUTURE, HAS NO PLANS "EXCEPT TO BE A COUNTRY EDITOR AND STAY ALIVE." . . . HIS NEXT ADVERTISING PROMOTION IN "THE PETAL PAPER": COTTON EYELET CLOTH, "IDEAL FOR SUMMER KLAN UNIFORMS." SO FAR THERE HAVE BEEN NO CROSSES BURNED ON HIS LAWN, BUT THE 35 YEAR OLD EAST AND HIS WIFE HAVE ALREADY LAID IN A SUPPLY

OF MARSHMALLOWS WHICH THEY FULLY INTEND TO ROAST IN THE HEAT OF THE FIRST CROSS THAT'S BURNED IN HIS YARD.

After reading the file, it was clear to me that the reporters and researchers had failed to make too much sense from my life. I was not inclined to be critical of their efforts, for, to be sure, I'd never been able to make sense out of my life either. I decided to undertake the task of recording what I was capable of, having to do with my background, environment and growing up, in what I'm convinced to be the poorest section of the poorest state in the nation. I am a firm believer that every person is a part of all he has met. With that in mind, I wondered how I got the way I am.

Chapter 2

If there is truth in the statement that "A coward dies a thousand deaths," and I believe there is, I have died ten thousand deaths, beginning with the dawn of consciousness in the year 1925.

It is to be expected that in one's memory there are unaccountable gaps. The first inward sensibility of life for me was far from being a gap, and I've spent most of my life wishing it had been; for, at that moment, I became a coward.

It was sometime in the early autumn. The weather had the slightest nip in it, the sky was gray, and the clouds were low that morning over the sawmill camp. There was excitement in my mother's boarding house. The workers talked about it at great length. The expression of sorrow was predominant.

I learned from the talk at the breakfast table that during the night a stove had set fire to the house in which a Negro family lived. Actually, it was a shack of two rooms, unceiled, unpapered, unpainted. How many of the family slept in the house I didn't know, but it was a large family. All persons had escaped, except a little girl, whose age was somewhere near ten.

As soon as it was good daylight, my mother set out to see the family, who were still standing in stunned silence around the burned house. Her intentions were good; her purpose in going was to help. Her mistake was in taking me with her. I remember we walked through a small valley and up a hill to reach the Negro family. The distance from the area in which the white employees lived must have been nearly a half mile.

The odor was sickening and horrible as we approached the hilltop. It had been hours since the death of the child by burning, but the odor of burned flesh lingered—for me it has lingered over thirty years. After speaking to the man and wife, my mother took my hand and led me to a blanket nearby. Someone pulled it back and exposed to view the burned, charred corpse of the child. So long as I live, I'll never forget the horror that came over me as I stood looking at that human form, so charred that it was not easily recognizable at first glance, although it did take on its proper form in seconds.

This experience was, for me, the dawning of consciousness, in the year 1925.

Since that day, every time the picture of that child comes to my mind—and for some reason it comes often—I die just a little, perhaps from fear of the horror I witnessed, perhaps from the ultimate realization that I saw in that child another child— me. While I was unable to put it into words at the age of four, I felt for many years, and still do, that "There, but for the grace of God, am I."

In any event, that was the beginning for me of "our Southern way of life." How often I've thought that such a beginning could be improved.

There are notable gaps in my memory from that morning in 1925, until I was about eight years old. However, there are a few moments I remember, but not in detail.

Looking at a map of the United States, one will note the state of Mississippi is at the bottom. (And in most every other way, too, but that doesn't show up on a map.) Looking at a map of Mississippi, one notes that Forrest County is located near the bottom, in the central area. The Forrest County line is approximately forty miles north of the Gulf Coast. Hattiesburg, the county seat, is exactly seventy miles north-northwest of Gulf-port.

Almost due south of Hattiesburg, some fifteen miles, High-way 49 made a sharp turn to the right. Down a slight grade and up a red hill was the sawmill camp. From the curve in the road the camp site was visible. It consisted of a group of houses along either side of the highway. ("Highway," in those days, meant a road that was graveled and was a fraction wider in certain spots than just a "road.")

I never knew how many houses were on the highway. A guess would be something like fifteen to eighteen. The company com-missary was on the left side of the highway, facing west, just a short distance from my mother's boarding house, which was located across the road.

Not visible from the highway, but to the right of it and back of our house, were the "nigger quarters." The houses were more or less lined up north to south on a small hill. A slight valley separated the "white" area from that of the "Negro." There was no road leading from the highway to the Negro area, rather a beaten-out path, muddy in the rain and dusty when dry.

The houses were shacks, both those of the whites and Negroes. There wasn't a single painted house, nor was there a single build-ing with wallpaper or paint inside. The houses, every last one of them, were built of rough lumber, each board six to eight inches wide. The wide planks were nailed onto a frame of rough two-by-fours. A strip of rough lumber about two inches wide was nailed over cracks where the larger planks joined together. Floors were made of a "dressed" lumber, of one-by-four-inch material. The roofs were of "tar paper," a black material of some sort, easily torn and punctured. There was not one roof in the camp without several leaks. It was an impossibility to put tar paper on a house top without punching holes in it. Every house had extra pails for use during rain.

Generally, the sawmill company dug a shallow well between two houses. That was the water supply. However, I must admit that my mother had a well all her own because she ran the board-ing house. I have no way of knowing, but I believe a well as deep as forty feet was unheard of. I remember that all the wells

18

were quite shallow and often ran low on water, and I've seen many months during the summer when water would have to sit for an hour or more before the mud and sand could settle.

The camp in which I lived in 1925 was typical of others in which I lived and grew up.

Aside from what I've related about the camp, there are four other things which come to my mind. First, a friend. I remember Tad Barber from a time near the incident of the burned child. He was the youngest son of the camp superintendent, Sol Barber. The house in which the Barbers lived was the largest in the camp, with the exception of the boarding house. I remember many rainy days with Tad. We would lie on the front porch (called a "gallery" in the usual Southern manner) and watch the water drain from the roof onto the ground. The water would make bubbles form in the gully below. With a stick, the two of us spent many hours bursting bubbles as they formed.

The friendship with Tad Barber was the most satisfactory I've known in my life. It lasted without a cross word until his death in 1943, on a bombing mission over Europe.

Second, I remember a damned fool. For some reason unknown to me, a woman in the camp took great delight in scaring the wits out of children. I was afraid of her because she'd put a paper sack over her head and begin chasing me. Why in the name of Heaven she wanted me, I didn't know. But once she caught me. I was almost hysterical, screaming, kicking and crying. She took me into her house and locked me in a small room, something like a closet or pantry. From the fear of being locked in that dark place, and fear in general, I suppose, I was almost limp when my mother found me and opened the door. There were heated words between the two women, but I didn't stay to hear them. However, the woman didn't lock me in a room again.

Third, a new Model-T Ford. In 1926 my father purchased a shiny, new, black Model-T Ford touring car. It was a beautiful machine. The top would let down, and sometimes did, whether you had such a desire or not. With the purchase of the Model T, I got my first taste of "being superior." It was a nice sort of feeling, at the time.

Fourth, I remember cheating on *Baby Ray*. *Baby Ray* was a

primer used in the teaching of reading by a private teacher in the camp. I was four years old when I began attending school. (I've often thought how ridiculous it was—a private teacher and an outdoor privy.) The whole of teaching was reading. If a child could read the entire lesson without missing a word, the teacher would paste a gold star at the chapter heading. A few words missed resulted in a silver star, and if you were poor, no stars of any color were given. I got gold stars when I'd studied, but when a silver star appeared in my *Baby Ray* book, my mother would be unhappy about it. I set my mind to work on the problem. It seemed logical that all I needed was a box of gold stars.

The sacrifice I made in order to cheat was noble, in a disgusting sort of way. By accident, I learned the commissary carried gold stars in five-cent boxes. I learned that the teacher bought her stars there. A five-cent box had enough gold stars in it to fill several *Baby Ray* books.

Every Saturday, my father gave me a nickel to spend as I saw fit. That five cents was always spent for candy. Confronted with something of a crisis, I gave up the candy and bought gold stars. It turned out that I was to have my first business adventure. Every day I'd paste a gold star in the little book, take it home and show my mother, and she'd be so happy about her intelligent son that she'd give me a few nickels extra during the week. That, in itself, was a profit; more was in the making. There were other children who had gold-star trouble. I had plenty; why not share them? I did. For each gold star I shared, I received a piece of candy, gum, or something someone had that I wanted.

Over a quarter century later I visited my mother and was looking through a collection of junk she'd saved over the years. In the collection I found my *Baby Ray* primer with its gold stars, dog-eared, moth-eaten, and I noted very few silver stars. I took great pains to put it back in the box—on the bottom.

Chapter 3

From the First World War until the early 1930s, something like 60 to 75 per cent of the population of the state of Mississippi depended on the timber industry for their livelihood. The remaining percentage of the economy was based on small farms, the Delta area being the exception.

During the 1920s the Southern Railway's New Orleans and Northwestern Division, running from Meridian, Mississippi, to New Orleans, Louisiana, had over thirty sawmill or logging operations on its line. Almost every village had a sawmill, some large, most of them small. Indeed, dozens of the towns in the state today were once sawmill camps.

By and large, economic matters were relatively simple: the rich got richer, and the poor had babies and worked for the sawmills. For the sawmill owners, matters were relatively simple. One seldom finds illiterate men forming labor unions, and illiteracy among the Negroes during those times has been estimated at about 65 per cent. From what I saw, it is my opinion that the whites weren't much better off during those years.

In any event, out of the sawmill era came what I now refer to as the "turpentine aristocracy." They are the second generation who've inherited the wealth of their fathers. In most cases they have sat on it; true, there have been notable exceptions. In looking back to those days, I am convinced the whole philosophy was simply this: Ignorant people are happy people.

In spite of the reams of copy written about the economy of Mississippi, declaring it to have been based on agriculture, for well over a quarter century the economic backbone was timber, the Delta area again being the exception.

Following the Civil War, thousands of returning Mississippians carved out small farms from the vast virgin pine forests. The pine forests were still owned, for the most part, by the Federal Government. Few Mississippians saw any possibility of tremendous wealth in pine trees. My ancestors thought small, lived small and died small. With Northeners it was different. They saw a dollar sign on every pine tree in the South. The bulk

21

of sawmilling was started by men from the North. Naturally, there were many exceptions, but the impetus given the sawmill business was basically Northern.

With the advent of the timber industry, numerous small farmers left their fields to work for the sawmill companies. It was a natural thing to do. Few had any cash money; few ever saw a dollar bill. It is my opinion that the economy of the state was based on two things—farming and timber. I contend that for many years, over a quarter century, as I've said, the timber economy was of greater value than that of farming. With the final rape of the forests, the economy reverted almost in full to agriculture. Those who had farmed prior to the saw-mills returned to farms. Thousands of others, unemployed, al-most desperate, began farming small acreages, especially in the southern part of the state.

The operation of logging camps was simple: get enough men, machines, mules, oxen, and whatever else necessary to cut a large tract of timber in the shortest possible time. Conservation was an unknown word in those days, and possibly for a good economic reason. The taxes paid by sawmill companies were paid to counties. The tax structure was determined by a Board of Supervisors composed of five men, each representing a beat, or district, in the county. Without exception, these men decided that taxes would be based on the amount of timber standing in the woods. It was only natural, therefore, that a mill owner should attempt to cut all standing trees, for with each fallen tree his tax payment would be less.

The final result in the southern part of Mississippi was that the land was stripped bare of trees; erosion set in; the lands were lost for non-payment of taxes. The rich had gotten richer; the poor returned to raising cotton, corn and babies.

As to the location of logging camps, at least the five in which I grew up, it was apparent that the management would first take into account the proximity of the company land to a railroad which could give service to the mill. With this determined, they would then decide where to build a camp site, compromising be-tween the center of the timber holdings and the railroad. The people who worked the woods didn't really enter into the picture, the camps being located without regard to the availability of schools, hospitals and other things often considered by present standards to be necessities.

After deciding on the location, the company would set to work building railroad tracks into the woods. Such railroads as were built are hard to imagine. The weight of the rails must have been about thirty or forty pounds to the foot. The roadbed was thrown up with scoops of dirt taken a few feet from the track side.

To grade a hill was something unheard of. They'd go over the hill, if it could be done; otherwise, they'd go around it.

I've seen rails disappear completely into the mud of the road-bed with the passing of an engine over them. Derailments were as expected as the sunrise.

When the tracks had been laid, the second stage of camp construction began: the actual building of houses for the families, better described as shacks. I could never see much difference between a dwelling for an ox, a mule or a man, except the man's mansion had a stove in it, purchased from the company commissary and taken out of his wages.

With the railroad built, along with the houses and a company commissary and an office, the rape was ready to begin. And rape it was, of men, machines, mules, oxen, and the tremendous virgin pine forests.

Chapter 4

In the summer of 1926, the camp south of Hattiesburg was cut out. I don't know the why and wherefore of my father's decision, but he decided to go to work for another sawmill company. That summer we moved about twelve miles farther into the woods, to a camp located near Maxie, Mississippi, which was to the south of the former camp. A two-track path led from Highway 49 into the woods. To blow out a tire was not at all unusual on that trail, what with roots sticking out of the ground as plentiful as rocks on the highway. My memory of that camp is poor. Yet I recall a few facts.

First, I recall that the camp was totally isolated; second, I remember well the fact that I had mumps. Also, I had blood poisoning in both feet at the same time. My father was building a chicken coop, and I was standing on top of it. A board was lying there with a large nail sticking through it. I happened to step on it. (Shoes? Only grown folk wore shoes, and not all of them.) I screamed, jerked my foot upward, jumped around because of the pain, and when I did I stepped on the nail with the other foot.

The treatment was simple. The camp's amateur medical experts said because of lockjaw (tetanus), they'd have to clean out the puncture caused by the nail. That, too, was simple. They got a long metal object of some sort, wrapped the end of it with cotton, soaked it with iodine, then inserted it into the holes in my feet. Instead of lockjaw, I got blood poisoning (septicemia). I don't remember the treatment used for that, but in spite of the treatments, I survived.

At the Maxie camp I became acquainted with a child about my own age, B. L. Harder. He was honest and straightforward. He felt that he was better than I because his father was a clerk and mine was a blacksmith. I didn't see it that way; so I proceeded to settle the matter with a poke at his nose. That sort of thing went on until 1934; it was never settled to his satisfaction.

Also, at the Maxie camp, I ran into something which, in my opinion, was of the utmost importance in my life. Each week a man came to the camp in a pick-up truck loaded with fresh vegetables and fruit. The commissary carried little or none of such items. The man was large, almost fat, and dark-skinned, with jet-black hair and eyes. He was pleasant to everyone, and exceptionally nice to me for some reason. My greatest delight was eating bananas; they were better than candy. The man always had several bunches with him. My mother would buy some, but the bananas I enjoyed most were those given me by the man. He knew how to pick the best ones in the bunch.

I would ride with him as he made his rounds through the camp, blowing his horn and ringing a bell to attract attention. That delight was short-lived, however. One day my mother had a talk with me. She said I had best not ride with the man any more. It was a crushing blow, and I asked why not. I was informed that the man was a "Dago." I had no idea what a "Dago" was. I shall never forget the answer I got. In simple, plain language, it was this: "Well, he's just different from us, that's all."

I inquired as to how he was different. "Just different, that's all. Just different from us." I wouldn't shut up and accept the facts of life; I kept right on asking questions about the man— and us.

I couldn't understand what was so different about him. I couldn't see it. After all, I pointed out, I liked him and he liked me, else he'd not give me bananas and other fruit. "He's a 'Dago' and he's different from us—and now that's all."

But it wasn't. I couldn't understand, said so and asked more questions. The conversation soon ceased to be a discussion and became an argument. I lost, and got spanked. Even with a blistered tail, I couldn't understand what it was all about. I saw only a man, a nice man who was kind to me and whom I liked.

Chapter 5

One thing about which I have been confused my entire life is my education, when it began, where, and also why. The parents at the Maxie camp hired a teacher to come, live there and teach their children. I recall having attended school in a house. I had started school by learning to read a *Baby Ray* book, but I have a faint recollection of additional subjects at Maxie. What they were, if any, I don't know. Anyway, I think it was there I was supposed to have "made two grades in one year," to quote my mother.

Less than a year after moving to the Maxie camp, we moved again. My father remained with the same company, Batson and Hatten, the home office of which was located in Lyman, Mississippi, about ten miles north of Gulfport.

About eleven miles west of Maxie is a wide spot in the road

named Carnes. The camp site was a fraction under a mile beyond the village of Carnes.

Carnes had two stores, a post office and a Smith-Hughes Consolidated School. In the fall of 1927, I entered a regular, state-county-supported school for the first time. It too had an outdoor privy. My troubles began, not because of the outdoor privy but because of the people.

The camp at Carnes was the largest in which I had lived. There were almost forty houses in all, for colored and white. A large number of sawmill kids entered school that year. We were "outsiders" to the local residents; the resentment was not great, but it was present, and one didn't need extrasensory perception to know it. As far back as I can recall, I've been plagued with a human weakness of a sort. If someone didn't like me, I didn't like him; and when I was treated by the teachers at the school, as well as by the students, like a bastard child at a family reunion, I found it unpleasant, to say the least.

The discrimination wasn't too great, but always present. Almost without exception, when an entrance line was formed we sawmill kids found ourselves bringing up the rear. I don't think I cared especially to be in front, but to be forced to the back was something else again. My reaction was to fight. Heaven only knows how many I started. I never won one of them, but I always felt a little better as I'd get up from the ground. Another thing I resented was the business of riding the school bus. Every morning a school bus drove by the camp en route to the school; in the afternoon it returned. There was enough room for all of us to ride on the bus, but we were not allowed to do so.

The school-bus matter irked me no end. I'm not proud of my solution to it. Instead of forming a union of the kids to protest to whomever one would protest, or, for that matter, instead of taking it to the Supreme Court, I became friends with a boy whose family was respected highly in the area. His name was Dave Dee. His oldest brother was the king of the bootleggers, a highly respected man. Dave was a nice boy, and we got along fine together. At his request the school-bus driver let me ride to and from school every day. I confess to having felt a bit superior to the other children in camp because of my "connections." I

26

could justify the maneuver by the simple process of reason. Was it not better to ride than to walk? It was that simple to me—but something wasn't right, else I'd not have bothered to justify my action by any means whatsoever.

Dave and I remained friends for years, as a matter of fact, until he was sent to the state penitentiary for bootlegging.

Except for the school-bus matter and the fights, I don't recall much about our stay at the Carnes camp. It was for less than a year. One other recollection of the Carnes Consolidated School has to do with a twelve-inch rule. The Coca-Cola Bottling Company would send the school a pencil, a tablet and a rule for each child. They did it twice each year. On the rule was printed: "A Good Rule: DO UNTO OTHERS AS YOU WOULD HAVE THEM DO UNTO YOU." I was impressed by these words. Admittedly, I didn't understand them fully, but I remembered them. I gave serious thought to the "good rule."

The following year, 1928, we moved to another Batson and Hatten camp, almost twenty miles away. The camp was in Perry County, south of another wide spot in the road, Janice. The camp site itself wasn't quite as far into the woods as the one at Maxie had been, but it was almost a mile off the highway. Janice wasn't the town that Carnes was. It had only one store, and no post office. The school was located at Oak Grove, three miles from Janice. From the camp to Janice was also almost three miles, if one took the road. Down the railroad and through the woods, the distance was nearer two miles. Along with several other children, I'd walk to Janice to catch the school bus each morning.

The attitude of the children at Oak Grove School was, to a degree, different from that of the children at the Carnes school. They weren't as resentful, it seemed, to those of us from the sawmill camp. Perhaps it was because there weren't as many of us at Janice as there had been at Carnes.

Superiority will show itself in people in one way or another. I found my grade taught in a church, the school having become overcrowded. Some of the children in the grades immediately below and above mine felt that by having been allowed to re-

27

main in the school building, they were in some unaccountable way a bit superior.

One boy had taken a keen dislike to me. The fact that my grade had been moved out of the school building was fuel added to the fire. His attitude was repulsive and distasteful, and that's putting it mildly. The boy wouldn't leave me alone. I had tried hard to avoid a fight with him. I'd not been in a single fight at the school since I'd been there.

The boy's name was Freeland. He had two nicknames; one was "Fatty" and the other "Race Horse." At noon one day he pushed my head into water from which I was drinking. Having reached my low boiling point that day, I added a third name to his list. We were in the school building, in a hall near the steps leading out the back. My comment to him was, when I'd wiped the water from my face, "Fatty, you're a fat, ugly son-of-a-bitch." To which he replied, "Yeah, and you're a red-headed, freckled-faced one."

With that intelligent exchange of compliments, I clobbered him. He fell down the steps. I followed him and when he got up I threw another haymaker. When he got up that time he had a piece of wood in his hand, and with it he split my skull. From the time the outdoor activity had started, the principal had been watching. I was bleeding freely and having trouble keeping my bearings. The principal stopped the fight. (And I might say that I was glad of it.) He dismissed Freeland, but I was carried into his office, bleeding head and all, and given a good licking by him.

The incident caused me an unusual amount of concern. When I'd started fights at Carnes I had expected punishment. I had no complaint to make. I did not cause the fight with Freeland, yet I got the punishment.

In less than a year we moved back to the camp at Carnes. Batson and Hatten had built a new boarding house which my mother was to operate. It was a large house, the design of which I've not seen duplicated since. There were ten or twelve rooms in the house. Like all the other houses, it was without paint, wallpaper or plumbing. I think, however, that for the first time in my life I lived in a house which was ceiled.

28

While we were at the Janice camp, Sol Barber, who had been camp superintendent and woods foreman at the first camp near Hattiesburg, had taken the same job with Batson and Hatten. We now had a medical doctor in the camp too, a man named Angus McNair. Additional families had moved in since we'd left the year before. I made new acquaintances, some good, some bad. The camp was a busy place. Additional railroad spurs had been built in the woods, and the company had sent up two additional Shay locomotives from Lyman.

Those new Shays were the most beautiful engines I'd ever seen, shiny black, powerful, wonderful. Actually, the Shay was a monstrosity in appearance; however, the locomotives seemed to serve their purpose. The entire drive mechanism was on the right side. The red engine, which I saw only when I would be at Maxie with my father, had drives on either side, operated from large chambers in which a piston was steam-driven. The Shay was operated in the same manner, basically, but the drives were mounted above the wheels, near the boiler, the pistons moving in a vertical rather than a horizontal direction. The piston strokes were considerably shorter, being geared for power rather than speed, and nothing I've ever heard, before or since, made so much noise and moved so slowly. Somehow, the whole thing seemed to compare to a one-thousand-horsepower aircraft engine in a turtle.

That fall, when the door opened at the Carnes Consolidated School, I was there. My mother went along with me and caused me great embarrassment. She explained, in my presence, that I'd had some trouble while there before, and would the new principal sort of keep an eye on me. The new principal, a Mr. Martin, certainly honored my mother's request, and in less than a week.

Every child at the school brought a lunch; some used paper bags, while others preferred tin lunch pails, which came in a multitude of colors. At noon one day, during the first week of school, I was walking toward the school building after having been engaged in a fight, using wet corncobs. I noticed a child sitting on the ground beside the path, eating his lunch from a pail. I will probably never know why I did it, but what I did I shall never forget. With deliberation, I planned to step in his lunch pail. I began to run, and upon approaching the boy I veered and poked my feet in the exact place I had intended. The destruction was complete.

The moment I'd ruined the boy's pail and lunch, I regretted it. I tried my hardest to justify it in some way. It was impossible. I didn't even know the boy. I had nothing against him; he'd done nothing to me in any way whatsoever.

As one would expect, the child was stunned. When he regained his composure, he reported me to the new principal. Justice was rapid, to say the least. Mr. Martin removed his belt and made contact with the seat of my overalls. I didn't make a sound, being guilty of the act for which I was being punished and not liking Martin because my mother had seen fit to single me out as some kind of little monster.

After he'd completed his work on my rear, I turned to him and quipped, "Do you think you've beat a little boy like me enough, you big, fat bully?"

What else I was going to say, I don't know, but I learned Mr. Martin had not quite finished beating a little boy like me. That second time I made a noise; it was not joyful, nor was it exactly unto the Lord.

The principal and I met again the next day. That morning before classes started I had looked up the boy whose lunch pail I'd ruined and demanded to know why he'd reported me to Mr. Martin. When he failed to give me a satisfactory reason, I took a poke at him. Thus Mr. Martin and I had an encounter for the second time in the first week of school. I didn't talk to him that time after he'd finished with me, but it wasn't that I couldn't think of anything to say.

Principal Martin probably bought more belts that year than he'd ever bought in his life. We simply failed to see eye to eye.

The years which followed weren't too bad for me; I cut down on my fighting, primarily because I was a coward, I think. I was getting to be a fair-sized child, and those with whom I fought could shake my teeth when they'd hit me. I do not mean to imply that I'd stopped fighting altogether. I averaged three or four a year through my freshman year in high school.

30

Dave Dee and I renewed our friendship the year of my return to Carnes, but I did not ride the school bus, except when it was raining. My decision was not based on anything resembling principle. I'd been reading the ads of Charles Atlas, the ninety-seven-pound weakling who had become the world's strongest man, or so it said in the advertisement. I decided to be another Atlas; hence my walking to and from school. There were times when I'd trot the entire distance. I was building up my muscles. Actually, while I was exceptionally tall, I was thin enough to hide behind any one of the telegraph posts along the railroad.

The year I entered the sixth grade a new principal came. His name was Elmo Rand; he was young, just out of college, and he made an effort to be a "regular fellow." I didn't care for regular fellows. I didn't trust them. Principal Rand played baseball with us, taking any position open to him after we'd chosen our teams. He arranged to have us play two or three games with other elementary schools in the area. On one occasion, we were to travel to Lumberton, a distance of seven or eight miles, to play a baseball game with the school there. I was proud of myself, having been selected to play third base. I was to ride with Mr. Rand in his car, a Model-A Ford sedan.

We were near the camp on our trip to Lumberton when a tire began to go flat. Mr. Rand cursed, calling it names even I didn't know, and I knew quite a few. I suggested meekly that maybe Sam, who worked at the commissary, could fix it.

Sam was a youthful Negro man. His full name I didn't know. He was pleasant, respectful, courteous and helpful. Sam's job was to help around the front of the store, operate the gasoline pump, sweep, mop and generally do whatever he was told. Mr. Rand pulled up to the front of the commissary, blocking the gas pump. Sam was busy with another car. He stepped over to Mr. Rand's car and inquired whether he wanted gasoline. Mr. Rand told him no, that he wanted a tire repaired. Sam said it would be a few minutes before he could get to it, and, if he pleased, would Mr. Rand move his car up a bit so as not to block the gasoline pump?

Mr. Rand flew into a rage. "No goddamned nigger's going to tell me what to do!" he screamed.

31

Sam made an effort to explain that he wasn't "telling" anyone what to do, but he didn't get a chance to finish his apology or explanation. The principal of the Carnes Consolidated Elementary School, Mr. Elmo Rand, set a wonderful example for the children under his wing that day. He flung open the door of the car, stepped out facing Sam, and swung a tire tool, hitting Sam across the side of his head, splitting it open. The Negro was knocked to the ground, unconscious. I thought he was dead, the way his eyes rolled upward in his head. That was among the more horrible moments in my life. I remember jumping out of the car and running into the commissary and yelling that Sam needed Dr. McNair, that he'd been hurt. I did not say how Sam had been hurt. Dr. McNair had to take several stitches in his head, but Sam eventually recovered.

Nothing was done about the incident. As a matter of fact, Mr. Rand was something of a hero at school after that. To be a "regular fellow" and to split the skull of a Negro who'd done nothing whatsoever was what heroes were made of in those days.

How often I looked at that man Rand after that—and wondered. I wondered many things, the answers to which I could not find. I wanted to do something for that Negro boy, Sam, but I didn't know what it could be. I wanted to talk with my mother about it, but I couldn't bring myself to talk with anyone. I never even mentioned it to Sam.

I was asked by my teacher to be in a program to be presented in the school auditorium. My mother was pleased and helped me with my lines; furthermore, she made the costume I needed.

The program was to be at night, so the parents could attend. We were flowers, each child being a different kind. Each flower had a little speech to make, explaining about itself. I had been chosen to fill the sweet-william role. A sweet william is a wild flower, purple in color, and it grows on a long stem. That was me, except the color. My hair was as red as hair could get, and my freckles were—well, they didn't lend themselves to a sweet-william appearance.

However, I studied long and hard learning my lines. My mother took great care with my sweet-william suit. Finally, the

32

long-awaited night came. Yes, I knew my lines; yes, I knew the drill; yes, I was prepared—so I told my mother and teacher.

The curtain went up. One child, a buttercup, did his part, moved to his appointed place on stage. Then another child made with the petunia bit, and on it went, until my time. I tripped onto the stage lightly, bowed to the audience and said, "I'm a sweet william, I sway in the breeze . . ." I swayed to and fro, back and forth, and the audience began laughing. I forgot my lines, so I started over. "I am a sweet william, I sway in the breeze . . ." There was a repeat, only the laughter was louder. I tried the third time—same result. I heard the teacher say frantically from behind the scenery: "Go to your place! Get into your place!" I got, but befuddled by the audience's reaction to a redheaded sweet william, I got into the place of the buttercup. That oversight resulted, and I don't know how, in the drill's getting messed up. More kids ran together that night than seemed to be present. It was one great flop, so the teacher informed me. I wasn't too unhappy about it. After all, the people seemed to enjoy it.

Graduation was only a few weeks away. One Saturday morning I was sitting on the back porch washing my feet for our weekly trip to Hattiesburg. A car drove up in front, stayed only a few minutes, then drove away. My mother walked back and told me that a classmate of mine had died that morning. I began drying my feet.

"All the boys in the eighth grade are going to be pallbearers," she informed me.

"What's a pallbearer?" I asked.

I was told. Suddenly I realized I was to touch a casket in which a dead person was lying. I recalled the little girl who'd been burned to death. I recalled the horror of that morning when I had smelled burned human flesh. I could see my grandmother as I had seen her dying, a shrunken, wasted, withered human being, and how I'd been asked to kiss her goodbye as she lay in her coffin. I remembered how frightened I was at the very thought of such a thing, and how I had run from the room, crying as if I would never stop. I saw in my mind the corpse of a man in the camp who had died, and how I had peeped through a keyhole one evening as he was being dressed for burial and how his feet had been drawn in an odd manner by rigor mortis, and how a pig had run under the house and made a bumping noise for which I couldn't account, and how I'd run almost a mile—until my lungs felt as if they would burst.

All these things ran through my mind as I sat there listening to my mother tell me what I was to do. This I could not do. I had to tell her that I wouldn't touch a casket.

I said I didn't want to be a pallbearer. But she was determined that I was to take part. I defied her, finally, and said she could kill me if she liked, but I wasn't going to do it.

From the time I refused until the funeral the following afternoon, I got four goings-over with a keen but strong switch. My father came to my aid, but it did no good. I was going to be a pallbearer if it killed me; my mother was happy when I finally gave in.

How badly I'd wanted to tell her that I didn't want to participate because I was afraid. How I had wanted to say, plainly and simply, that I was frightened to be anywhere near a corpse. I wanted to talk to my mother about it, to explain, to confess. I couldn't bring myself to admit that I was a coward, and that's what I thought I was.

We had the funeral. The weather was hot. The flowers smelled awful. I was sick. Everyone was happy. Indeed, I observed that a good time was had by all.

A few weeks later, at graduation, the school saw fit to deck out an empty chair with a wreath of flowers. It was final tribute to our departed friend, someone said. I learned immediately that my position on stage was to be by the empty chair, and I balked at the idea. I argued that such a gesture was in poor taste (only I called it something else), and had we not done everything mortal beings could do for the dead classmate? I lost the argument. People love to suffer too much to miss a chance like that. I sat through the ghoulish graduation, right beside the spirit of my deceased comrade. Being sick of the whole affair, when I went forward and received my diploma, I did not return to my chair. I marched as straight off the stage as I could go. I walked home, where my mother was waiting for me. She was curious to know how she could explain my act to her friends. I didn't tell her; I couldn't explain my action to her.

I had managed to get through elementary school, but it was late the following day before I could sit down with comfort.

Chapter 6

With the closing of school in early May, my life began. I spent the summers fighting with B. L. Harden, who lived across the road from me; we were still trying to decide whose father was superior. To be sure, we both knew; but the best way to convince a person was to bash in his skull. Except for our daily fight, B.L. and I roamed the woods. We dug caves, caught crayfish and snakes, picked flowers, stole push-cars, played baseball, and shot marbles for keeps. Most of our pleasures were sinful, especially playing marbles for keeps. We did that out of sight of parental authority.

One of our great pleasures was to float a raft we'd built on the pond where the engines stopped for water. Someone had put two alligators in the pond, so it became quite an adventure to tempt wild animals in traveling those uncharted waters as we carried medicine or food to stranded souls at wherever the isolated outpost happened to be at the time.

A family lived two houses up the road from us. They had more children than anyone else in the camp. The mother's face filled me with pity. I saw her, worn from toil, sad-eyed from chasing her brood, pale and sickly from staying pregnant all the time. Her oldest child was a boy about two years older than I. I liked him in a backhanded way, but he was the worst sneak I've ever seen. Mortimer McPhail was a bully, and because of his size he had no fear of his bluff being called. The summer found the two of us playing together, B.L. having caught the smallpox. One rainy afternoon Mort and I were wrestling on the floor in a room in the McPhail house. He had thrown me. As I lay there, in no hurry to get up, Mort decided to fall on me, which he did without warning. I heard a sharp crack, as if a board had broken. We started to get up from the floor to see what happened, and then it was apparent what had broken—my left leg.

As soon as Dr. McNair had finished with me, my mother saw fit to work me over. I had been told not to play with Mortimer McPhail, and I was served right for having not paid heed to my instructions. There was some talk about the Devil's having got hold of me.

After the leg had healed and I was able to take long walks, I went to the blacksmith shop one day. My father and the other blacksmith, Walter McLarder, were in front of the shop. My father was a few yards away from McLarder, whom I had stopped to talk to. On the ground between the two of us was a large piece of iron. I asked Mr. Mac if the metal was hot. He said one way I could find out was to stick my foot on it. I was barefoot, as would have been any self-respecting logging-camp boy, but what was bad was the evident fact that my brain was bare, too. Without any hesitation, I popped my whole foot on the piece of iron. I removed my foot and several layers of skin remained on the metal. Only a second before my arrival, Mr. McLarder had cooled the red flow of the metal by putting it into water; that piece of iron was just short of red hot.

The shock was delayed, and before I began to scream, I looked directly into the eyes of that man and said to him, "You're a goddamned, no-good son-of-a-bitch." Had I not been in such pain, I believe I'd have picked up something and tried to kill him. But the pain set in, and the thought of murder passed.

My father rushed over, looked at my foot, looked up at Mr. Mac and said, "Walter, dammit, you should know this boy is too little to know about things around here." He was angry, I could see that, but he said no more. He lifted me in his arms and walked almost a mile to our house. I don't know what was said after he returned to work, but after that no one was kinder to me than Walter McLarder. He brought his violin to me and began to teach me to play. I was in bed, flat on my back, but I had a means of worrying everyone. I never learned to fiddle very well.

In my entire life I've seen my father angry twice; and only twice have I heard him curse. Once I'd heard him curse because of his Model-T Ford. To crank a Model T in the winter is nothing short of an engineering triumph. You began the night before by draining the radiator. (Anti-freeze in those days wasn't put into a radiator; the men drank it.) The next morning you boiled a large container of water and poured it into the radiator. In the meantime, while the water was heating, you jacked up the right rear wheel. With the water poured in the radiator and the wheel off the ground, you were almost ready. The spark lever was closed, the ignition turned on "Battery" (and how the coils would sing and hum) and the cranking began. Once, after such an effort, my father's Ford started, jumped the jack and pushed him against the back of the garage. I was inside the car, my job being to jerk down the spark lever, pull up the gear lever on the left side and regulate the gas lever. With my father pushing on the advancing Ford, I heard him say to me, "Turn the damned thing off!" The incident at the blacksmith shop was the second time I'd heard him say a word not acceptable in any church.

During that same summer I first heard a phrase that was to haunt me. Mortimer McPhail was the boy again. One day we were playing together and he asked me if I were an adopted child. I didn't know what the word meant, and said so. "Well, you know, like Mr. and Mrs. East ain't your real mama and daddy," he said. Of course, it was silly, and I told him it was. Later, other kids asked me the same question until I became worried and upset about it. I felt an unexplainable sort of "apartness," as if I were an outsider, an intruder. It was something Mort had made up, of that I was sure. After all, had I not caught him in many lies? But the seed was there, planted firmly, and it grew for many long, miserable years. Again I failed to bring myself to talk with anyone about it, although the question was always in my mind.

My mother had a Negro, Ella English, who helped her with the boarding house. Ella was the wife of Isom, a big man, strong, a real sport. When Isom would come in from work at night he would get dressed up and start a crap or poker game. Isom was a friend of mine, a good friend. He treated me as if I were a man. He called me by my name, instead of addressing me as "White Boy" as did most other Negroes in the camp. Once I asked Isom why the people called me "White Boy." He said, "I just reckon a nigger knows his place around this camp." I explained to Isom that while I was white and he was black, I had nothing to do with it in either case. He said he knew that, and maybe we'd better not worry about it too much, that maybe it was more important for him to show me how to make a nine the hard way with a pair of dice he had. I never learned to make a nine in any way, hard or easy.

Isom was, I fear, too much of a sport. He was a nice-looking fellow when he was dressed in his Sunday suit. He had a large mouth, and two of his front teeth were gold, and they stood out like the rising sun.

One morning someone came to our house and said Ella wouldn't be at work that day. It developed that Ella had caught Isom with another woman and had stuck an ice pick into his heart. My friend was dead. I wept, but I couldn't hate Ella; I knew what had been going on. I'd heard Ella and my mother talk, but I hadn't realized how serious such a thing could be with some women.

I walked across the spur line of the Illinois Central tracks to the "Nigger Quarters." I went directly to Isom's house. Ella was weeping as if her heart was broken, and it was, I'm sure. I heard her say over and over again, "I killed Isom because I loved him." That struck me as somewhat unusual, to say the least.

I went inside and found Isom in his Sunday suit, laid out on a table made of wood. He was not in a casket. He looked about as he always had; his lips were parted slightly and those gold teeth were shining through. I have always thought Isom would have enjoyed knowing that on his eyes were half dollars. I know what would have happened to them had Isom been alive. He'd have started a crap game. I wanted with all my heart to say goodbye to a friend, to the first person who had ever treated me as if I were an equal, as if I were a man. I didn't know how to say goodbye to Isom. I've always remembered him with a warm spot in my heart.

I've often wondered what happened to Ella for killing Isom. I have never heard anyone say. It was not spoken of at the boarding house, not in my presence.

Ella did not come back to work for my mother. Instead, Tee's mother came to work at our house. Her name was Mattie Williams and Tee was her son, whose age and size compared to my own. Tee was to become my best friend for the few years we knew each other. As a matter of fact, my regard for Tee was to lead me to a good bit of trouble, some of which I still suffer from.

To begin with, I would invite Tee to ride on the raft with me. Inasmuch as I was half owner, I felt no need to clear an invitation with B. L. Harden, the co-owner. One day my partner saw fit to tell me Tee couldn't ride on the raft, pointing out, of course, that he owned more of the raft than I, and, besides that, Tee was a "nigger." We settled the ownership with our fists, and it was decided that the raft was a fifty-fifty deal, but B.L. screamed at me as he ran home, "Tee's still a nigger."

I don't want to leave the impression that I didn't know what the word "nigger" meant. I knew, and I will add this as information: I was in high school at Pleasant, Mississippi, before I ever heard the word "Negro" and I didn't know what it meant. I remember quite distinctly asking about it.

Tee may have been a "nigger," but I could see no difference in the two of us. It mattered not one iota to me; first, Tee was a friend, and I enjoyed his companionship and that was all there was to that. It was the same as with the "Dago" at the Maxie camp. I didn't give a damn. No one objected to my having Tee for a playmate, except B.L.

In looking back, it seems strange that not once did I ever inquire as to where Tee went to school. I cannot recall any school for Negro children having ever been in the area. I don't think they went to school.

Inasmuch as I accepted Tee as a friend, and was accepted by him in return, it seemed natural to me that I could ask him to spend the night with me at my home. This was the natural course of things. B.L. and I spent nights with each other almost weekly,

39

either at my home or his. So why not ask Tee? Always, naturally, I would ask my mother for permission to invite anyone to spend the night. I'll never forget that conversation.

The answer from my mother was a flat "No!" It was quite a surprise to me that she should say no, especially when I thought that she had allowed Mortimer McPhail to spend the night with me a time or two. The questions began, an argument resulted, as usual, and finally I got a tanning. My mother told me the reason why Tee couldn't stay with me (after I'd made her angry enough) and it was quite simple, provided anyone understood, which I didn't. "Tee," she said, "is a nigger. That's why he can't spend the night, and that's all there is to it."

My reasoning was simple. Tee was my friend. That was that, I concluded. Needless to say, Tee was never an overnight guest at my home. I was glad about one thing. Tee and his mother were not present to hear the words that had been spoken.

It should be pointed out that my mother was a good woman, generous, kind and religious, as she understood it. I've known of her getting up in the dead of winter and walking through the night to help some person in the camp who was ill. I can recall numerous acts of kindness by her, favors done to both white and colored people. I am of the opinion that her belief in her Lord was such that had it demanded her life, she'd have given it. To her, being a victim of so many things, a "nigger was a nigger."

After the closing of the camp, everyone moved away, and my contact with families there ceased, except for the Barbers. I've never known where Tee's folks moved. One place he's been for a long, long time has been on my conscience.

Chapter 7

Revival meetings always started in the same way. We sat still, most often with our heads bowed slightly. Then with the sense of timing of a seasoned actor, Brother Hull would lift his arms upward toward Heaven and the tent top and would say in a hushed, sincere voice, "Now, turn to page fifty-two in your hymnals and let us sing 'Revive Us Again.'"

While his arms were raised, we would stand, getting to our feet without unnecessary noise. Then the piano would blast forth and rock the tent. We opened our mouths and made a joyful noise unto the Lord, which I'm sure He heard without any trouble whatsoever.

> "We praise Thee, O God! for the Son of Thy Love,
> For Jesus who died, and is now gone above.
> Hallelujah! Thine the glory. Hallelujah! Amen.
> Hallelujah! Thine the glory, revive us again."

With the "Hallelujah" refrain, the tent shook. For a brief moment, my sinful little heart was gladdened.

Following "Revive Us Again," there would be two or three other songs from the *Cokesbury Hymnal*. Then, in the same way he'd been doing for years, Brother Hull would commence:

"I know there is sin with you. I see hearts heavily laden. I see you need saving." (Of course, he'd saved a large number of the same sinners the summer before.) "You cannot escape the eye of the Lord," he would usually continue. "For He knows the fall of the sparrow."

Forever and always I began to get a bit frightened at this point. My mind would wander as I listened to the words of the Lord being spoken to me, and I knew they were directed right at me—an awful sinner. Well, let's see, what sins had I committed since the revival of the past summer? Yes, I did plan to kill Mort McPhail for breaking my nose. True, I'd called him a son-of-a-bitch, but he'd deserved it. I wondered if the Lord took into account the fact that Mort was indeed a son-of-a-bitch. He had snatched the basketball from my hands as I was about to throw it. The shot was mine by rights; everybody agreed to that. Without giving the matter much thought, I'd taken a good, healthy poke at him, landing it square in his mouth. It had knocked him down—and that was where I'd discovered the sin of seeing movies. I had seen Tom Mix, Tim McCoy and others poke a man as I'd done, and the fight was over. I had been misinformed. After a second of astonishment, up rose Mort and—well, finally someone pulled him off me.

I squirmed as I sat under the tent, my eyes on the sawdust, not daring to look up at Brother Hull. It was true, I had limited credit on my side. I had decided to give up calling people sons-of-bitches. Mort had helped decide that for me. Could that be to my credit? I still thought it—only I was afraid to say it any more. No. No credit for me; after all, as I thought in my heart, so was I. I didn't think too well of so many people. I'd squirm a little more, digging my toes into the sawdust.

I would notice my black, dignified Sunday shoes; noting them, I'd feel worse and would peek out of one eye at Brother Hull, who was looking right at me. Always he was calling my sins to my attention:

". . . and in your hearts there is covetousness," he'd say.

Of course, I knew what that meant. I wanted something that wasn't mine; I knew all about that. Like those shoes at the commissary. They were the most beautiful shoes I'd ever seen, and have them I must. The only way to get them was to pay for them myself, and a dollar-fifty wasn't a minor sum. I was well aware of that. I had managed to get the shoes, but in getting them I had sinned.

The summer before, I had sort of felt the spirit move a little, but not to a frightening degree. Anyway, I decided to save ten per cent of the money I got and give it to the Lord. I kept a simple set of books so I'd know where the Lord stood. I had wanted those yellow shoes like Isom's, and to get them I borrowed some of the Lord's money, which I was going to return, but without interest. Naturally, I had to tell my mother about it when I came home with the new shoes. It was a terrible sin—just terrible.

I had to repay the Lord, since I'd promised (my mother said), and I couldn't wear the shoes to the Summer Revival. It seemed like a high price to me, to pay for nothing. My mother had nothing to worry about. I got caught in the rain one afternoon with the yellow shoes, and that ended them quickly. They fell apart.

I stopped squirming for a moment. Hadn't the Lord punished

me for whatever sin I'd committed? Wasn't it His rain that had ruined my shoes? Had I not replaced His money? The preacher could lump it. I'd sinned, yes, but for sinning I'd paid. What was the price of a little sin, anyway?

Then came the part about dancing being a creation of the Devil himself. That was no problem, since I didn't dance. But smoking was a terrible thing in the sight of the Lord, said Brother Hull.

I began to squirm again. True, I wasn't a confirmed user of sinful tobacco, but I had smoked a little with Isom and others. They hadn't said it was sinful, but they weren't speaking the words of the Lord, and I knew that. As a matter of fact, I'd heard it said that Isom was a "no-count nigger and got what he deserved." While I resented such reference to my friend, I couldn't help but agree that Isom had been a pretty bad sinner.

After a good hour of sweating it out, and I thinking several times the Lord was likely to take me any time with a bolt of lightning or something, Brother Hull would call a halt to the sermon for that day. We'd be dismissed with a prayer not less than ten minutes long. In my less reverent moments, I'd wonder to myself if perhaps the Lord didn't get tired of bowing His head, too. I knew I did.

That was about the way I'd react to the first meeting of the annual Summer Revival, suffering something terrible for whatever sins I'd committed since the last one.

Chapter 8

As one approached the camp from the east, the first sight revealed a few scattered houses to the north, just off a graded road at the top of the hill. Down the hill there was a sharp curve to the right. At the curve a graded road continued straight into the largest area of the camp. To the left of the dirt road was the commissary; continuing in a straight line, you saw the first house, also to the left, which was ours. The houses continued

43

for perhaps a third of a mile, then the road turned to the right sharply, making an elongated horseshoe when followed back to the state highway.

Another graded road turned off the highway about a hundred yards from the front of our house and intersected the camp road between the commissary and the house. This closed the open end of the horseshoe. In that area between our house and the highway there was a good seventy-five yards of usable space for various activities. Facing the inside of the horseshoe, the usable space was perhaps two hundred yards deep. It would appear, of course, that the entire area would be available to use, but after the two hundred or so yards, you began running into cow pens, chicken coops and the like.

As a result of the over-all layout, and since it was almost the center area of the camp, the baseball games, boxing, basketball, movies and revival meetings were held directly in front of our house.

Each summer we could depend on two tents being put up in the area, though not at the same time. One would house the "picture show," the other revival meeting. As a general rule, the show arrived first and usually stayed for three or four days. All the movies were Westerns, usually starring Tom Mix, but occasionally Tim McCoy or Hoot Gibson. It was always a happy time when the show truck pulled into camp. For the most part, the question was, first: who's in the show? Followed by: how many reels, five or six? A six-reeler was a bonus of sorts; it was quite long. I always managed to get a pass for the first night because I'd get a job helping put up the tent. The other nights were a problem. I had to depend on a handout from my mother, and if I got into any sort of trouble, I was punished by being kept at home. By and large, the mothers had a bunch of little angels for the better part of a week each summer. I remember washing my feet at night without even being threatened.

One summer the revival got to camp before the movies, and I recall how the "picture show man" griped about a lack of attendance, blaming it on the preaching. How could he expect a bunch of folks who'd just been revived to go to a wicked picture show? He didn't understand our religion at all. The movie oper-

44

ator had said something about the "damned preachers being the ruination of the world," and he swore dreadfully.

The movie fellow didn't make the same mistake twice. Thereafter, he got to camp before we all got religion. Business was better like that. By the summer following his mistake, I'd forgotten my sacred vow not to attend a wicked show. I could always repent, and often did.

I was never as happy to see Brother Hull pitch his tent as I was to see the "picture show man." Having been seasoned to the annual revival for every summer as far back as I could recall, I accepted it without rebelling. The revival lasted much longer than the movies. It took God longer to get things straightened out than it took Tom Mix.

The preacher was a kindly old man, a Methodist, whom we all called Brother Hull. I'd never known him by any prefix other than "Brother." He always stayed at the boarding house, delaying our meals by his long blessing of the food. I saw no point in it, and always looked around while the blessing was being asked. I saw a few others looking around, too, but when they got caught, they'd bow their heads quickly. A time or two my mother caught me with my head unbowed, and I got her sermon in addition to the 10:00 A.M and 7:00 P.M. ones by Brother Hull. I always wondered how I got caught with an unbowed head if my mother's head hadn't been not a little unbowed also. I asked about it, but I didn't get far with that line of questioning.

Brother Hull and I had a few talks about saving my soul. To me, the kind old man talked in riddles. The business about the Father, the Son and the Holy Ghost confused me. I inquired about it, and the explanation confused me more. I seemed to be pretty wicked, inasmuch as I was a rather big boy and still hadn't given my heart to Jesus and the Methodist Church. I couldn't understand how anybody wanted such a sinful and wicked heart as mine. While I didn't put it in these words then, I look back and think my reasoning was relatively simple. Anything that would have me as a member, I didn't want to be a member of, because I knew me better than it did, and that isn't saying much for either party.

Also, in looking back, I find that my belief in God continues to grow deeper with each passing year. Were there no other evidence of God, I'd have to believe in Him because I don't know how else I survived those revival meetings and fundamentalistic teachings.

Whether or not a person had been saved the previous summer mattered little; the good Brother Hull always entered the camp and found it infested with sinners, large and small. My mother and Brother Hull knew the Will of God, and there was no question about that; what's more, they knew what God had in mind with reference to me. I think everyone knew God's will with reference to me, except me. I had no idea.

I was confused about many things, things around me, but mostly about things within me. I went to the services twice a day, every day, and the more I went, the more questions came to my mind. I resolved the Father, Son and Holy Ghost theory in a rather simple manner. I decided these Three didn't make much difference anyway; after all, They didn't work for Batson and Hatten, nor did I go to school with Them or know Them in any manner whatsoever.

Thirty-odd years after my un-Christian confusion at Carnes, my dear friend, Easton King, a newspaperman here in Mississippi, remarked one evening over a bottle of bourbon that "There's absolutely one thing you can depend on, and that's that there are no absolutes." King would probably have been bounced from the tent had he said a thing like that at the Carnes camp meetings, provided, of course, that any of us had known what "absolute" meant. There were absolutes; indeed, there were absolute absolutes. Brother Hull knew what they were, he told us. It boiled down to this: "If you ain't fer the Lord, then you're ag'in Him, and if you're ag'in the Lord, you're fer the Devil." Brother Hull said, as my mother had told me many times, that anyone who smoked, dranked, cursed, gambled, wanted things which weren't his and didn't go to church was on the wide road to "hell-fire and damnation."

I believed it. However, believing it didn't make it easy to live with. So many things I was told tied me down, and that made me uncomfortable. It worried me to think I was defensive when I heard someone say that my friend Isom was a wicked, sinful

46

man. I knew what the word of the Lord was, and yet I refused to accept the fact that Isom was going to hell. Why should he? He was my friend, and anyone who'd been kind to me didn't deserve to go to hell. But he was supposed to, by the word of the Lord, and that I knew, because Brother Hull and my mother said so. I got the impression that a good person, a Christian, especially a Methodist, would never be taken from this world in the manner Isom had gone. Instead, he'd die in bed with his shoes off, and certainly Isom didn't die with his shoes off—just his pants. (I've often thought that should count for something.)

In one of our talks once, I inquired of Brother Hull about why Jesus had wept. I don't recall anyone having told me that God and Jesus were the same, but I could never decide on any difference in the two. My question was: "Brother Hull, it says in the Bible 'Jesus wept'; I wonder why God had to cry?" The good man explained that it was because men were so wicked and sinful. Pondering that, I inquired if God didn't have the power to keep men from being wicked and sinful, and, if so, why not just put a stop to sinning and stop crying about it? Brother Hull told my mother. She had a talk with me, in the presence of Brother Hull. I was informed that until I reached my twelfth birthday she was responsible to God for the sins I committed. I didn't want my mother going to hell because of me, and I worried an hour or two about my sinful ways.

I must confess that while I wasn't too happy about my mother's getting my sins chalked up against her, I used it to my own advantage many times. When my mother and I would have a difference of opinion, which was too often, I'd "get even" by going out and sinning all over the place. I'd smoke—sinful. I'd steal Coke bottles from the commissary and break them on the railroad. I'd sit and curse as long as I could think of words; then I'd repeat myself. What's more, running out of known sins, I'd commence to sit and think evil thoughts. Why not? I'd ask myself. When she finds out the sins against her, she'll let me have my way about a few things. It was simple logic.

Eventually, I lost that battle, too. I learned that the sins I'd committed in my mother's name were retroactive and would be charged against me when I was twelve. I thought, "Ain't this a hell of a mess. They must have more bookkeeping in Heaven than at the commissary." There was no way to be free; I was told I could not escape the Lord, that He knew the fall of the sparrow. Often at night I'd lie in bed and cry because of my difference of opinion with the Lord. How many lonely hours I've spent because I couldn't help being the way I was. These things I didn't discuss with anyone, because every time I'd try, I found where I'd been doing something against the will of God.

There were other problems with the Lord. I decided once to be a Christian, even if it killed me. I kept up with the Lord's ten per cent with a keen sense of responsibility, knowing full well that if the Lord knew about a sparrow, He'd get me if I cheated in keeping His account. Often I'd make as much as fifty to seventy-five cents by selling peanuts. The Lord's share would be held out and properly recorded. One time I set my peanuts down and played baseball, and a shower came up and ruined five bags. That was twenty-five cents, gross. I deducted the amount from the Lord's part. Later, before I learned never to talk to Brother Hull, I told him what I'd done. I explained to him that I figured if the Lord wanted His in peanuts, it was all right with me. I was made to give the Lord His money back.

My father seldom spoke. He attended to his business and stayed out of that of others. I doubt seriously that a total of all the words I ever heard him speak would fill three of these pages. He was exceptionally kind and gentle. Of course, he was a sinner; he never spent over ten minutes in his life without a wicked pipe stuck in his mouth. Most of his words were in defense of me. On the business of saving my soul, he was on my side. I overheard him talking to my mother once and he said in his soft, kind voice, "I think it best you and the preacher leave the boy alone. He'll find out what he needs to know when he needs to know it." For a few days they left me alone, but I suppose they couldn't deny the will of God too long.

It was most difficult to resist the pressure as the revivals continued year after year. I say in complete honesty that by the end of a two- or three-week tour for God, Brother Hull had me frightened silly. Always, but always, Brother Hull would stop the singing as the doors of the church stood wide open awaiting the

sinners to march forward and give their hearts to Jesus. With
the joyful noise stopped, he would proceed to relate that just the
other day at some place or other where he was reviving a group
of sinners, he had begged a certain young man to step up for
Jesus' sake, and the fellow had refused. And lo, Brother Hull
would say, the man who had refused to be saved and thereby
get a passport to Heaven went out of the meeting and met with
an awful accident and was killed that very night.

Then the singing would begin once more, and sinners would
march up and shake the preacher's hand and give their hearts
to Jesus. It was a frightening thing to me. Knowing how very
wicked I was, I often left the tent to walk a few yards home,
knowing full well I'd never make it. How lonely I was! How
long I'd lie awake at night! How I wept, but not for the sins of
man.

When I was about eleven or twelve, I could resist no longer.
I knew I'd lost another battle. With the promise of a new suit,
and with the threat of going to hell, and with several nudges in
the side, I walked the sawdust trail. I gave my heart to Jesus
with hesitation and reluctance—and with disgust for myself.
There must have been much joy in Heaven that night, but there
wasn't any joy in my heart. I had sold out.

After I got my new shirt collar wet from the sprinkling, I
gave serious thought to becoming a minister. When I think back
on it, I am surprised. All one summer I read the Bible with care
and sang hymns to the top of my voice and quoted Scripture
without provocation. The worst thing I did in the name of the
Lord was to get into a fight. A fellow much older and larger
than I told me that Jesus was just another man and there wasn't
anything to that religion stuff. In the name of the Lord, I hit
him. I presume it was also in the name of the Lord that he beat
hell out of me. That was the last person I attempted to convert.
I've often thought that I, being a Christian, was going to love
him, even if I had to crack his skull. It didn't work—seldom
does, I've observed.

I was still lonely; questions nagged at me day and night. I
refused to discuss the matter with anyone, knowing that what I
had to know would be learned when I had to know it.

49

I did not develop my religion-sex theory at the time of my conversion, but I wasn't too old when certain ideas entered my mind with reference to the two. In recalling some of the revival days, I began to put little pieces into place.

There were insignificant comments made in my presence. A good dip of snuff made for long hours of sociability, and most of the women in the camp dipped snuff. Since it was a sin to drink, play cards and enjoy life in most ways, the women held quilting parties. At these parties, ten, twelve, even fifteen of them would seat themselves around a quilt, fill their lower lip with Garrett's, then proceed to sit and spit for a spell. Often I'd be forced to accompany my mother because of weather, a broken bone, burned feet, or some other reason. I sat quietly and listened to them. I picked up such information as to how Jane and Henry got married in August and their baby came in April; and other couples were commented on in the same hushed manner. Since then, I've been interested in the close connection between sex and religion.

In the early spring of 1934, the timber had been cut and families began to move away from the Carnes camp. My father was kept on for a while because he could do machine-shop work as well as blacksmith, and repairs were needed on various equipment while the tracks into the woods were being pulled. Finally, in early summer, the work was finished. All the track was up; all the buildings had been sold, and my father was unemployed. He was without money, too. Earlier, the bank at Lumberton had closed and what he had had was lost.

At the age of thirteen, a stage of my life came to a close. I was a graduate of the Carnes Consolidated School, a doubting Christian, and for the first time in my life I knew what it was not to have a dime.

My father only smoked his pipe and kept his counsel.

An era had come to a close. The rape of the virgin pine forests had been complete. The days of the giant sawmills, the scattered logging camps, would be no more in south Mississippi. With the close of the logging era, Federal-State hard-surfaced, two-lane highways inched their way through the region. Labor unions were beginning to organize in a few towns; instead of branch

50

water to mix with their corn liquor, Mississippians were beginning to use 7 Up and Coca-Cola. With the end of the logging era, progress began in earnest in the Magnolia State.

Chapter 9

The house into which we moved when we left the Carnes camp was, by 1934 Mississippi standards, not a shack; however, even by those standards, it was as close as one could come to it.

It was a frame building of four rooms, built like a box, with a corrugated tin roof. On one side was an enclosed, shedlike room. It was falling apart, but so was the rest of the house. In this area I set up my first laboratory.

The location of our new home was about a half mile off the U.S. highway, approximately four miles south of Pleasant at a railroad freight stop named Barton. Inasmuch as no one had written a history of Barton, Mississippi, I could only guess by the appearance of things that it had at one time been the site of a logging camp. However, when we moved there it was a farm owned by a "company up North," wherever that was. The house into which we moved had obviously been intended as a sharecropper's home. The management of the farm was under the direction of Ray Willies, who certainly proved to be a friend of ours. While I knew about money, having used some of the Lord's, I was not aware of the seriousness of the situation at the time. I heard my parents speak of money, its shortage and the loss in the bank, but I failed to realize how badly off we were.

Chester Hare, whom I'd known as far back as I could remember, was a big, red-faced, serious man. He was in the piling business. He'd buy timber and cut only those trees which would make good utility poles.

Instead of returning to the farm on which he was born in Lincoln County, Mississippi, where he owned a small farm of about eighty acres, my father had decided to go to work for Mr. Hare. In midsummer of 1934, my father and Mr. Hare had gone into the woods south of Carnes for the purpose of marking trees to be cut. While looking over a tree in the woods that day, my father felt a prick on his left leg. He'd spent many days in the woods in his life and thought the prick to be a briar. He paid no attention to it, and only moved his leg. The prick continued to irritate him, and again he moved his leg, still not looking down at the ground. Finally, after feeling the prick three or four times, he noticed it wasn't a briar at all. He saw the stubby body of a moccasin protruding from his overall. Without becoming excited, my father reached down and took the head of the snake into his hands, placed his ax on the tail, then stretched the snake, turned loose suddenly, and the snake snapped away from the calf of his leg. Then, with the deliberation with which he did everything, my father took his ax and chopped the snake into several pieces.

By nature, the moccasin is a water snake and is one of the three poisonous snakes in this country. However, the "copperhead," a species of the moccasin, is often found in the hills. The poison of the snake works on the blood cells, breaking them down, and often causes death. Bites by the snake have resulted in death in less than twenty-four hours, depending on the treatment and the time elapsed before treatment. In the case of my father, the time elapsed was three or four hours, which was much too long.

Practicing medicine in Pleasant was a wonderful old country doctor, S. L. Olden. Dr. Olden was sent for and met my father at our house upon his arrival. He began the treatment by splitting my father's leg and attempting to pump out as much of the poison as possible. Under the circumstances, it wasn't much. Then the good doctor began to apply hot epsom-salts water, soaked into gauze. That was the extent of the available medical knowledge. Dr. Olden sat with my father for almost twenty-four hours. Dead-tired, he'd return to Pleasant for a little rest, and then come back to my father's side. Dr. Olden was a frank and honest man. He told my mother that he didn't see how my father could possibly live more than thirty-six hours. However, he didn't stop his efforts for a second.

For a week my father was on the brink of death. We didn't

52

know from one hour until the next whether he'd live. My mother spent most of the time crying, saying she didn't know what she'd do if she lost Jim. As for me, I was just plain mad. The whole business didn't make sense. Here was the best man I'd ever known, a man who spent his life at hard work, a man who was kind and generous, lying there dying from a snake bite. There was no sense to it at all. Had I not been told that the Lord loved all His children, and especially those who minded their own business? While it was true that my father seldom attended church, I'd seen him so many times get up from his bed in the cold winter and go to the aid of people he hardly knew. What the hell kind of fellow was the Lord, anyway? My father had done nothing to merit such suffering—to the Lord or anyone else. I was angry and upset, and the pieces of the puzzle wouldn't fit into place any way I viewed them. My reaction was simply "To hell with the Lord, if that's the kind of person He is." To think such a thought was frightening. Confusion is a forerunner of anger, and I was confused.

My father, except for his heart, was not a large man, possibly about five feet eight or nine inches tall, but he was a powerful man, strong through his shoulders and back. Once I'd seen him hold off an advancing Model-T Ford; another time I'd seen him lift one end of a rail, and for him to lift a cross tie was a matter which required no effort whatsoever.

Yet this wonderful man lay in the room next to me and begged God to let him die—such was the pain he endured. For the most part, he was in a coma the first week, but during his waking hours—how he suffered. I wept often as I'd hear him groaning in agony, begging for death. I wept because I was angry. I wept because I hated suffering of any kind by anyone, especially my father. I wept because I was unable to give him relief from the suffering.

Many were the times I was faced with a decision of the greatest importance, even for an adult to make. I wanted my father's suffering stopped, and the only way, it seemed, was to bring about his death. I gave it serious consideration; I'd give him something, anything to relieve his suffering. Then, and for what reasons I know not, I couldn't bring myself to do it. In a way much less real, I suffered with my father.

Finally, after about two weeks of agony, my father began to improve. His weight had dropped and he looked like a ghost. His leg had swollen so much that Dr. Olden feared it was going to rupture. I'll never forget the appearance of his leg. From the place of the bite, in the calf, upward to his hip, my father's leg was the color of copper. Whether this was a natural color of swelling or the result of the poison, I never learned. Improvement was slow. It was almost two months before he could stand, and then not for long, because of weakness from having been in bed.

In the meantime, the situation had become just short of desperate with us. We had no income, no savings, and tremendous bills had piled up. Whether or not my mother explained to Dr. Olden about his fee, I don't know, but I talked with him and told him that we couldn't pay him and that I didn't know when we could. He was most kind and understanding, and explained to me that a human life was not measured in terms of fees, that if ever we could pay him, he'd appreciate it, inasmuch as doctors had to live, too. When hunger is a bedfellow, a child learns fast about money. I've never forgotten the kindness of Dr. Olden, country doctor of Pleasant, Mississippi.

As it was, my mother had a cow and a flock of chickens. They helped more than I thought possible for anything to help. I would gather eggs, along with milk and butter, take them to Pleasant and swap them for basic needs, such as flour, salt, and sugar. With the help of my mother, I raised a garden and we had vegetables. The matter of house rent was another thing. I spoke with Mr. Ray Willies and explained the situation to him. His reply was "Well, I won't tell anyone you're living there."

Once, while talking with Dr. Olden about paying him, I heard him say something that escaped me at the time, having never heard of such a thing. He explained that the day would come when a working man would be protected by insurance against accidents. He said that sooner or later employers were going to be forced to share in responsibility for their employees. I'd never heard of such a thing, nor had anyone else in the sawmill camps; if they had, it was a subject not discussed in my presence.

During that summer at Barton, I had set up a laboratory consisting of nothing much, which I'd made of whatever material I could find. What I was seeking, I don't know. A little ignorance goes a long, long way. However, the tung tree was a recent import to the area, and the nuts, or fruits, of the tung were poisonous. I recall having worked weeks on a fly spray, using tung nuts as a base. I mixed the mess with kerosene, and while it wouldn't kill a fly, it was effective on mosquitoes. It was some time before I learned my experiment was a failure, that kerosene will kill mosquitoes without the benefit of my tung base. I dissected frogs, lizards and anything I could lay hands on, the one exception being snakes. About the only thing I learned was that I didn't learn anything, but it was years before I'd admit that.

Actually, my experiments were, insofar as I knew, the result of my interest in medicine. As far back as I could remember, upon being asked what I wanted to do when I grew up, my reply had been "I want to be a doctor." I'd stood in great wonder at what I'd seen Dr. McNair at the Carnes camp do with broken bones. Once he had let me watch while he sewed up a knife cut on a Negro man. I had felt the sharp sting of the needle as he had worked, but to be able to do such a wonderful thing was to my liking.

It was, all in all, a lonely summer, that one.

On the twelfth day of September in the year 1934, there passed through the doors of the high school in Pleasant, Mississippi, the most ignorant child in the long history of the institution—not only the most ignorant, but probably the most stupid: me.

I had not looked forward to going to high school, except for the fact that there was a laboratory in which I could work with "store bought" equipment.

I found that the only course which would allow me into the lab was in general science, taught by S. J. Brooks, who was also the football coach. Coach Brooks was a nice, pleasant man, but he was not a teacher. The football business being what it was, he had little time for classroom interests. In addition to the general frustration from which I suffered in new surroundings, I didn't have a single textbook, for in those days a student had to purchase them at the bookstore. It was impossible for me to buy a book, having no money. Coach Brooks would loan me his textbook when I'd ask for it; however, my poverty embarrassed me, and I seldom used his book.

It was a disappointment that I wasn't allowed to take both biology and chemistry my freshman year. I had argued the matter with the person in command, but to no avail. I resented being told what I could and could not do. After all, how could they know anything about me? I wasn't interested in anything other than those courses which would afford me time in the lab. The general science course offered nothing by way of lab work, except a flashlight and a tennis ball whereby the solar system was explained.

Every day I found myself among two hundred people, more or less, yet I found myself alone. Why such terrible loneliness? Was it because I was so awfully ignorant? Because at thirteen I was the youngest child in the entire school? Because for the entire year I had two shirts, which my mother had made from the same piece of cloth, and only one pair of pants? (Because of this, I was asked by other students if I ever changed clothes.)

The year moved slowly. I'd become accustomed to many things, but never did I become adjusted to such references as my being "a Beau Brummel," "a fashion plate," "the best-dressed person at school," and other like remarks. I found them hard to take, but I did without a single fight. I don't know why I didn't strike back in the only way I knew—perhaps because I was afraid. Perhaps I took the ridicule because I had begun to wonder about so many things I'd been taught that didn't stack up. I had been taught that God would take care of those who didn't have. Of course, I had entertained grave doubts, but that first year in high school provided me with proof that someone had misled me. God had nothing to do with it, was my conclusion. Those who had—took. Those who didn't have were reduced to one pair of tennis shoes—that was me, my leather shoes with the genuine leather heels having worn beyond repair.

56

How did one go about taking? I didn't know; I only presumed there was a way and that sooner or later I'd find it.

What with being driven more and more inside myself, and with my introduction to the solar system, I concluded with great care that God did not exist. I related my conclusion to a class one day, explaining carefully that the very existence of a solar system disproved the existence of God. I took care to avoid any mention of my personal feelings. I was quite scientific about it. After I had denounced God as a figment of the imagination of weak men, my troubles began in earnest. The reaction of students, and teachers as well, was not understandable to me. Why should they make fun of me because I thought what I did? Could I help it if I had discovered something they didn't know? Having taken what I considered a reasonable point of view, it was only natural that I defend it, which I did. Every day of my life I reached the boiling point, but not once did I resort to fighting. I stood alone, and it was a lonely stand, but to back down was out of the question.

For a number of reasons, therefore, I became an atheist.

My freshman year dragged on, and I grew in loneliness, bewilderment and confusion, but not in learning; and of more importance, not an iota of wisdom was mine to claim. Finally, in May of 1935, my freshman year closed. My score was three F's and one D, the passing grade being in agriculture; also, in one year I had become an atheist, an introvert, and had acquired an interest in astronomy, which I still have.

In addition, I had serious doubts about the innate "goodness" of man—especially me. I had a strong suspicion that we were all bastards, and I knew for a fact that God didn't love us.

While I was making an academic and social splash that first year at the high school in Pleasant, two relatively important things were in the process of happening. Up in north central Mississippi the Snopeses were taking over, laying hands to everything that wasn't nailed down. In south central Mississippi, the Easts continued to lack the imagination of the Snopeses. Nonetheless, my father continued to improve, getting back his strength slowly.

Again that summer my mother and I planted a garden,

milked the cow, and I sold whatever we could produce. During the year my father was laid up from the snake bite, Sol Barber, whom we had known since the days of the first sawmill camp, had secured a contract with the Hercules Powder Company of Hattiesburg to furnish them with stumps. Hercules was a naval-stores operation, producing resin, turpentine and several hundred by-products from pine stumps. Pine stumps were plentiful. I often thought that all we had were pine stumps and boll weevils.

Mr. Barber approached my father and suggested that if he and Lynn Barber, one of his nephews, would go into the stump-hauling business together, he would let a sub-contract to them. My father gave the matter thought, decided he was up to it, and the partnership was formed.

My father did not have a truck, although one was necessary to the stump business. However, a few years before moving from the Carnes camp he had bought a 1929 Chevrolet coach, and, except for some ancient furniture, that was all he owned.

My father traded the car in on a Ford truck, the roughest thing I'd ever seen, and Lynn Barber and J. C. East became capitalists. They worked so hard hauling stumps that it was three years before they went broke.

Shortly after going into the stump-hauling business, my father decided we'd move into the village of Pleasant. So the East family moved to town, into a three-room house not more than thirty yards from the cemetery. I never became accustomed to walking past it on dark nights.

Chapter 10

We moved to Pleasant in the late summer. I needed clothes and had decided it would help if I had a few books in school that year. I approached Jesse Wild and asked about a job. He was a large man, slightly fat, with a dark complexion and jet-black hair.

"What the hell can you do?" he asked.

"Well," I replied, "I don't know—but I can try anything."

"Do you know how to cut ice?"

"No, sir."

"Can you read scales?"

"No, sir."

"Can you lift a hundred pounds of ice or cottonseed meal?"

"I don't know."

"You're a dumb little son-of-a-bitch, ain't you?"

My face felt flushed. Several persons standing around the store laughed. Among them was Jesse's son, Jesse, Jr., who was about my age. My impulse was to loosen several teeth in each mouth there, beginning with Jesse Wild. I was bewildered, confused, angry. I muttered something like "Yes, sir, maybe so," and turned to walk out.

He called me back and said I could work for him if I'd work hard and learn to do the things he'd asked about. I thanked him and began sweeping out the store.

The stores in Pleasant ran along the highway, which was parallel to the railroad. All the stores faced the tracks. Southward, the business section began with a grocery store, then a garage, then an alley, a drugstore; a road intersected the highway, then on the corner another grocery store, a barbershop, another grocery store, the post office, an alley. The Jesse Wild General Merchandise enterprise began at that alley and extended for approximately sixty-five feet to another alley, across from which was another garage.

The building that housed the store and market had been built by Jesse some ten or twelve years earlier. On one side of the store was a barbershop and on the other a restaurant. Both businesses were under the roof of the main building, with the store in the center. The restaurant, twelve feet wide, ran the depth of the entire building, but the barbershop was only about half the depth, because behind the barbershop Jesse had his office, and behind that was a storeroom. The building was approximately sixty feet deep.

Entering the front door of the Wild store, one saw to the right an assortment of dry goods, bolt cloth, shoes, hats, thread, but-

59

tons, pants, shirts, underwear and numerous items of the like. The grocery section took up the left side. First was an enormous candy case, then a small showcase in which tobacco was kept. After the tobacco case were a few feet of empty counter. Behind the entire counter shelves were filled with packaged items such as cornmeal, rice, sugar, coffee, and beans of two or three kinds. At the end of the counter, a door opened into the restaurant. Looking farther back, beyond the counter, one saw such items as horse collars, trace chains and an assortment of hardware. On the counter another glass case contained smaller items— pocket knives, fish hooks, etc. At the end of this area a door opened into the meat market. It was screened, but in spite of that the flies had a field day. In addition to the flies there were several creeping and crawling critters around. The back door of the market led out to a sausage mill and the ice house. Jesse's office, located almost behind the dry-goods counter, was a small room, but Jesse had managed to get a chair and a couch in it, besides the usual roll-top desk and a safe.

I'd not been employed two days when a big, black Buick stopped out front one afternoon. I was refilling the drink box and puttting ice in it when Jesse yelled at me to "go see what them people want." Jesse and his son sat within ten feet of the parked car, doing nothing. I stopped my work, dried my hands, and went out.

"Do you have a couple of good cold Cokes?" the driver asked.

"I'm sorry, sir, they ain't real cold. I just put them in the box a few minutes ago—but they're pretty cool," I replied.

I heard Jesse snort. The man thanked me and asked if Mr. Wild were in. He got out of his car and went into the store, where he carried on a polite conversation with Jesse for a few minutes. Then he returned to his car and drove away.

Jesse, in angry tones, screamed at me: "Goddamn it! How dumb can you be?"

I didn't answer. After all, I didn't know.

"Do you know who that was in that car?"

I shook my head.

"Can't you talk?"

"Yes, sir," I said. "I don't know who the man was in the car."

60

"That was Frank W. Foote, the president of the First National Bank in Hattiesburg. That's who he was, by God."

I didn't know what I was supposed to do about it.

"Jesus," Jesse continued, "but you're a dumb bastard."

"Yes, sir, you said that."

"By God, when anybody wants a cold Coke, you've got cold Cokes to sell. Do you understand that?"

"Well, Jesse, these in this box ain't cold. I could have got them at the restaurant, I guess, but I just didn't think about it," I explained.

"Jesus!" You goddamned dumb fool! I've got cold Cokes for sale. You get them out of my box. Next door, hell!"

Junior piped up and said about the same thing that his father had been saying, leaving out the profanity.

Upon the comment by Junior, I couldn't hold it any longer. I walked over to him. "If you open your big, fat mouth just once more, I'll break your damned neck."

Jesse was beside himself. He continued ranting.

I had a dime in my pocket. When he stopped cursing me long enough, I said, "I'll be glad to pay for the drinks I didn't sell, Jesse," and I handed the dime to him.

I felt his open hand slap hard against the side of my head. It sent me sprawling on the floor. I picked myself up and walked back to the storeroom and sat on a sack of feed and wept. I thought I'd never be able to stop weeping. Slowly, as I did stop, my bewilderment turned to anger. I began to think how I could kill him. Then I realized, suddenly, that to kill him was not the answer. I didn't know the answer, but to take human life wasn't it, no matter what.

He kept my dime.

I worked from 6:30 A.M. until Jesse decided that everyone in Pleasant had gone to bed for the night. Often it was eight or nine o'clock before I could go home.

I swept out the store first thing every morning. After that, I worked the drink box, draining water and refilling it with bottled drinks and ice. Then, with that finished, I'd have the pleasure of cleaning the market, where a huge icebox held something like 300 pounds of ice. The first two blocks I could manage, but the one that went on top was difficult for me to lift. I caused further trouble with my boss by cutting the ice into two pieces and lifting them without too much trouble.

He did not like this arrangement. He instructed me not to cut the ice any more, but to get it up there as best I could. It was impossible for me to lift a hundred pounds of ice head-high. I did the best I could, which amounted to dropping a hundred pounds of ice from about chest-high to the floor. It shook the entire building and shattered into countless pieces. The two Wilds rushed back to the market from their chairs in the front of the store. I didn't offer to buy the ice.

After a week's employment with Jesse Wild, I waited on Saturday night to get my pay. I didn't know what it was going to be because I'd not asked. I had needed work, and I was in no position to quibble when I was hired. Finally, Jesse staggered from his office where he'd been drinking for hours.

"What the hell do you want?" he asked of me.

"Well, I thought it was payday."

"You honestly think you deserve pay?"

I didn't answer.

"I don't think you do," he said. Finally, he continued, "I'm paying you fifty cents a week. How many drinks did you drink this week?"

"Two," I told him.

"Okay, that means you get forty cents." With that he gave me the money and ordered me to be sure I made a ticket for anything I got in the store: drinks, candy, etc.

He give me no chance to explain that I'd paid for the drinks when I drank them.

I planned numerous times to kill Jesse Wild. I knew I could never kill him, but it was a pleasure to think about it. I vowed to get even with Jesse—some day I'd do it. I could wait; I could keep my temper when I'd think about the great pleasure I would have.

Junior Wild was another matter. I wasn't sure I could hold my temper where he was concerned. I didn't plot against him; I didn't think of that faraway day when I could get even. I decided I had no choice but to put up with him. My needs were

62

real. School was about to open and I wanted another shirt and a pair of pants. How I wanted to buy a pair of shoes that weren't tennis shoes.

The stump-hauling business wasn't going too well, as nearly as I could gather from bits of conversation I overheard. My father had enough trouble without my asking him for things I wanted.

I continued to work at the store for fifty cents a week. By the time school opened I had my new pants and two new shirts, but the same old tennis shoes had to do.

During school, before and after classes, I worked at the store. I'd get to work at 6:30 A.M. and do my chores; then I'd walk the mile from the store to the school. Any number of times Jesse would send Junior to school in the truck while I finished sweeping and cleaning up at the store. I'm sure the walk did me good, but such cannot be said for the feeling I had about not being asked to ride. After school I went directly to the store and worked until it closed at night. With the coming of winter my duties increased. In the mornings I had to build a fire in the potbellied, wood-burning stove in the store. On Saturdays I was often sent out to Jesse's farm to gather enough wood to last until the next Saturday. I was much happier when in the woods by myself.

With the opening of school in September of 1935, I had a new English teacher, a dear and kind lady, Miss Thelma Berry. During the first year I'd missed the pleasure of reading from a literature book. I didn't have one to read. Miss Berry insisted that I borrow hers several times. I did, and fell victim to the words written in the book. Except with Miss Berry, I was as withdrawn as possible. With her, I could talk about any number of things in which I'd become interested. I was especially taken by the Romantic poets, and of those my favorite was Shelley. Miss Berry and I spent many hours which gave me great pleasure—I enjoyed groping for a thought, a fleeting idea. Finally, a proud day in my life came: I had saved enough money to buy a literature book. I experienced that wonderful feeling of owning something that gave me great pleasure.

As sympathetic as Miss Berry was, I could never bring myself to talk with her about many things that bothered me. Why was it, being an avowed atheist, that I read and reread the Proverbs? What was more and, to me, much worse, I enjoyed reading them. I also wanted someone to explain to me how a man like my father—a man who had never in his entire life done an injustice to any living soul, a man who had worked with his hands and back to provide for his family, a man who had never lied or cheated anyone—how was it that such a man had nothing, was bitten by a snake, almost died and was not over the ordeal even then, compared to a man like Jesse Wild, with whom lying and cheating and grabbing were a way of life and who was probably the wealthiest man in the town—why the difference? I could not find the answer. I wondered about virtue being its own reward—could be, I decided, but it did nothing to pay for school books and leather shoes.

By the skin of my teeth, I got through school that year, and with one book.

After school was out in the spring I made a decision which startled me. I decided I would stop working for Jesse Wild. I quit. I decided I'd go to the woods camp with my father and Lynn and their crew of Negro workmen. For working in the woods I would get fifty cents a week, plus my room and board.

My tour of duty lasted one week. My father decided I wasn't careful enough with blasting caps and dynamite to be allowed to remain. He also decided that the work I was doing was too heavy for me.

During that week in the woods I came to a conclusion about the stumping business and the way my father operated it. He was going broke. First, he worked as hard as any man he had working for him. Second, he would take money from his pocket and give it to any man who asked for an advance on the next week's salary. More times than I like to recall, I saw him give money to his men from his pocket, saving just enough to buy groceries for the week. I was opposed to it, but I said nothing.

Finally, I had no choice but to return to work for Jesse Wild. However, I had decided I was not going to take any abuse from him.

All I wanted was to be treated like a human being. The old

routine soon resumed. After one especially stormy incident I was angry to the point of exploding, but I thought I was holding it fairly well until I heard myself telling Jesse, "Some day I'm going to get even with you, you big blabber-mouthed bully." I was startled not by what I'd said—I'd been thinking it for months—but by the calmness and determination with which I'd said it.

To say that these were unhappy days is to put it mildly. I was miserable. How did a person get to be treated like a human being? What did one have to do?

There was some pleasure, however. Jesse's wife, a kind and lovely lady, had a set of books in which the great literature of the world was printed. Mrs. Wild let me borrow one book at a time. When I'd finished reading it, I'd get another. I first encountered Goethe, Schiller, Plato and Voltaire in those books. The only happiness I experienced was late at night, reading at the kitchen table by the flickering yellow light of a kerosene lamp.

The exact time it began is something I don't recall, but Jesse Wild and I engaged in a battle of wits. One of many disgusting things I was a part of was selling melted-down ice at the same price as if it were full weight. Ice was purchased in Hattiesburg in 400-pound blocks. It was hauled to Pleasant in a one-half-ton pick-up and stored in the ice house behind the store. Jesse sold ice for seventy cents a hundred. From fifty pounds on down it cost the customer about one cent per pound.

Often a 400-pound block of ice would melt down well over fifty pounds, yet Jesse said it would be cut as if full weight. "After all," he said, "I've got ice and if anybody gets it, they'll pay my price." I found it harder and harder to cut a piece of ice into ten or fifteen weights and sell it, knowing full well that it was far short of what the customer was paying for.

The battle began. What I did was relatively simple. I'd take the ice into the market and weigh it and sell it for whatever the price should be, not for what it was supposed to be.

One day the customer happened to be a Negro man, Calvin Jones, a Baptist lay preacher. I tied a piece of string around the small block of ice for him, looked at it and decided it was a good ten cents short of what it was supposed to be.

"Well, Calvin," I said, "this will be fifteen cents. I think it's a little underweight."

He thanked me and turned to walk away, when Jesse's booming voice sounded from the market door. "How much did you charge him for that ice?" he demanded to know.

"That's a two-bit piece of ice," I said.

"I know what it is, but how much did you get?"

Calvin hesitated; I told him to go ahead, that I'd take care of the matter. I didn't reply to Jesse's last question. I stood on the ice-house porch, not knowing exactly what I should do.

"Goddamn it," he shouted, "get your stupid ass in here."

Calvin turned to me and said, "I'll pray for him, young man."

"You do that. And you might include me in it, too."

I did not rush into the market. I took my time, not to aggravate Jesse, but rather because I knew too well what to expect. Jesse held open the door and, like a condemned man, I entered the market, stopped, leaned against the refrigerator and looked at him.

He began by demanding to know what price I'd charged Calvin for the ice.

"Fifteen cents," I told him. Had I had a dime of my own, I think I'd have lied and given Jesse the twenty-five cents. I handed him the money I had.

"Fifteen cents! Goddamn! Fifteen cents for two bits' worth of ice!" He shouted these words at me.

"Fifteen cents," I muttered. "That's all the ice was worth, Jesse. It had melted 'way down." I waited for the storm I knew was coming just as soon as Jesse could talk, or scream, as the case usually was. His black eyes were unblinking and his lips trembled as he stood glaring at me.

"Calvin Jones," he began, "ain't nothing but a goddamned preaching nigger!"

"That didn't change the weight of the ice," I replied.

I never knew whether his fist or open hand struck me, but he struck, knocking my head against the refrigerator. My ears rang, and tears welled in my eyes. I was hurt physically, as well

66

as hurt from humiliation. I did not fall. I stood and stared at the man hovering over me. I didn't know what to say, and if I had, chances are I'd have cried had I opened my mouth.

"You're a no-good, smart-aleck, little adopted bastard," Jesse said to me. "I ought to kick hell out of you, that's what I ought to do, by God."

The word "adopted" stung like an arrow.

"Well, Jesse, it takes a man with guts to do his duty. You ain't nothing but a bucket of guts. Start kicking, by God. Kick hell out of me."

He said not a word, but turned and walked toward the front of the store. As I looked in that direction I saw several men watching. No one spoke. I walked toward the front, a few steps behind Jesse. At the cash drawer I stopped and handed the fifteen cents to Junior and said it was for Calvin's ice. With that I walked out the front door and went home, vowing never to go back.

I spent the balance of the day alternating between anger and self-pity. I spent considerable time, too, wondering about the word "adoption" and what was behind it, what it meant to me. In my heart I knew something was wrong, but what, I wasn't sure. I had no way of knowing. To ask was out of the question; I could never ask either of my parents, or anyone else.

Over the years, since first having heard the word, I'd noticed certain things. We went to Columbia, Mississippi, three or four times each year. My mother's family lived there and they were hell on reunions, having family gatherings at every opportunity. I disliked the things; they bothered me. However, I had noted several things which disturbed me and caused me to wonder. Some of the relatives were overly kind; others never spoke to me, except to tell me to get out of their way or give me an order to do something. Also, I couldn't fail to note that of the eighty-odd who usually gathered at my grandmother's house, I was the only person with red hair, fair complexion and bored with the whole affair. I tried hard to be happy at such gatherings, but I was not a part of them. I withdrew instinctively.

Chapter 11

The next morning I felt better and returned to work at the store with a new and healthier disrespect for Jesse Wild.

Except for one other incident, the summer passed and I survived.

The incident had to do with picking pears. A man with a large truck came to Pleasant in search of green pears, and Jesse arranged to buy them for him, for a fee. One morning I went to work, and Jesse asked how I'd like to make three or four dollars in one day. I was happy at the prospect. Along with three or four other boys, I was to pick pears and be paid by the bushel; thus, the harder I worked, the more I'd make. We worked all day, gathering from several orchards out in the country. I worked like the very devil, counting my money as I'd dump each hamper of pears into the truck. We returned to Pleasant that night, and my income was a little over two dollars for the day's work. The man with the truck told us to go on in the store and get a drink, that he'd be in and pay us. I was exhausted but happy at having earned so much money. That was the most I'd ever made for a single day's work. We pear pickers each uncorked a large root beer and waited. We continued to wait— and wait. When the man didn't show up, we went outside to see what the delay was. The truck was gone!

I had suffered many disappointments, but I'd never before been so tired and disappointed at the same time. We returned to the store, crushed. Then I remembered that Jesse knew the man and would know where he was from.

"Jesse," I asked, "could we use your pick-up and try to catch up with that fellow? You know which way he went."

"Those drinks will be a nickel apiece, boys" was his reply.

"Jesse . . ." I started.

"Jesus, you're stupid," he said to me. "All you boys have learned a lesson today. Never trust anybody out of sight." He laughed long and loud.

"You think it's funny?" I asked.

68

"Hell, yeah, I think it's funny. If you had any sense you would too."

I didn't grin on Saturday night when I learned I'd been docked a day's pay from my fifty-cents-a-week salary.

There were a few things which failed to amuse me.

During the summer we had moved from the three-room house by the cemetery to a four-room house by the railroad. It wasn't much improvement. The financial situation had not changed, but when school opened that September, I had two books for the five subjects I took.

One of my subjects was biology, and I ran into trouble right away. A biology book was the most expensive of those I needed, and I could not afford one. Too, the teacher and I had a difference of opinion. I could not draw a cell. I could see pictures of cells, but to duplicate them was impossible for me. I contended it was useless to draw cells when I could see them pictured in other students' textbooks. I stated my view on the matter with force and conviction in class. As a result I was asked to drop the course. I declined the invitation, stating my views on the subject of my rights with the same force and conviction to the superintendent. I was suspended from school for two weeks. The suspension had a disastrous effect on my grades. I flunked plane geometry as well as biology.

My attitude was one of cynicism, bordering on bitterness. My interest in literature continued to grow and I read a good bit in the library, the contents of which were limited. My chief interest was in biographical books. I read of such men as Da Vinci, Edison, Lincoln, Lee, Jackson and Franklin, and for Franklin I could never develop any great interest or respect. It was interesting to me that Franklin was looked on as such a great man when I knew well he'd stolen many of his little stories from Indian literature, which I had read in Mrs. Wild's books of the world's great literature. I ran into several items which were identical, except that Franklin had changed the situation and characters to fit his time and need. To me this was dishonest, and I questioned it in talks I had with Miss Berry, who had continued to be nice, even kind to me, but was somewhat bewildered by my attitude toward almost everything.

69

Not once during my days in school did it seem a bit odd that I was reading literature instead of science subject matter, in view of my avowed aim to become a doctor. My grades in English were a sight to behold, so Miss Berry said. We'd have a month of grammar, which I failed each time, and the grammar would be followed by a month of literature, in which I did fairly well. The F's and A's would be balanced out and I'd usually get by with a D.

At the end of my third year in high school, I again decided not to work for Jesse during the summer. My clothing situation had improved somewhat. I had managed to get a pair of leather shoes, not nearly so sporty as my yellow box-toed ones had been, but serviceable nonetheless. What with two pairs of pants and four or five shirts, I decided to be independent. With school out, I decided to become a mechanic. Joe Simmons and Gene Reynolds owned the Pleasant Motor Company. I talked with Joe, and he said I could come to work and see if I liked it, but he couldn't pay me anything at first. That was okay with me; independence comes high, I figured.

Joe was a kind man who seldom spoke an unnecessary word. He was a good mechanic and had infinite patience with engines and with people. I liked Joe as well as any other person I knew. I liked the work in the shop. I received a great amount of satisfaction from being able to make minor repairs on engines; to make an engine run because of my efforts was indeed a thrill. I made mistakes, but Joe was kind and patient and showed me how to avoid the same mistake twice. I was surprised at the end of the first week when Joe gave me fifty cents. I told him I couldn't take it, that it was not in our agreement. He said he figured I was worth as much to him as I was to Jesse Wild, whom he didn't seem to like especially.

One day Jesse walked into the shop, called me over to the side and said he needed me at the store. He'd pay me one dollar a week if I'd work for him. Like Oscar Wilde, I could resist everything except temptation. I talked with Joe about it and he said it was all right with him if I went to work for Jesse, but if I wanted to come back and work in the shop I'd have a job there.

So it was that I broke my vow again. I returned to the same

never-failing routine of being Jesse's scapegoat. For a dollar a week my responsibilities increased. I was often sent in the pick-up truck to Hattiesburg to haul ice back to Pleasant. I learned to handle a 400-pound block of ice with skill. I had to learn or break my back, and I was never fond of back-breaking work, though I had had some experience with it. The battle of wits continued between Jesse and me. I found that he was drinking more and more, and to me it was a sickening sight. I found he was cheating more and more, and to me that was disgusting. The cheating was a problem for me, and a very serious one. How could I, with full knowledge of what I was doing, cheat a man who needed every cent he had to take care of his family? I was often a first-class bastard, but cheating for Jesse was something I couldn't bring myself to do. So, I undertook to play God. When I knew Jesse had cheated a person in some way, I'd give him extra measure in whatever it was I was selling him. Not only did I continue to sell ice by its weight, but I sold meat, cloth and groceries in a like manner. Naturally, I did not make my dishonest honesty known to anyone.

Part of my job was to weigh out various grocery items, such as sugar, coffee, beans, rice, cornmeal and certain seeds. We sacked those items and stacked them on the shelves in ten-, fifteen-, twenty-five- and fifty-cent bags. In weighing the items, I would always add a dash extra, and not once did it keep me awake at night. Another thing I'd do was to give an extra piece of candy to kids. If they wanted five one-cent pieces, I'd give them six. I did this for months and no one knew about it. Justice was not abstract with me; it was real and personal. I have no idea as to the number of times I'd seen Jesse weighing bulk groceries short three to four cents. I'd stand and watch him as he did it. He knew I saw what he was doing; inevitably he'd turn to me, wink and at the same time make polite conversation with the poor customer whom he was cheating. Not once did I mention this to anyone. The closest I ever came to it was with a young Methodist preacher. He was new to the town and had learned that I was the village atheist. It was his duty to save sinners, so I was a good place to start. After telling me all about the good in God and His mercy to mankind, I asked one simple question: "How do you explain the fact that God lets a lying, cheating bastard like Jesse Wild live?" He did not know what I was talking about.

It was to be expected that Jesse should catch me sooner or later; he did. One day some honest kid commented that I'd given him six pieces of bubble gum for a nickel and returned the extra one. Jesse overheard the child and asked me about it. I said I had made a mistake. He questioned my ability to count and nothing came of it. Two or three farmers soon followed with comments like "them corn seeds I got the other day went farther than any four-bits' worth I ever got here before." A lady commented one day about a half-dollar's worth of sugar, saying the price of sugar must have come down. Jesse put the bag on the scales; I was caught, and there was no excuse. I didn't offer one.

The long and short of it was that he weighed every bag on the shelves and all that were overweight were charged to me. He cursed me for everything he could think of, and some of his best terms he repeated several times. But he didn't strike me. I've often wondered why. Of course, I had to stop playing God for a while—I couldn't afford it—but I slipped back into my old ways as soon as Jesse turned his back.

The summer was long and hot. As slowly as it passed, however, it was more rapid than my getting out of debt for having played God. It was the time school opened in the fall before I'd paid the price of my folly.

I didn't understand my attitude toward school during the first part of that year. I didn't like anyone. I didn't want to be around anyone, and it was mutual. The only person to whom I was halfway civil was Louie Taylor. Louie remained my friend, in spite of me. I was ready to argue with anyone about anything and without any provocation whatsoever. Still I enjoyed reading books of my choice. As much as Miss Berry meant to me, I refused to write a book review she'd assigned. I argued with her, stating that I'd be glad to review any three books of my own choice, but not one of her choice. She didn't argue; she gave me an F. That year I took a course in manual training, which was woodworking, and the first thing I had to do was to square two blocks of hardwood. I worked for over a month and failed completely to get one piece of hardwood squared. I sawed, I planed, I sandpapered, I cursed. Finally, I threw one of them through a plate-glass window and stalked out of the classroom. Superintendent Bruce had words with me; I promised not to do it again and I also promised to pay for the window, which I did on the installment plan.

Another course I took was American history, and at the age of sixteen I learned that the South had lost the Civil War. It's unbelievable, but that is a fact. I was surprised at the news, but not especially alarmed. I wasn't interested in history; my interest was sitting in the back row, looking out the window, and chewing Beech-Nut tobacco and spitting out the window. Superintendent Bruce and I had a conference about chewing tobacco in class. He was nice about it, but firm. Perhaps the two of us would not have come to a parting of the ways had it not been for a teacher I had in chemistry. Item one, I didn't like the man. Item two, the feeling was mutual. We seldom spoke, and when he asked a question of me my stock reply was a simple "I don't know." That, unfortunately, was quite true. Neither of the two books I had that year was a chemistry book. I made a discovery in the chemistry class. It was by accident that I learned about mixing ferrous sulphate with hydrochloric acid. Such an odor—there is nothing like it. The odor clings; it's almost impossible to get rid of it. After my discovery, I was never without a small bottle of the ingredients, and I would set off little stink bombs in the auditorium, a classroom, or wherever I found myself inclined not to visit. The chemistry teacher knew who was responsible, but he was without proof. That did not make our relationship a compatible one. One day, not long after the opening of school, he was beside himself. He accused me in the classroom of being the person who was doing it. I demanded that he prove it. I was furious, and one uncivil word led to five hundred others. Finally, in a fit of temper, I screamed at him to go to hell. With that invitation from me, he slapped me across the side of the head. I was seated; with my ear ringing, I arose and hit him with my fist in the stomach. My departure from the classroom was hasty. Knowing what was to happen, I went directly to Mr.

73

Bruce's office and told him what I'd done. I explained the matter in detail. Frankly, I didn't expect sympathy, and it was just as well, for none was forthcoming. While I was there, the chemistry teacher came in and told Mr. Bruce that if I stayed in school he was leaving. Failing to resist the opportunity, I said goodbye to him.

It happened the other way around. A goodbye was in order, but it was I who was leaving, said Mr. Bruce. At first, he threatened to have me put in the State Training School at Columbia. The school is for children who are too young to be sent to the state penitentiary at Parchman. After some thought, Mr. Bruce decided to expel me. He asked how I'd like that. My reply was not pleasing to him. "Well, Prof," I said, "that's one way I'd be rid of that son-of-a-bitch you have teaching chemistry." Mr. Bruce asked me to bend over a chair in his office; I obliged without comment, and he proceeded to raise a welt on my rump with his belt. After exhausting himself, he decided to suspend me for one month. I demanded to know why he didn't have me hanged.

"When you come back to school," he said, "if your attitude is the same, you'll wish I had hanged you."

My mother was quite upset and went to the school to see Mr. Bruce. He was nothing like I'd anticipated. I figured he'd tell her what a jerk she had for a son. Rather, he explained that he thought I needed a little time off to do some thinking for myself. Of course, he told her that I'd struck a teacher, but he had asked me to take off a month from school and think some things through. My mother didn't understand, not fully. My father just looked at me for a few minutes; finally he said in his quiet, unruffled voice, "Takes a little time to grow up, don't it, Boy?"

It did.

I had begun working in the garage with Joe Simmons after school every day, and with a month in which to do nothing, I went to work full time. I enjoyed it, as I had earlier when I was with Joe. If I could ever have understood the timing of an auto engine, I might have been a mechanic. Timing baffled me. While I enjoyed my work in the shop, I suffered untold hell from fits of depression. I enjoyed the luxury of self-pity without being able to afford it.

74

At last I came to the conclusion that life wasn't worth the effort, and the best thing any sensible person could do was to get out of it by killing himself. I devised ways and means of committing suicide, always taking into account that everyone would feel sorry for me. I'd kill myself and that would make them suffer. I took a bottle marked "Poison" from Dr. Olden's office and decided to drink it, whatever it was. The doctor knew I was suffering from something, although he wasn't quite sure what, and when he missed the bottle from his shelf, he came to see me. He wasn't sure I'd taken it, but he asked me point-blank. I answered in the same manner and told him what I was going to do with it, and, as best I could, I told him why. He listened with concern and patience while I told him how unhappy and depressed and lonely I was.

"And you want to take a human life, yours?" he asked.

I nodded.

"I thought we talked about human life once," Dr. Olden said.

"We did."

"I took a sacred vow once never to give poison to a fellow human."

I looked at him.

"Son," the kind doctor continued, "nothing in this world is so great and wonderful as the gift of life. That is a gift of God and no one has the right to take it."

"But, Dr. Olden, you didn't give me the bottle. I stole it from you."

"I'd feel as bad if you drank it, no matter how you came by it." He extended his hand, and I returned the bottle to him.

"I'm sorry," I said.

"Do you still intend to study medicine?"

I nodded.

"Have you read anything about the progress being made in brain surgery?"

"No, sir," I answered, "but I'd say it's about time someone made some progress wi*¹. ᵤe brain. God didn't seem to do very well with it."

"I think God did right well, but He might have been a little careless in whom He gave them to."

Dr. Olden and I engaged in a conversation relating to progress in brain surgery. He explained to me, in words I understood, the marvels of the brain. He was a patient and kind man. At that moment I decided to become a brain surgeon.

A few days after the conversation with Dr. Olden about the bottle of poison, he stopped by the garage for gasoline. I was filling his tank when he walked around to me and asked how I was feeling.

I assured him that I was fine.

"You look tired and run-down to me," he said. "Haven't you lost weight?"

"Yes, sir, but not much."

"You didn't have much to lose." He smiled. "Come by the office the first chance you have."

The following day I went to Dr. Olden's office. He explained to me that he thought if I'd drink a bottle of beer each day it would give me an appetite and that perhaps I'd feel better.

"I've already talked with your mother about it. She understands. While you're here, would you like to read any of my books?"

I was delighted to have the chance to read medical books and told him so, expressing my thanks.

"Well, take one on females first," he said, getting a book from the shelf, "because I know you're a boy and I remember when I was one. Read about sex and babies and the like and get it over with."

Then he put his hand on my shoulder and looked me straight in the eye. "I want you to remember one thing. I want you to remember that sex isn't vulgar. The reproduction of the race is another gift from God which some men don't appreciate. The function of the female is basic in the scheme of things with the Maker. She should be appreciated as such, and for a lot more, too."

I didn't say anything, feeling a tinge of guilt. I think the doctor knew.

"Dr. Olden," I asked, "about drinking a bottle of beer every day, don't you think that will cause talk?"

"Son, remember another thing. What people say isn't of any

76

consequence. Always do what you have to do and don't mind what anyone says. But always try to be right in what you're doing."

With the drinking of beer each day, I became not only the village idiot and atheist, but the child most likely to go to hell. Any number of persons were openly critical of me for drinking beer, but I did it. They didn't seem to understand that I didn't like the stuff, but looked on it as so much medicine. I remembered what Dr. Olden had said to me, but I wasn't long in deciding that his advice was much easier given than taken.

It was about this time that Jesse Wild installed a refrigerator counter in his meat market. I still carried in my pockets the makings of a "stink," iron and acid. One day about noon I went into the store, through the market. Jesse Junior was the only person in the store; he was up front. When I entered, he said something to me about my entering through the back door, which was where I should enter. I boiled, but held my temper. I told him I wanted a five-cent piece of cheese. He told me to cut it and bring him the money. That was what I had expected.

I cut the cheese, and while I was about it I put a small amount of iron in a jar top and poured acid into it, hiding it behind a slicing machine which was next to a wall. It was safe from discovery. By the time Jesse returned from lunch, his store was indeed something to smell. Word spread like the wind and everyone who wasn't busy dropped by to see what was wrong. Jesse was frantic. I told Joe Simmons what I'd done and he advised me not to tell anyone else, but to sit tight and see what happened. The entire afternoon at the store was spent in cleaning out everything, the refrigerator counter, the old icebox, everything. Water was heated and everything was scrubbed with strong soap. Jesse had the cleanest market in Mississippi, but the odor continued. He threw out a pan of sausage, not being sure about its freshness. He pondered the possibility of a dead rat between the walls. Yes, he recalled putting out rat poison a few days ago, and could it be possible that a rat had got in between the walls and died? He just didn't know. The odor began to die out late in the afternoon. There was considerable relief on the part of the Wild boys. I saw to it that their relief was short-lived. Early the next morning I found the chance to refill the container without being caught. The clean-up campaign began once more. The Wilds, both father and son, were ready to weep: No one had bought a single item from the market since the day before, and to them a dime meant as much as their right arms.

I continued to add acid to the container as it was needed. I stood around and expressed my great concern, offering a suggestion every now and then. Jesse was so frantic that he had Junior go back and scrub the sausage mill with hot water and soap. That was probably the first time it had been really clean since they'd been in business. Joe Simmons and I enjoyed the situation fully. Finally, courtesy demanded that Joe go to the store to express his sympathy; he returned to the garage in a hurry and called me to the back.

"Jesse is getting ready to have the walls torn out. He thinks it's a dead rat between the walls. What are you going to do?"

"Help him tear the damned place down," I replied.

Joe was concerned. "Have you thought about what Jesse would do to you if he ever found out what you've done?"

It had not entered my mind.

"Boy," Joe said earnestly, "that crazy bastard would kill you."

Not too much discussion was needed to convince me of that. Before the wrecking got under way, I was able to get the jar top out without being detected. The odor died out quickly, at least quickly enough to save the walls. I was relieved, because the possibility of getting killed had made me uncomfortable. Too, it had not occurred to me that someone from school could have come in and identified the odor for what it was. In such case, the evidence against me would have been circumstantial, but Jesse never seemed to need too much evidence to hang a crime on me. It was over; it had been great fun.

After the elation produced by the stink bomb wore itself out, my loneliness was almost complete, and I again considered suicide. I was afraid to die, but to live was awful. The situation was more than I could handle. I was numb from living. Dr. Olden's books were interesting enough, and the books I borrowed from Mrs. Wild were still more interesting to me, but the numbness was ever-present, in spite of the books I read. I lived in the little town; I worked and went to school there, but I was not a part of it. I was not a part of anything. Except for the limited time I spent with Tad Barber, I was alone, no matter how many persons were around.

After the Christmas holidays I was permitted to return to school. I caused no trouble. Mr. Bruce and I became good friends. He never mentioned any of our differences to me, but showed me all the kindness and consideration possible. Miss Berry asked me to try out as feature editor of the school paper. The invitation was a surprise to me, but I wrote a piece or two and was given the job, which I kept until I graduated. The junior class did a play every spring. Miss Berry directed it, and I was invited to take a part.

It was during rehearsals that I began to get interested in girls. Backstage was a good place for such an interest to develop. It happened that I was impressed by a sophomore named Frances Sellers. She was a good-looking girl, believe me. The rules and regulations at the school were such that little time was permitted for such pleasant things as necking. I had a long talk with Tad about the situation, explaining to him that I had decided to "make" the girl. He gave me the benefit of his experience. I hit on a plan whereby my dishonorable intent could be made a reality. Frances was a good Christian who went to church every Sunday and to prayer meeting every Wednesday night. I asked if I could take her to prayer meeting one evening. She was delighted, having tried for months to convert me. The appointed evening came and all went well en route from the school to the church in Pleasant. I was tingling with excitement, having sneaked a feel without rebuke. I had it made; I was sure of that.

The Pleasant Methodist Church was a barn of an old building. It seated approximately two hundred, and that night there were about fifty persons present, possibly more. Frances and I sat about the middle of the church. Tad seated himself directly in front of us. The business at hand got under way. The pastor began praying. When he finished, he didn't say "Amen," but left it open for the next person who wanted to pray. Several prayers followed the pastor's. I was looking around at the people and thinking how silly they were. To my great surprise, Frances began to pray. I bowed my head, not wanting anyone to know I was with her. She asked the Lord for several blessings, the nature of which I don't recall. About the time I thought she was finished, I noted a pause in her prayer. The pause was but for a moment, however. She came back loud and strong: "And, oh, yes, Lord, please, please help P.D." After the shock of it, I thought for a moment that was right nice of Frances. She stopped, and from Tad I heard, "Yes, Lord, for goodness sake, help P.D." I looked up and noticed several persons looking at me. Again I bowed my head. Frankly, I was embarrassed. I did appreciate Tad's effort. Finally, the prayer returned to the pastor and he asked the Lord to help me, too. This was too much. After an eternity, the meeting was over. I saw Frances back to school, and that ended that. I'd had it.

The next day Tad inquired how I'd made out.

"Tad, my friend," I said, "I think the Lord misunderstood you, either that or He sure as hell didn't answer your prayer."

Anyway, that was the last time I was ever to attend a prayer meeting.

School closed in June and I was surprised to learn I'd passed chemistry with a D. The same was true with manual training. But it had been a hectic year.

Chapter 12

The summer came like thunder. First, my mother was taken ill suddenly and an operation was essential. My father was somewhere in the woods, and I didn't know how to get in touch with him. I asked Richard Campbell, a kind man who was the rural mail carrier, to drive her to Columbia. He did and I got help from relatives who lived there. I hitch-hiked back to Pleasant to meet my father when he came home for the weekend. It was a long battle for my mother. She was several months in regaining her health. After the danger was past, I returned from Columbia, where my mother was staying with my grandmother, to Pleasant and went to work for Jesse Wild again, at a salary of three dollars a week. With the hospital bill and the loss of time from work, my father went broke. He had borrowed money against his truck and it was lost. Later in the summer, he became the night watchman for the town of Pleasant. His pay was small, to be sure, and we never had any cash, but we did have groceries, inasmuch as the merchants paid a *pro rata* share of his wages.

No sooner had I gone back to work than Jesse and I began our battle once again. The first thing I got caught doing was taking rocks out of a bin in which dried beans were stored. How rocks get into dried beans is something I don't know, but they are always present. One day I had caught up with my work and I was idly picking out the rocks and putting them into a paper bag. Jesse saw me and exploded.

"Jesus," he exclaimed, "what the hell are you up to now?"

"Just taking out the rocks, Jesse."

"Ain't you got enough sense to know that I bought them rocks right along with the beans?"

"But, Jesse," I began, "the rocks—"

He interrupted. "You put them rocks back in the beans, that's what you do."

I put the rocks back without saying another word.

"Now, you go out in the back and get as many rocks off the road as you've taken out and thrown away. You pick up the dark kind like in the beans and bring them in and put them in the bin."

"Jesse, I haven't thrown away any of the rocks," I said.

"Don't argue with me; just do what you're told. I'm not in business for my health."

I loaded the bean bin with black rocks. Later, when the lack of witnesses permitted, I removed the rocks.

Jesse had always drunk regularly, but that summer he stayed drunk. He engaged in everything from which he could make a dime. Among other things, Jesse began to sell liquor, which was illegal in the state of Mississippi. It was bootlegging, pure and simple. He made me take his car into the woods a few times, take pint bottles from boxes we would find there, put them into

81

paper bags, return them to the store, and place them in the refrigerator counter storage space. I had argued with him about having to do the job, which I knew to be illegal, but the result had been the same as always. Jesse heaped his abuse on me and when I had told him I wasn't going to do it, he said he'd fire me and would get the other merchants to fire my father. Under the circumstances, I handled the booze as instructed.

The crowning blow during that summer came when Jesse told me to drive a school bus loaded with soldiers to Biloxi one evening. Jesse had rented a bus from a Negro man for twelve dollars. He sold round-trip passage to Biloxi for five dollars. About twenty men decided to make the trip. I was told to drive the bus, to leave Pleasant about 5:00 P.M. and stay in Biloxi with the men until they decided to return. Also, Jesse said there would be "a little something extra in it for you." I made the trip, returning to Pleasant at about 4:00 A.M. I was dead tired, so I went home and went to sleep. At 6:00 A.M. Junior came and woke me and said his father wanted to know why I was late for work. I asked Junior to tell Jesse that I'd been back from Biloxi only two hours. About half an hour later, Jesse came and woke me and told me to get to work, that I was an hour late. I went.

When payday came, I was expecting "a little something extra." When I didn't get it, I reminded Jesse of the trip.

"By God," he said, "that's right. Let's see, you left three hours before closing time and were an hour late for work the next morning." He scribbled with a pencil on the back of a sales book for a minute or so. "Now, deducting the time you had off from work, I figure you owe me fifty cents. You want to pay me now or do you want me to take it out of next week's pay?" he asked.

He said it, but I couldn't believe my ears. Could it be possible he was serious? I stood in disbelief.

"Answer me," he demanded. "What you want me to do?"

"Jesse, you no-good, lousy, drunk, cheap son-of-a-bitch, I want you to die," I answered.

He did nothing; I had expected him to slap me. However, later he told my father what I'd said to him.

"You mean to say the boy called you names like that?" my father asked.

"He sure as hell did," Jesse said, "and what are you going to do to him?"

"Nothing, I guess."

"By God, why not?" Jesse demanded to know.

"Well, Jesse," said my father, "I hate to know the boy uses such words, but I can't punish him for being right."

And that was the end of that.

The summer moved with unusual slowness. Like all summers in south Mississippi, it was hot, humid and depressing—and, for me, lonely. I became more and more withdrawn, cut off from warm, friendly human contact. The one saving factor was my fourteen- to sixteen-hour work day, which produced the blessedness of such complete exhaustion at night that I would sleep instead of lying awake and indulging in self-pity. When Jesse couldn't think of anything for me to do, I would often spend Sunday afternoon with Tad Barber. We especially liked such afternoons when it was raining. We would lie in the hayloft of the Barber barn and dream, each telling the other of the worlds we were going to conquer. Such dreams! Such hopes! I doubt Tad knew of my state of mind. Possibly he didn't know of it because with him I could talk about most things, although there were exceptions, of course. While Tad didn't especially care for poetry, he would listen with apparent interest while I tried to explain, mostly to myself, the beauty of the English language.

Tad and I were as close as I've ever been with anyone. When a third person would show up, I went into my shell. I was no longer a part of that intangible something which was his and mine. I always wanted to talk with him about the question of my adoption, but I could never bring myself to open the subject.

Those were pleasant moments, and much, much too short. Often I found myself saying a prayer in which I thanked God for a friend like Tad and for those few Sunday afternoons. The incongruity of an atheist's praying didn't occur to me.

My resentment and anger mounted where Jesse Wild was concerned. Whether I hated him is something I didn't know. I disliked him; I resented him; he disgusted me—but hate him? I often wondered about it. Perhaps I didn't have the energy to hate, and it does require considerable energy. I had cursed

Jesse to his face, without suffering any ill effects, but it was not much satisfaction to me. The tightness, the pressure within me, was not relieved.

One afternoon a man came into the store and asked to see Jesse, saying he wanted to pay his account. Jesse was in the restaurant drinking. I walked through the door opening into the restaurant and found him standing beside the counter, quite drunk. He was angry for some reason; his face was flushed and his eyes blazing.

Noting my presence, he bellowed, "What do you want, you little son-of-a-bitch?"

"Mr. Sauls wants to pay his account," I answered.

Without any warning, either by word or movement, Jesse swung his full weight toward me, striking me across the face with his right hand. The blow was hard, the suddenness of it caught me off guard, and I was sent sprawling backward. I finally hit the floor about six or eight feet from where I'd been standing. There were several people standing around in the restaurant. Someone laughed a shaky, nervous laugh that died quickly.

Inside my mouth the taste of blood was present. I felt my face and mouth and discovered the bleeding was inside, the result of a cut lip. Blood wasn't present on my mouth or face. I was angry, but not with the explosive kind of anger I'd so often felt. I had one desire, to strike back, to hit Jesse. My movements were calculated, even thought out before I arose from the floor. He was too tall for me to do damage to his face. His stomach or side was the place to strike if I wanted to get in a blow with my full weight, which was more than a hundred pounds. I approached him slowly, displaying no outward sign of what I felt inside. As I approached him, he lifted his left arm upward and backward in a position to hit me again. The opening he left was all I needed. With the full force of my weight and my anger and my resentment, I struck him in the ribs, just under his raised arm. He staggered to the side, clasping his hands to the spot I'd hit, and as I went through the door I heard beer bottles falling to the floor, Jesse having knocked them off the counter.

He did not return to the store that afternoon. I was worried,

84

but not afraid. My anger, while boiling and surging within, was kept in check and my mind was clear. I figured ahead and kept a Coca-Cola bottle within reach the remainder of the day. I cannot begin to explain it, but after I'd cooled down, I felt a certain peace of mind, a certain satisfaction, a lessening of tension of mind and body. That night I slept well. I felt guilty about nothing whatsoever. However, as a simple matter of precaution, I made it a point the next morning to be five or ten minutes late for work. When I walked in the store, Jesse was sitting beside a window looking at the street. He looked up at me and for a few seconds didn't say a word. Finally he said, "Do you know you broke two of my ribs yesterday?"

I didn't know it, but I was delighted with the news. "Jesse," I said, "I just want you to know that my only regret is that my hands aren't bigger, that's all."

Nothing more was spoken between us. Later in the morning I was cleaning the market when Junior saw fit to walk back and talk to me.

"Didn't you know Daddy was drinking yesterday when you hit him?" he asked me.

"Yeah. I know he was drunk."

"You shouldn't have hit him. You took advantage of him, that's what you did."

I didn't speak; I listened.

"Well, by God," Junior demanded, "don't you have anything to say?"

"Junior," I said, anger mounting in me, "I'll say this to you. My hand was only big enough to break two of that slob's ribs. You're about half as big as he is, so I figure I can break at least four of yours and, with luck, maybe more. Now, you want to hear anything else?"

I guess he didn't because he walked out of the market, went to the front of the store and began a conversation with his father. I didn't wonder if they were talking about me; I just didn't care somehow. I felt good that morning.

In addition to what has been related about the summer of 1938, two incidents remain in my mind. Summertime is revival time, especially at the Methodist and Baptist churches. Late one afternoon a group of boys about my age suggested we attend church that night at the Negro Baptist church, the one where Calvin Jones was lay preacher. I didn't especially want to go, but it was seldom I was asked to go anywhere with anyone, so I went. We sat outside the building, watching the activity through a window. The church was filled with people. They opened services by singing. There was no piano accompaniment. The music was made by a mixing and blending of voices, low and high, the cadence arrived at being quite rhythmical. I enjoyed it. The visiting minister began the sermon. As he increased the intensity of his message, the people in the congregation joined in, chanting in a musical way. The over-all effect was one of rhythm. The boys with whom I was sitting began to make remarks about the people in the church.

"Jesus!" someone exclaimed. "Look at 'em jumping up and down." Everyone laughed.

"Some of them niggers will get the Holy Ghost in a minute," someone else said.

There was laughter again. Such remarks continued, first from one boy, then another. Whether or not they were heard by the people inside the church, I don't know. I felt awkward and flustered by it all. While I disapproved of the church—not just theirs, but all churches—I felt they had as much right to their kind of worship as did anyone else. I suggested that we go, saying that, after all, we didn't have any business being there. My remark caused some discussion among the boys. They told me to go if I wanted to.

I wanted to, so I left. The whole business disturbed me greatly. How it was wrong I did not know, but I felt that going to the Negro church and sitting outside and laughing and making remarks was wrong. Too, I thought of what would happen should Negro children sit outside the white Baptist church and act the way we had, laughing and joking about the services. Why had I not said more? Why had I not said all I was thinking about our being there and scoffing at people honestly trying to worship? Why had I not done something to get the other boys to leave, too? Why was I afraid to do more than make a mild remark and go away as if the situation would vanish when I could no longer

86

see it? The only answers I had for my questions gave me little comfort as I walked home even more lonely than I had been before.

The other incident that remains with me was a trip I took to New Orleans with Joe Simmons. Joe asked me to go with him and drive back a car he was going to buy. It was my first trip out of the state of Mississippi, and I was anxious to go. We arrived and Joe gave me fifty cents to buy my lunch. He had something to do and told me to do as I pleased until the middle of the afternoon. I had two or three hours to spend by myself, so I walked the streets looking at everything in sight. I had never before been in a city and I was delighted and a little bewildered by it all. Somewhere near the French Quarter, I was ambling along when I heard a woman's voice.

"Hey, there, white boy," she called. Looking around, I saw no one. Again the voice was heard. Still there was no one in sight.

"Up here," I heard the voice say. I looked up and saw a Negro woman with her head stuck out of a third-story window. I looked around to see if she was talking to someone else. She wasn't.

"Hey, white boy, you got a dollar?" she asked.

I shook my head.

"How much you got?"

I didn't answer.

"Well, why don't you come on up?"

I was at a loss. I didn't know what to say to the woman. This was something for which I was completely unprepared. I stood there looking at her.

"Come on up," she insisted. "Maybe you got fifty cents. Fifty cents will do, white boy."

I had no desire to go up. I wasn't sure what I wanted to do. Questions entered my mind about the situation. My impulse was to tell her I had fifty cents and I wanted her to have it. I felt only compassion. I was sorry for the woman. I don't think I stood in moral judgment of her; rather I was most sad that a woman had to make a living by selling herself to any passerby who had the price. I turned and walked away, not looking back. As I walked, a thought entered my mind—at least she didn't have to work for Jesse Wild. I felt sad, but not nearly so much as I had at first.

Chapter 13

In spite of the fact that I had worked the entire summer, the opening of school in September found me broke. I had bought a few clothes and one pair of dress shoes. Once again I did not have money to buy books. Notwithstanding the lack of books, I made out well enough my senior year. While my grades were nothing I'd care to brag about, I did pass. The nine-month session ended without my striking a single teacher or throwing anything through a window. Again Miss Berry asked me to take part in the class play. That year I behaved fairly well backstage, not wanting to get prayed for again in public.

Mr. Bruce had transferred to a school in the central part of the state. The new superintendent was R. B. Runnels, an elderly man who had spent his life in the public-school system of Mississippi. Mr. Runnels and I got along well enough. He did have a habit of which I disapproved. At assembly, which was twice a week, he always had the student body read the Twenty-third Psalm in unison and followed that with a pledge to the flag. While I didn't mind either, I did get awfully tired of it twice a week for thirty-six weeks. Following the pledge, Mr. Runnels would ask a student to say a prayer. Whether he knew of the trouble God and I were having, I don't know, but on one occasion I was called on to pray. I was baffled. Indeed, I was dumfounded. I could feel the blood rushing to my face. Other students were looking at me as I sat still and silent. What to do? I had a reputation to preserve. The question was a simple one: how to get out of this and save face. It seemed an eternity before I could think of anything to say. Finally, with every eye in the school on me, I said, "Mr. Runnels, if you please, I don't pray in public."

While I did not have trouble with teachers, I did have minor trouble with a few students. Had I not been a coward, I'm sure the affair would have ended in a fight. Teen-age boys are interested in sex, and the older they get, the more they brag about their prowess. Hardly a bull session existed without the subject of sex coming up sooner or later. Monday bull sessions seemed always to be the most interesting and lively because the boys who lived in the dormitory always spent the weekend in Hattiesburg, where most of their homes were. At a session on a Monday about mid-term there were several of us in the dormitory room of Ed Sanders. While I had a big mouth, I did more listening than talking. After all, I had read Dr. Olden's books and remembered what he'd said to me about sex. At the bull session that Monday, Ed began telling us about his weekend at Hattiesburg.

"Well, Ed," someone asked, "how'd you make out? Did you get any?"

"Sure," Ed replied, laughing, "I got me a can of snuff and went down in the nigger quarters. Hell, fellows, that's all you have to do up there. Just give 'em a can of snuff. Them niggers are always glad to give a white man a piece."

I listened, but I was not laughing. Somewhere down deep inside me I began to boil. I couldn't hold it. Almost in a rage, I said, "Ed, you're a damned liar."

There was silence. Ed looked surprised. "What's the matter," he asked, "didn't you ever get a little?"

"Damned right I have," I answered, lying through my teeth, "plenty of times. But one thing I've never done is to rape a woman."

Ed became angry, as did some of the others.

"Well, what the hell is it to you?" asked Ed. "Suppose I layed all the niggers in the county, what's it to you?"

"Ed, by God, any time anybody is done a wrong it's my business," I answered.

"You must be a damned nigger lover," Ed said, looking at the other boys.

To be called a "nigger lover" was a fighting matter. I did not feel inclined to fight. I was too involved, despite my anger, in

89

trying to figure out why I'd blown my top. I was especially concerned with having blurted out that a wrong to anyone was my concern. I had no idea why I'd said it. There were two things for which I was thankful as I left the room without saying another word. One was that I had not gotten into a fight; the other was that no one had asked me to explain my statement. I tried for days to understand my resentment at the Monday bull session, and I also tried to figure out what I'd meant by my remark. I could not get it into focus. Somehow it had to do with human life, and I recalled the remarks by Dr. Olden in which he had said many times to me that nothing was more valuable than a human life, that it was a gift from God, who had made us all. Somehow, to my mind, all this business tied together; how was something I couldn't get into words.

In my reading during the school year, I had run into the word "Pantheist." I had found the idea of God and Nature of great interest. Over a period of time I came to the conclusion that perhaps, after all, there was a God, but, if so, God was seen in the nature of things, not in a church building of any denomination. I had also gotten around to wondering about the business of God's making man. If so, and maybe so, then who had made God? No one had the answer to that question. To ask it was to invite a lecture on the most fundamental of religious attitudes. Finally, I came to the conclusion that there was a God, but He wasn't anything like I'd been led to believe. At that time I didn't go any further into the matter.

I continued to work for Jesse Wild during the afternoons and on Saturdays. Still, I was always broke. Occasionally, Mrs. Bush at the post office would find an odd job for me to do, and I'd always take the money she gave me and go to Hattiesburg to the movies. I loved them; I could forget myself at a movie and for a couple of hours be someone else, doing wonderful and great things. It was on a trip to Hattiesburg one afternoon that I was to be as shaken as I'd ever been. My mother had a cousin who owned a jewelry store. Out of habit, I always stopped in to have a word or two with him. That afternoon someone was in the store and Jack called the man over and said to him, "I want you to meet Jim and Birdie's adopted boy."

90

I couldn't speak. A simple "Hello" wouldn't come. All I could think to do was get out of the store. I wanted to run. My mind was in a whirl. The difference I'd noted at the family gatherings, the dark-haired, dark-skinned cousins and uncles and aunts, my red hair and fair skin with freckles, the treatment by the family—some kind, some not—so many thoughts, so many questions, too.

But Jack French knew! I wanted to ask him questions, but I couldn't bring myself to speak. I walked out of the store, down the street, and hitch-hiked a ride to Pleasant. I was still numb when I got home. My mother wanted to know if I was ill. I was, but not from an illness I could talk about. Why hadn't she told me? Why had never a word been said to me by either parent? It was beyond me. After the numbness wore off, anger set in, but I could not talk with anyone, not even Dr. Olden, no one.

The year moved on and finally graduation day was close at hand. There were so many things to buy, especially a class ring and invitations; cap and gown were to be rented. These things were out of the question. I didn't mention the ring to my parents. I was the only kid in the class not to buy one. Other children asked me why I didn't want a class ring, and I was hard pressed for an answer because I was ashamed of eternal poverty. I lied, saying first one thing, then another. Out of my salary from Jesse I had managed to save enough to buy twenty invitations. The question of renting a cap and gown was to be taken up, and I didn't have the necessary three dollars. At a class meeting held to discuss the matter, I asked for the floor and stated that I had decided not to rent a cap and gown. The class president said that everyone had to have a cap and gown, else he couldn't graduate. I took the floor again and told that I had more than the sixteen required units, and I didn't give a damn whether I graduated or not. Miss Berry then took the floor and requested that I stop cursing and told me to see her after the meeting. I couldn't imagine her having me expelled or suspended, but what else could she want? The answer was soon in coming. That wonderful and kind lady didn't say a word to me about my language, but explained how she wanted everyone to graduate together,

91

to walk onto the stage and be proud of having finished his school work.

"For many of you here," she said to me, "this will be the only time in your life you'll graduate. And I'm ordering a cap and gown for you. You're entitled to graduate with your class."

"But, Miss Berry," I explained with hesitancy, the words coming hard, "I don't have the money to pay for them. I've not had a single book this whole year."

"No one has mentioned money, except you," she said. I didn't say anything. "Someday you'll have the money and you can give it to me." I couldn't say anything. I wept. It was an act of kindness and I'd not expected it. I couldn't hold back the tears. Miss Berry left me alone, not speaking another word. I had not intended saying anything to my parents about the matter, but I talked with my father and told him that I'd planned not to graduate with the others.

"Your mother would be mighty disappointed" was all he said. The next day he gave me the money to pay for the cap and gown. I don't know where or how he'd gotten it. He didn't say.

Graduation was a bore. I was uncomfortable, the weather being hot and humid that June night. While the commencement speaker was talking, I sat with a handkerchief in my hand mopping my brow. Finally, the names were being called out. My turn came, and I walked forward to receive my diploma. I'll never forget the tremendous applause when Mr. Runnels handed me the diploma. The audience, like me, must have thought I'd never make it. When the applause died down, I turned to the audience and bowed low. They applauded again, even louder. Mr. Runnels motioned me to sit down. I did, but I wanted to continue taking bows. After all, it wasn't everyone who could spend five years on what should have been a three-year job.

Chapter 14

My father had taken a job in Columbia after my graduation and my mother was excited at the thought of returning to her home town with all her family within shouting distance. With nothing else to do, I decided to stay in Pleasant and work for Jesse Wild. I don't think my father was too happy about my staying or his moving, but the decision had been made. An uncle who was in the moving business moved them, and my parents took two rooms in my aunt Ollie's house.

In the meantime, after two weeks with Jesse, I landed a better job in Pleasant. Jim Odom, a son-in-law of Sol Barber's, had put in a new garage. He approached me about working for him, taking care of the front, selling gasoline, running a small sandwich shop, and being general flunky. The salary was ten dollars a week. I was bubbling over with joy. I figured it out that by taking a room with Joe Simmons at his home and cooking my own food at the café, I could live on about five dollars a week. This would leave me five to apply toward going to college in the fall. It looked as if I'd have all the money I needed to enter college. I bought my own food and cooked it at the café. I was living well, all things considered. Jim and I got along well together. We had only one difference of opinion, and it had to do with a hamburger. Someone had ordered a hamburger and I'd cooked it and put tomato, lettuce, pickles, etc., on it and sold it for a dime, which was the price quoted on the menu. Jim was unhappy about the extras I'd put on the hamburger and expressed views on the subject of how to make hamburgers. I didn't argue with him; I complied.

The job didn't last long, nor did any of the jobs I picked up after I went to Columbia to be with my parents. Discouraged, I went to New Orleans to enlist in the Navy and was rejected because of a kidney infection. Finally, the summer ended, but rather than having a pocketful of money to get started in college, I was dead broke. I had checked the catalogues of all the schools in the state and found that Pearl River Junior College in Poplarville was the least expensive. I could enroll for twelve dollars, but I was a long way from having that much money.

One day I happened to be in Hattiesburg for some reason or other, and I decided to see if the bank would make a loan to me so I could enroll at PRC. I had never been in a bank, but I walked into the Citizens Bank of Hattiesburg and asked to see the president. I'm sure G. W. McWilliams was as baffled by me as I was by him. He was patient while I explained to him my story, my ambitions and my plight at that moment.

"Young man," he said to me, "of all the people in America, who do you think was the greatest?"

"Abraham Lincoln," I answered, wondering what that had to do with a ninety-day loan of fifteen dollars.

"I'll let you have the money," said Mr. Mac. "Can you get someone to sign your note?"

Why I said it, I don't know, but I said I thought Jesse Wild would sign it. Mr. Mac gave me the paper and instructed me to bring it back when Jesse had signed it. I knew I'd made a mistake, but it was too late. I felt I had no choice but to try. I hitch-hiked a ride to Pleasant and asked Jesse if he'd sign a fifteen-dollar note for ninety days. I explained to him that I had a job lined up in Poplarville with a grocery store, which was the case, and that I could pay back the money to the bank. His answer to my question was brief and to the point.

"Hell no," Jesse said. "I wouldn't sign a goddamned thing for you, now or never. I don't owe you one damned thing."

While I was disappointed, I was not surprised. "Jesse," I said in the nastiest way I knew, "I want to thank you. You are a kind and generous son-of-a-bitch." I walked out of his office and was never to see Jesse Wild again.

I learned by a newspaper account of his death four years later, and I tried hard to be glad, but I couldn't. At the same time, I could not feel any sadness. While I was far from grief-stricken, I felt bad about the death, because it was the death of a human being, not because it was the death of a person who'd browbeaten and humiliated me for years. Such an objective approach in a subjective person is hard to get into focus.

Too, I wondered for some time about the insignificance of the

94

life of Jesse Wild. What good had he done? Had anyone bene-
fited by his having been born? If so, who and how? I could see
no purpose, no reason for his having passed through this thing
men call life.

On that September day in 1939, I left Jesse's office and
caught a ride back to Hattiesburg, undecided as to what I should
do. To tell Mr. Mac that Jesse wouldn't sign my note was to say
that I was unreliable, and a bank doesn't make loans to any such
person. It was quite a decision to make; finally, seconds before
closing time, I went into the bank and told Mr. Mac what had
happened, leaving out my nasty remark to Jesse. For a time he
sat and thought and looked at me. I got up to leave. As I did,
he told me to sit down, that he was going to let me have the
money. Mr. Mac pushed a note to me and asked me to sign it.
He asked no questions as to whether or not I could pay it from
my job in Poplarville. As I left his desk that day, he said to me,
"God bless you, son. I wish you the best of luck."

At half past noon on Saturday, October 9, 1954, Mr. Mac
died in a hospital in Jackson, Mississippi. To me, G. W. Mc-
Williams was not just one of the state's best bankers but one
of the kindest and most humane and understanding men I have
ever known.

My pocket bulging with the bank's money, I returned to
Columbia and packed my tin suitcase, which didn't take long.
At that time I had two pairs of shoes, one leather and one tennis;
four pairs of pants, two cotton, two wool; four shirts; and a few
pairs of drawers. As I had to wear one each of my wardrobe
items, I had plenty of space in the suitcase, and in that space
I packed home-canned jellies, jams and preserves, made from
peaches, plums and blackberries. I set forth to get a college
education, fortified with such edibles, plus fifteen dollars in
cash. I hitch-hiked from Columbia and got as far as Lumberton
when dark caught me. From Lumberton to Poplarville, a distance of about twelve miles, I rode a bus. It was dark when I
arrived, and I was starving. Near the bus station there was a
small café operated by a lady and her daughter. Checking the
menu, I found that a bowl of Irish stew was fifteen cents. With
an additional five cents I bought the largest root beer they had.

95

On twenty cents I feasted. That night I didn't know it, but I was to consume a large quantity of stew before the year was over.

I was unfamiliar with the college way of operating. Lugging my stuffed suitcase from downtown to the school left me exhausted. The distance was a fraction less than a mile, but I was loaded with jelly and jam.

I had not expected trouble, but immediately I ran into it. An assistant in charge of one of the boys' dormitories said I had to be registered before he could allow me to sleep in one of the rooms. I pointed out that it was too late to register, that I was going to do it the next morning; my argument fell on deaf ears. I thanked the man and departed, but I didn't go far, only around the building and back into it. I soon found an unlocked room and went to bed.

The next morning I registered and became a college man in pursuit of a medical degree. As a potential medical student, I had chosen courses in English Literature, American Literature, American history, French and spoken English. The latter turned out, to my amazement, to be a course in public speaking. While I didn't elect it, I found that I'd also have a class in military science and tactics once a week and that I'd drill for an hour three mornings each week.

Soon I began to have trouble with the military.

An area of disagreement developed when I persisted in wearing tennis shoes to drill. It wasn't all stubbornness on my part; I had only one pair of dress shoes and didn't want to ruin them wading around in wet grass.

The job I had in town required me to go to work after class each day and work until midnight. The result was I'd sleep through ROTC drill most days. First, the company commander, a cadet captain, started to raise hell; it went from him to the cadet major, then to the cadet colonel, then, as I'd expected, to the Regular Army colonel in charge of ROTC. Not too many words passed between any one of them and me. I said simply that I wasn't going to drill, that I'd come to school for an education, not to be a soldier. The colonel commented that my grades did not seem to merit my attitude, pointing out that I'd been kicked out of two classes. It was a relatively simple matter for them. The colonel reported me to the administration and I was suspended automatically for one week.

Upon returning to school, I went to the colonel and explained my position, telling him that I had to work to go to school and asked if I could be excused from ROTC. The answer was an emphatic *no!* He didn't argue, nor did I. My mind was made up about the military matter. I didn't like it and I wasn't going to do it. Somehow I made it through the first semester, skipping ROTC just short of being suspended again.

Later I approached the colonel again and made my usual plea to be excused from ROTC. The answer was the same. I became angry and in the finish of the discussion I was so angry I called the colonel a stupid son-of-a-bitch. I'll never forget the expression on that man's face. He didn't believe it, so he asked me what I said. I knew my position was bad, and my temper was under control, so I said, "Nothing, Colonel. I didn't say anything at all."

"Colonel," said the cadet major, who was also present, "what he said was that you were a SOB, and the ROTC could go to hell."

Having lied unsuccessfully, I exploded: "And you, you sneaky, dirty bastard, are a son-of-a-bitch, too." I turned and walked away. The more I thought about it, the angrier I got. Finally, I went to the business office and bought four stencils. Then, on a borrowed typewriter, I composed four pages of nasty vitriol about matters military. I spared no one, especially the cadet officers. I skipped all my classes, devoting my day to my first publishing venture. Finally, when the sheets were finished, mimeographed, stapled and ready for distribution, I took them personally over to the dining hall and handed them out to students as they entered.

It was a short, simple matter. The next day I was expelled for good.

In early 1941, I went to work for Greyhound Bus Lines in Hattiesburg, in the baggage department. No intelligence was required, only a strong back; I qualified quite well.

The manager of the station was a chubby, blond young man with whom I got along very well. Shortly after I went to work he approached me and said he was short on cash and would be most grateful if I'd let him have some money until payday. I didn't have any cash and told him so. He suggested that I borrow it from a loan company; he'd sign the note and repay the money to them. I didn't want to do it, but how could I refuse the boss?

I borrowed one hundred and fifty dollars and gave every cent to him. A month or two later he suggested I borrow a hundred dollars from the bank and let him have it as we'd done the other. Again I hesitated, and I considered the matter again. He had made the monthly payments on the installment loan. That was okay; he was all right. I said yes, I'd do it.

One day an auditor came and made an audit which lasted for two full days. On the third morning my friend, the manager, was not to be found. No one has heard of him since.

I soon made two decisions, one of which is explicable; the other is not. First, I decided not to pay the installment note to the loan company. Why I decided the way I did is still beyond me. I contended, and in complete honesty, that I didn't get one cent of the money, so why should I pay it? At the bank I had made arrangements to pay off that note on an installment basis. I cannot explain why I should decide to pay one and not the other, but such was my decision and until I was threatened with a lawsuit, I stuck by it. Finally, I paid off the loan, not because I felt any responsibility, but out of fear of being sued and losing my job.

The second decision I made was to quit Greyhound and take a job with the Southern Railway System in their ticket office. Whether or not that was a mistake is open to question, but it was to prove interesting at times; indeed, most of the time it was interesting. From the day I reported to work at Southern Railway, I didn't fit. It was April 18, 1942, when I began and August 1, 1951, when I left, and that's a long time not to fit. Somehow, through it all, I never cared whether a train was on time or not. I was not entirely displeased when I was drafted into the Army in 1942.

It can be said truthfully that the Army and I got off to a bad start; truthfully, it can also be said that the situation showed no improvement as time passed.

Chapter 15

It would be difficult, perhaps impossible, to determine the influence events preceding my induction had on my attitude while in the Army. Prior to my twenty-first birthday, which was in November, six months before I was drafted, my mother had insisted that I spend my birthday in Columbia. I seldom went to Columbia—the place held unpleasant memories for me—but I went like a dutiful son. My mother wanted to tell me about my adoption, at least all she knew about it. First, she explained that she may have made a mistake, but it had been decided long ago that I wouldn't be told until I was twenty-one. As she knew the story, it went like this:

On the first day of December in 1921, she and my father had gone to see a woman in a hotel in Columbia, having been told by a doctor that the woman had a son she wanted to give for adoption. They had gone to see the woman, who gave no explanation as to why she wanted to give her child away. My mother and father, being childless, were not too concerned with the reasons why. The necessary papers were drawn up, and the adoption was made legal. Where the woman had come from was unknown and it was unknown where she went. However, in less than a year my parents were called on by the father of the woman who gave birth to me. He said simply that his daughter wanted the baby back, and he was willing to pay any reasonable amount if he could have the child. The Easts said no. Still later, the brother of the woman called on my parents and made an attempt to recover the child for his mother. Again the Easts said no.

The father of my blood mother was Richard T. Battle, a farmer from a community in the western part of the state. The brother was Dr. Larson Z. Battle, who practiced medicine in a Delta town. They made no trouble for the Easts, only suggested that a child was better off with its blood mother. Still, the Easts learned nothing about my blood mother. Her father and brother offered no information, and the Easts didn't ask.

Anyway, that was about the extent of the information my

mother was able to supply. She said that Dr. Battle was still practicing medicine in the state.

While I had more than suspected for many years that I was an adopted child, hearing the actual story from my mother literally knocked the props from under me. I thanked her for telling me, and asked no questions. My state of mind was difficult to define. I was resentful toward a woman whom I'd never known. I almost hated her. How could a mother give away her child? What kind of woman would do such at thing? I was confused and resentful and disgusted. As hard as I tried, I could not get the woman off my mind. It could not be explained. I could not begin to understand such a woman as my real mother had been. I wanted to know her, and at the same time I never wanted to see her. Frustration was my fate; there were too many questions to which I could find no answers. While my temper had always been near the boiling point, I found it more and more difficult to control. Explosions were frequent. It was in this frame of mind that I entered the Army at Camp Shelby, Mississippi.

Chapter 16

Ten million men in this nation went through the same induction procedure as I did. I doubt seriously, however, that any of them were moved about with such regularity as I was. In less than twelve months I was transferred five times, the Army having a difficult time finding where I'd best fit into the scheme of things.

My fifth transfer was to Camp Butner, North Carolina, located near Durham.

When I arrived in Durham it was raining, and it seldom stopped for the first two weeks of my stay. The camp was new and the streets were mud.

To relate my feelings about the camp is impossible. I was confused and angry and sick and disgusted. I could not get anything focused in my mind. Why? Over and over I asked the question. Why, since I had to be in the Army, could I not at least be sent overseas where I might feel that I was doing some small amount of good, instead of being aimlessly shipped hither and yon about the United States, from one meaningless job to another? The rain and mud didn't help my attitude, nor did the attitude of the company commander help my feelings. I was supposed to have been sent there as the company clerk, but before the Fourth Service Command could supply me, the captain had secured a clerk from some source or other. In short, they had nothing for me to do—except to make carbon copies and wash dishes. It was a half mile to the PX from our area, and I walked it every evening and got loaded on beer. What a lonely, miserable feeling it is to be some place and not know a single other person with whom you can talk.

For several months I'd been having complete and total lapses of memory, a condition for which I had no explanation. The memory lapses continued, getting more frequent, and it was obvious that they were increasing in their length. I was frightened as well as miserable and lonely and angry and confused.

I'd hardly arrived at Camp Butner when I received a letter from my foster mother in which she told me of the death of my mother. I don't know how she knew, but she said my real mother had died in Houston, Texas, and was buried there. I think I tried to have two reactions to the news of the death. I tried to be happy about it, but failed; and I tried to feel some sort of pity, and also failed. I think I felt nothing; I was emotionally numb. In any event, I was unable to clear the matter from my mind.

One afternoon I was walking to the PX for beer and the next thing I knew I was standing in the middle of the street with a driver of a truck shouting at me to get the hell out of the road before I got killed. I had no memory of anything whatsoever, except having set out for the PX. I returned to the company headquarters and requested permission to go to the hospital. The captain wanted to know where I hurt. I didn't hurt anywhere, and that brought on more talk. I refused to tell him what had been happening; frankly, I was embarrassed by it, not being able to explain it in any manner. While we were a medical company, there wasn't a doctor in it that I ever saw. Finally, after batting my head against the wall that was my commanding officer, I got permission to go to the hospital. His final thrust was "Anybody who's sick and don't hurt anywhere must be in pretty bad shape." Arriving at the hospital, I was sent to see First Lieutenant Felix Goldberg, M.D. Dr. Goldberg was a psychiatrist.

He was as small a man as I'd ever seen. His hair was jet black and his eyes watery blue, deep set and wide apart. Dr. Goldberg gave me a sedative that night and for the first time in months I slept a restful sleep. He asked very few questions on our first meeting. The following day he got down to business, asking probing questions about family, schooling, economic background and countless other things. I did not lie to the doctor; I did, however, discover the difference between the truth and the whole truth. Some of the questions I could not bring myself to talk about. Not once did he press me for an answer. I continued to get sedatives every night for about a week. The memory lapse occurred only twice in the first two weeks I was in the hospital. I asked to be released from the hospital. He advised against it, but said if that was what I wanted, he'd approve it. In less than two weeks I was back in the hospital again, as frightened as I'd ever been. To be walking along and not know anything about what's happened for heaven knows how long is indeed frightening—at least it was to me.

The fact that I was hospitalized added to my confused state of mind. Over a period of several weeks Dr. Goldberg must have reached a conclusion with reference to me. One morning he called me into his office and asked me if I'd like to go home. I thought he meant on a furlough. He said it was his opinion that I was temperamentally unsuited for the rigid discipline demanded by the military. He explained how he thought I must have felt about it, but he added, "I'm in somewhat the same position as you, in a manner of speaking. I left my native Germany, my family and friends, and came to the United States. I want to do everything I can to help my people, and I'm here safe and sound in this country. Every day the Nazis are killing Jews, and some of them may be my relatives or friends. What

102

can I do to help them? I'm not a general, but maybe by helping here in the hospital I'm helping those people in Germany. Maybe by working for the railroad you can make a contribution to the effort, too. I have been able to adjust to my environment; you haven't, and that is no reflection on you. Sometimes we can't adjust to situations in which we find ourselves. In Germany I could not adjust to Hitler, but my desire to help was not killed by the way I have to fight. Nor will yours be. I want you to go home and rest for a month or two and then go back to the railroad. Too, there's a doctor in New Orleans who may be able to help you get your balance."

I was concerned and asked if I was nuts.

"Far from it," he said and laughed. "You are only trying to escape something which you cannot become adjusted to. Some people do it with alcohol; others use narcotics. Since you are neither an alcoholic nor an addict, you have tried to drive out reality by temporary lapses of your memory. It is not a serious thing, not now. But it could easily result in a complete breakdown if it continues. Go see the doctor in New Orleans when you get home. He has more time to help you than I have, I'm sorry to say. I think for your own good and for the good of the Army your best place is out of the service. You'll be a while getting used to the idea of not being in. But for God's sake don't start letting that get you down."

Dr. Goldberg was right; I've still not become accustomed to my failure as a soldier at a time when I was needed. With reference to Dr. Goldberg, I've often thought of him, tried to understand the man. One thing has remained in my memory. While I was in his care in the hospital, the doctor often asked me to join him in the recreation room. He would sit at the piano for an hour, sometimes more, and play. While I don't know whether he was a good pianist or not, I enjoyed it. What I've wondered about is the question of who was getting the treatment, the doctor or the patient. Perhaps it made no difference.

Chapter 17

Returning to Hattiesburg was a mistake. The memory lapses continued, but in time they tapered off. Having returned home, I was often asked why I'd been discharged. To explain the matter was beyond me—that is, to go into the facts that I hadn't been intelligent enough to adjust to the circumstances in which I found myself. I hit on the idea of saying simply, "I had a nervous breakdown," and letting it go at that.

I waited almost a month before deciding to return to work at the railroad. In the meantime I'd gone to New Orleans to see Dr. Charles Hooker, a psychiatrist. He thought it was all right for me to return to work, but he wasn't a railroad doctor. Before I could go back to work, it was necessary for me to have a physical examination by the company doctor. I went for that and was greeted with a flat refusal to allow my re-employment.

I was making no progress with Dr. Hooker. The fault was mine, of course, because I refused to talk with him freely. I could not bring myself to relate the blow that I'd suffered because of Tad Barber's death on a mission over Europe, and especially I could not bring myself to talk about my family. The question of why a mother would give away a child haunted me day and night, but I discussed it with no one. At home I would take long walks by myself. I was of the opinion they were good for me, and I found them to be relaxing to a degree. Over a period of time I began to wonder if I wasn't wasting time and money with Dr. Hooker by not telling him of the things which bothered me. Finally, with considerable pain and anxiety, I related the fact that I was an adopted child and, with his probing, I told him the story as it had been told to me. His advice was that I get in touch with blood relatives, especially Dr. Battle, inasmuch as he was obviously interested in me since he had made an attempt to return me to my mother. For weeks I hesitated, debating the question of whether or not I should do as Dr. Hooker had suggested. I should make it clear that for over a year the thought of suicide had been close with me. To do the act took a kind of courage I did not have, but I thought of it constantly. Finally, in desperation, I reasoned that I had nothing to lose by getting in touch with Dr. Battle. I couldn't be more in agony, no matter what his reaction might be. I called him on the telephone and identified myself. He knew who I was and expressed considerable pleasure at hearing from me. A meeting was arranged at his suggestion; we met in Jackson a day or two later.

Larson Z. Battle, M.D., was a tall, slightly stooped man, gray, with a serious face, but still a kind face, and with eyes that always seemed to have a grin in them. They were eyes that had seen much and were concerned with much. He was waiting for me in a hotel lobby, and as I entered the building I knew who he was as if by instinct. I think his response was the same, based on his act of rising and walking directly toward me with his hand extended. Here was a man to whom I could talk. I knew that without having to think about it. Dr. Battle, my mother's brother, was the first blood relative I'd ever known. We were friends without sparring to find out what the other thought. It was a new experience for me, and rather a strange one, too. We spent the entire day in conversation. I was not hesitant in asking questions of him about my mother, nor was he hesitant in answering them, no matter what the question or how personal or cynical it was.

Basically, he told me the story of my mother. It was quite obvious that the memory of her was painful to him, but for reasons which differed from mine. His pain grew from a concern, mine from a lack of concern.

My mother's name had been Laura; she was the youngest of five children, all of whom had grown up on a farm. At an early age she had shown an interest in poetry, making an attempt at writing. She also had a talent for music. Later, she entered Mississippi Woman's College in Hattiesburg, and after numerous ups and downs received a degree in music. While in college she was expelled twice because of temper tantrums, the result of which had been a general cursing out of everyone in sight. Both times Uncle Larson had gone to her and had helped her cool off. Both times he had managed to get her back in school. She had been a frustrated person her entire life, failing to find

105

an outlet for what was inside. In a state of frustration and anger at her father she had married R. P. Thompson just after graduation from college. Her husband was a farmer. From the marriage a girl was born. Before her birth my mother returned to the home of her father and obtained a divorce immediately after the child was born. The daughter was reared by grandparents and by Uncle Larson. My mother taught music and finally began to give concerts in cities in the South. Her temper was something she could not control. Once in New Orleans she had become angry before a performance and refused to play; the result was that all tickets had to be refunded. She was not a manager's delight. In New Orleans she had been married again, that time to Dr. M. D. Hopkins. Becoming pregnant with me, she had become depressed and subject to terrible outbursts of temper. Finally, she decided to leave my father and return to her parents' home. En route from New Orleans, she had given birth to me in Columbia, Mississippi, on November 26, 1921. She found herself in desperate circumstances. She didn't want her husband to know where she was; at the same time, she didn't want her father to know she'd left her husband. Being of her temperament, she had decided to let the Easts have me, a decision she was to regret until the day of her death. For a long time she didn't tell her parents of my birth. When she finally did, my grandfather tried to get me from the Easts. After divorcing my father, she married Thompson for the second time. From the second union a boy was born. My mother's pattern held true. She left Thompson and gave the second son, named Ray, to Uncle Larson to rear, which he did. After her third divorce, she moved to Houston and lived with a sister and taught music until her death.

From Uncle Larson I learned that my father had died a number of years ago. He knew little about him. I learned that my sister, as well as my aunt, lived in Texas; also, that my brother was serving in a paratroop outfit overseas. Uncle Larson said my mother was one of the most tragic persons he'd ever known; she had failed to find any outlet for her creative desire, and, in so failing, she destroyed. He felt more or less responsible for her. He felt he could have helped her had he not been so

106

engrossed in his own efforts. Having to work his way through medical school, he had little time to give his sister. He felt guilty about that.

At the meeting in Jackson he asked me to come to his home and stay with him. I had told him of the trouble I'd been having; he seemed to think it quite natural and assured me I had nothing to worry about, as my memory lapses would pass in due time.

Back home in Hattiesburg, I tried to get back to work. Again the company doctor wouldn't allow it. Since I had time and a railroad pass, I decided to go to Texas to visit my sister. I went, not knowing what to expect. She was a nice, pleasant girl, but a complete stranger to me. We got along well enough. But my aunt! What a pain she was. Karlene told me that our mother, when ill with cancer, had had to take quite a bit from her older sister, who had recounted all her sins to her. Karlene knew of me, but had no idea where I was. She told me how much my mother had suffered because of her act in Columbia in 1921. One day Karlene drove me out to the cemetery to my mother's grave. I hesitated to go, but as I stood in the cemetery beside the grave I felt the deepest compassion I've ever known, before or since. It wasn't as if I'd suffered a loss, because you can't lose what you've never had, and I'd never known the woman as a mother. I felt a great desire to weep, but tears wouldn't come. I think it was pity or compassion in the broadest sense of the word. In any event, I didn't hate the woman, and I was glad to know that. It was, as a matter of fact, a relief of some sort. For the first time in my life, I knew full well I didn't hate my mother.

I returned home, and later went to north Mississippi to spend two weeks with Uncle Larson. He had a small clinic and allowed me to stand around while he worked. He had two sons and one daughter. None of his children had any desire to study medicine, and Uncle Larson was disappointed because of it. I told him of my early desire to become a doctor. I also told him what had come of it. Before I returned home, Uncle Larson told me if I would go to medical school he would help financially and in any and every other way possible. I thought about it for some time, finally deciding that I didn't have the kind of mind to do it. I could not retain facts. I've always been deeply grateful to him, and wished I could have availed myself of the opportunity. While he and I got along fine, his wife and daughter caused me considerable trouble. They seemed to resent my being there, both having had an obvious dislike for my mother. We couldn't get along. Because of those two women I cut short my stay with Uncle Larson. I didn't tell him why; I don't think it was necessary.

I was genuinely fond of the man and visited him many times, limiting my stays to a day, sometimes two. He had a great understanding of human nature and an equal ability to accept people for what they were. He laughed most of the time, but never out loud.

As the summer passed I improved. Before going into the Army, my weight had been about one hundred and sixty. It had dropped to one hundred thirty pounds. Slowly, I was gaining it back. My memory lapses became still less frequent; however, my temper wasn't anything to brag about. As I was and am a coward, I didn't get into fights, but there were many times I came close. I didn't sleep well, but I was sleeping better than I had been. My nerves were on edge, and I was worried about money, or the lack of it. That, of course, was nothing new.

Finally, after more than six months from the time I was discharged by the Army, the railroad's doctor allowed me to return to work.

After returning to work I decided to become an outstanding young man. I knew what it took, so I set out to be a jolly good fellow. I joined a civic club, worked at it, spoke to people whom I couldn't stand and who couldn't stand me, made contributions to worthy causes, and stayed sober. I did everything along that line except to go to church and kiss babies. It was sickening, but I was fairly successful, success in that line being what it is. I was invited to join the country club. I had arrived; but, unfortunately, I couldn't afford it. I was so busy being a success as an up-and-coming young man that I had gone in debt head over heels. In looking back on that year, I thought I was a happy man who enjoyed every second of it. I must have been sicker than anyone thought.

Later, after a brief period in the ticket office in Hattiesburg,

108

I accepted a job as a traveling passenger representative on Southern Railways' two streamlined trains, the "Southerner" and the "Tennesseean."

For the first few months I was assigned to the "Tennesseean," running between Washington and Memphis. Before being promoted to the "Southerner," on the New York-to-New Orleans run, I made a number of trips from Washington to Memphis on the "Tennesseean." One of the duties of a passenger representative was to make a comprehensive report at the end of each trip. Usually I couldn't think of anything to report. However, once in Knoxville, while stopped over for twenty-four hours, I shared a hotel room with a fellow employee. Undressing, I noticed he laid out a blackjack and I asked what use he found for it. I was told that "them niggers sometimes need to be put in their place." To that gentleman a blackjack seemed the proper instrument with which to do it. I thought it a bit stupid, but said nothing to the man. My report for that trip included the comment: "From Corinth, Miss., to Memphis, Tenn., I found it necessary to put two niggers in their place by slugging them." Of course, it wasn't true, but I couldn't resist the temptation to make the remark. On my word, nothing was said to me about it at the office.

After being promoted to the "Southerner," I had several words said to me at the office in Washington. Actually, my days as an "up-and-coming young railroad official" were numbered, but I didn't know it at the time. Still unable to think of anything to put in my reports, I'd include the most outlandish things I could dream up. One report I sent in said simply, "On this trip the train was wrecked and everyone was killed." Another report of mine carried the statement: "I traveled from New York to New Orleans and back to Washington and didn't open my mouth to a single person. The train was on time, and I was glad, glad, glad! Do you hear? I was glad!" Naturally, I was asked to explain each such report. My bosses didn't understand them, but they had nothing on me.

An item which I could not comprehend was the treatment of Negro passengers. I accepted the fact that they had a separate car, but it seemed downright silly to me that in the dining car there was a curtain between tables. On one side of the curtain a white passenger would be eating, and less than two feet away a Negro passenger would be eating, the curtain up between them, of course. It didn't seem to make sense. I made no, complaint about it. However, one thing came up about which I did complain. In New York, the Pennsylvania Railroad had a certain allotment of seats on the "Southerner." They would sell them to Negro passengers, assigning them a seat in a car reserved for whites. When the train would leave Washington, as soon as we'd crossed the Potomac River, it was the duty of the passenger representative to move the Negroes from the white car into the Negro car. I did it a couple of times, feeling disgusted with myself. I'd had no trouble with any of the Negro passengers when I had asked them to move. However, one man asked me a question I couldn't answer. When I'd asked him to move he'd asked me, "Why?" The only answer I could think of was that it was a "company rule." He informed me his money had been green, the same color as that of every passenger on the train. I couldn't argue with him; I knew that, and it caused me to question myself and others like me. As a result of our discussion, I decided it was all right with me for the Negro man to sit where he was. In short, I refused to make him move. For that I was reported by the conductor, the hostess and some of the passengers. I gave my boss the same answers the Negro man had given me. I thought they were quite sound, and I defended the Negro passenger and myself. I could not account for my behavior in the matter of arguing the defense of that unknown Negro man.

While I had offended my employer, I knew full well that all I had to do was to repent, so to speak, and say, "Yes, sir, I'll see that it never happens again." I could not bring myself to repent; to do so would have been completely dishonest, and I knew it. I received a stern warning. I still contended, and to his face, that the reasoning of the Negro passenger was better than that of my boss. I knew my time was limited; the railroad officials had no choice but to can me sooner or later. So I beat them to the punch. I quit a few steps ahead of being fired.

During the time I was traveling for the railroad I had something of a shock on one trip. Leaving Birmingham, heading north, I was walking through the train and as suddenly and as

110

unexpectedly as a bolt of lightning, the thought entered my mind: Jesus is not God! It was in those exact words. To say I was not stunned somewhat would be erroneous; I was stunned completely. I stopped and stood for a long time looking out the train window. I had given no thought to God for years. How, then, did the idea creep into my mind? God was the last thing on my mind, and, insofar as I knew, I was probably the last thing on His. I'll admit I was frightened at the thought, and why I didn't know, for had I not been a good atheist at one time? To tremble at questioning the divinity of Jesus was beyond me.

After getting over the shock of a thought's having entered my mind, I began to read everything I could lay my hands on. I discovered some delightful men. I had read a fair amount of literature but had never delved into the minds of the philosophers—men who had been plagued with similar questions. One idea led to another, from God to man to government to evil and good, to education and mind and matter and heaven knows what. The only thing I'd wanted to know about was God. I suspect I drew more conclusions with less to base them on than anyone in modern history. As soon as I'd get one idea worked out, someone would present another idea and shatter my seemingly satisfactory shell. Finally I reached the same conclusion that Socrates had reached over two thousand years ago—that I really didn't know anything. But Socrates had said he knew nothing, and I was not as sure of myself as that. I wasn't sure about anything.

When I was in Washington I spent most of my time at Brentano's searching their shelves for God. We were not too well acquainted, I fear. From my efforts came one conclusion by which I've stuck—that nothing is more important in this life than man, that there is a tie-up between God and man in man's daily living and his treatment of his fellow man. Man is not God, but in man's decency there is a part of God. Admittedly, my thoughts didn't go deep, but to me they were important, something by which I could try to live.

Having resigned my "glad-handing, good-fellowship" position in Washington, I returned to Hattiesburg and the ticket office.

Chapter 18

By the middle of July of 1951 I'd had it with the railroad. I was so miserable and sick of the whole thing that I thought one more day would kill me, or make me kill myself. On the fifteenth day of July I sat down one morning and wrote my resignation, giving two weeks' notice and asking if I could have my two weeks' vacation starting then. At first my superiors were surprised and wouldn't believe me. Slowly, I think, it dawned on them how happy they really were and they allowed me to leave at noon with a full day's pay.

Nine and one third years earlier I had started work for the railroad as a clerk at eight dollars per day. After that lapse of time I resigned from the railroad as a clerk at sixteen dollars per day. A number of persons were interested in knowing why I'd resigned. They couldn't understand why anyone with my seniority and security would suddenly give them up. And, unfortunately, I couldn't explain it to anyone. I didn't know why I'd done it; after all, I was in debt, as usual, and had no prospect of another job. Frankly, I never did know why I quit.

In the early winter I decided I wanted to work for myself, but I didn't know at what. I heard that a local labor union, the Coke and Chemical Workers, was interested in getting out a paper of its own but had no one to do it. I contacted the chief steward of the organization and we worked out an arrangement. It would be a percentage deal. I was to get two thirds of the net profits; he was to get one third. He wanted me to handle the entire business, subject to his approval.

From the start, the paper, *The Union Review,* did quite well. It had the blessing of the company, and from the first issue it showed a profit. My only interest in the paper was to make money. I found out quite early we would have no editorial policy other than loving the Lord and hating sin. By his own modest admission, the chief steward's column made the paper. That's about all there was in it; the balance of the copy was canned. However, the chief steward and I got along fairly well. When I'd feel the need to rebel at some of his actions or comments, I'd consider the money I was making and curb the desire. The chief was, in a loose manner of speaking, an interesting man. I once decided he was the kind of person who'd never use a rapier, not if he could get his hands on a club. He had a desire to be right, and in order to end a discussion to his satisfaction he'd not bother to strengthen his argument; he'd simply strengthen the volume of his voice.

My plan was to present him with a complete audit at the end of each month. I wanted him to know how I was running the paper, where the expense money went, everything. He'd look over the books and comment about the expense of a two-dollar engraving, or something equally unimportant. I am honest in saying that it reached the point where I was afraid to go to the bathroom without first talking it over, or listening it over, with the chief steward. The situation did not add to my personal happiness, but then I would think about the sweet smell of money and find it easier to accept the facts of life. I've never had the chance to discuss with a prostitute how she justified the business, but somehow I don't think I have to talk with one to know.

The paper went along well enough. All I had to do was make as much money as possible and give away one third of it. One summer it was decided at a union meeting that I would be given a title. They voted to make me "Assistant to the Chief Steward in Charge of Public Relations." As a result of that kindness it was suggested I take a job at the plant. It was thought that my being among the men who "actually owned" the paper would promote good relations. They got me a job in the labor pool. My duties were to dig holes in the ground, using pick ax and shovel and, should a crust of concrete cover the area, to make use of an air hammer. I've seldom been so thankful for anything as I was when the company had to reduce their force and I was cut off as an economy measure.

After that happened, I approached another local union, the Garment Workers, and proposed a deal with them to put out a paper. I was able to "own" that one myself and had to kick back only ten per cent of the net profits. I was then operating two union papers, and at a profit. The second paper was not nearly so profitable as the first. While the captive audience was greater

113

in numbers, their pay rate wasn't nearly so high. It was no trouble to me, however, and most of it was clear profit due to the fact that I let *The Union Review* pay the contract price on printing and then I'd lay out pages so they could be picked up and run in the *Local Advocate* at a greatly reduced rate. At one period of time during the operation of the union papers I managed to get out of debt completely for the first time in my life. I was uncomfortable, unaccustomed as I was to being free of debt. I was saving every cent I could from the papers. While I wouldn't admit it, I knew that the chief steward and I would come to a parting of the ways sooner or later. I resented more and more the fact that I was treated as something of an irresponsible child. I think human nature was expressing itself in my case. The more money I had in savings the more I resented certain attitudes and treatment.

For some time I had been engaged in the printing business, having bought a job press and put it in my garage at home. I worked at it in the time I had. I considered going into the job-printing business, but I didn't have the necessary capital. One day I learned of a weekly newspaper for sale about twenty miles from Hattiesburg. I went down to see about it. The price was twelve thousand dollars. There was a friend to whom I talked and he suggested we buy it, saying he'd buy half of it. There were two stumbling blocks. First, I didn't have six thousand dollars, and, second, I didn't want a partner. Things moved along quietly, but in my mind I kept the idea of a weekly newspaper fresh. It was in the summer of 1953 that I decided to see what could be done in the little town of Petal, just across the Leaf River from Hattiesburg, a distance of about three miles. I was making good money with two papers; so it stood to reason I'd make even more with three. Little did I know that I'd lost my mind on that point. After a preliminary survey I saw the possibility of a small paper. It would have to be printed on contract, inasmuch as a paper there could never support a shop of its own. The merchants in Petal welcomed me. A real home-town, weekly newspaper for Petal! They talked in terms of volume advertising, and I listened in terms of having finally found a means of getting somewhere from nowhere—admittedly, a long

114

three miles from Hattiesburg and about thirty miles from the Carnes logging camp.

In thirty-one years I had not gone far, but in the Magnolia Jungle it is often difficult to travel rapidly. The undergrowth is often dense. While I'd not traveled far, I had managed to do one thing: I'd escaped attending family reunions and the contact with that large number of persons with whom I had nothing in common.

Part Two

Chapter 19

There is one basic prerequisite to establishing a weekly newspaper: you have to be simple. That qualification I met without question.

However, there were questions which I asked of myself, and, being simple, I received answers in kind. The first question was "For what purpose do you want to start a weekly paper?" The answer was simple, sound and good: to make money. It seemed logical to assume that if I made six hundred dollars a month from two papers, putting them out every other week, I'd make twelve hundred dollars a month by the addition of a paper once a week. That was the theory.

What was needed to begin the publication of a weekly was another question. I decided not too much was needed—some money, an office, a place to print it, and a formula for success. I had less than $3,000, but decided it was enough. I rented a building in Petal and moved my job press and office equipment into it. I had a printing contract with *The Chronicle Star*, a large weekly in Pascagoula, and I'd discussed the paper with Easton King and we'd reached an agreement on the printing. And the formula? I had that, too—a good one. I had checked a large number of the weekly newspapers in the state and had seen the trend in their operation as to policy, news coverage and format. It was quite obvious that the formula for success could be summed up in these words: Love American Motherhood and Hate Sin.

Had I bothered to look deep into my mind and heart that late summer of 1953, I might have had different answers, but, to be honest about it, I didn't want any other answers. The ones I had were good; indeed, the state had over one hundred newspapers operating on the formula. Why should I be a screwball?

I had signs painted on the glass front of the building. I had the inside of the building painted. I arranged with a half dozen ladies to report community news. I glad-handed from hell to breakfast, winning friends and conning people.

I submitted to membership in the local Kiwanis Club, and each Tuesday I attended the meeting and dutifully ate the green peas and mashed potatoes, shook hands, smiled and listened to my peers discuss the weather and the world situation. In fact, I wore a large button, about three inches in diameter, on which my name was printed. I suppose that was aimed at eliminating strangers. It did; we were just one big, happy group calling one another by our first names.

After less than a month of such pleasantness I began to put my button into my pocket instead of on my coat or shirt. A fellow Kiwanian asked me one day what my first name was. I replied, "You can just call me mister." Along with several others, the fellow failed to see the humor. I was asked to wear my button—and I did.

I had a desire to write a column, and I wasn't sure why, except that I could mention names and keep everyone happy. Everyone's happiness and my success went hand in hand; I knew that. In a manner of speaking my ability to arrive at names was comparable to Adam's, as related by Roark Bradford. The Lord asked Adam why he'd named an elephant what he had, and Adam replied, "Well, Lord, it just looks like an elephant." First, I had arrived at a name for the paper by listening to people discuss a previous paper in the village of Petal. Everyone had referred to it as "the Petal paper." Why not name the paper what people are going to call it anyway? I did. And the column I wanted to write had to be named. I took two factors into account. First, my name, and second, the fact that Petal was east of Hattiesburg. The name of the column came out "East Side."

When I began to get down to business I found my ideas differed ever so much from the ideas of the majority of Petal's businessmen insofar as volume advertising was concerned. To most

120

of them volume advertising meant ten to fifteen dollars' expenditure per month. In my preliminary talks I'd not tried to get them to sign a contract, and that had been one more mistake in a series I was making.

Those were hectic days, long, hot and dry in more ways than weatherwise. I was working at ad layouts, copy, selling and glad-handing sixteen to eighteen hours each day of the week. While in the process of getting the new paper off the ground, I had not neglected the other two. The sweet smell of money was there, and I kept at it.

The Petal Paper, Volume 1, Number 1, Thursday, November 19, 1953, was what I had expected it to be: a sheet designed to keep everyone happy, even me. The six pages carried thirty-nine ads of varying sizes. All the news stories were local; in addition, there were a few features. The front page carried a four-column picture of the local football team, and that fit my theory of how to succeed at operating a weekly paper: mention everyone's name.

The "East Side" column was my pride and joy. I ran it two columns wide and set it in 10-point type. In the first issue I began a series of short features which I titled "Citizen of the Week." Of the entire series I recall only two which were worth while, insofar as the person's being worth a write-up. In the first issue I did the feature on Dr. J. E. Pou, a fine old man who had devoted his life to the community. Later, I did a feature on Dr. A. T. Tatum, another person worthy of mention. The other "Citizens of the Week" were the village businessmen, whose sole contribution, like mine, was to figure how to make a dollar from the citizens of the area.

In addition I had arranged with several ministers to write a column each week for the paper. "Prayer and Meditation" was aimed at those Christians who were afraid not to read any printed word about Jesus. The editorial page carried five safe pieces. They ranged from the cause of forest fires to the fact that businesses had no choice but to be fair because of competition, to the Great Baby Boom, and then to the cattle population of the nation. Of course, the outstanding editorial was the one I wrote having to do with the policy of the paper. Titled simply "A Statement of Policy," it went like this:

The primary purpose of *The Petal Paper*, which you are now holding in your hand, is to be of service to you.

Service is a word through which a number of businesses have stuck their hands pretty far down into the pockets of the American people. Needless to say, any business must operate on a profitable basis, or cease to operate; however, there is a great difference in the two approaches.

This paper will always serve you at the least possible cost. By that we mean that no charge will be made for items you want to insert, except, of course, in the case of advertising.

We have no bones to pick with anyone; therefore, there will be no crusades, except when it is to the public interest.

If one has the stomach for it, that's not a bad policy for a newspaper to have. On Thursday, November 19, 1953, I wasn't the least bit ill, either. Later I took another step in fence-straddling by writing an open letter to the people of Petal and running it on the front page. I wrote:

Almost from the first day the office of *The Petal Paper* was opened, we have had the question of "Incorporation" called to our attention. We have heard parts of both sides of the question, and are convinced the question certainly has two sides, both with good points.

Now, we have been asked by advocates of both sides what we thought about the question of Incorporation. We think it's a good subject, an intelligent subject, and feel that it should be discussed not only in the barber shops, the grocery stores, the service stations, but in your paper, which, after all, is the place for such a discussion.

As a newspaper our job is not to discuss the question; our job is to report your discussions, be they pro or con. As a newspaper our job is not to make news, but to report it accurately and as unbiased as is humanly possible.

It would be most difficult to beat that for fence-straddling. Had Joseph Pulitzer established a prize for "Pleasing Everyone" I feel certain I'd have won it twice in the same year. Too many Mississippi editors have cast-iron guts; nothing makes them ill. As for me, I was probably the only one with a stomach made of solid brass. As profitable as it was, I didn't sleep well at night, but

122

not because of conscience; rather, I wasn't sleeping well because of trying to figure new ways and means of getting my hand farther into the pockets of people. I didn't want to slight a single one of them. And every Tuesday I ate my green peas and mashed potatoes and smiled until my ears hurt.

With three papers going at the same time, my work habits continued the same, sixteen to eighteen hours a day. In order to stand the pace I began taking Dexedrine. It gave me a boost and kept me alert. At night I failed to rest because of the effect of the stimulant; in order to sleep I was forced to take sleeping pills. It became a cycle, almost a way of life.

In opening the office in Petal, I had not only forgotten to hang up the Kiwanis Code of Ethics but, more importantly, I'd neglected to consult with the chief steward who controlled the union paper. I saw no point in telling him of my plans to start my own paper. Certainly I was not neglecting the paper in which he was interested; his cut was good each month. However, around the middle of December he called me in to see him and told me that he wasn't asking for my resignation, but if I wanted to resign it would be all right with him.

The paper was making money, I had no desire to give it up, and I told him so. Had I attempted any sort of honesty with myself, I'd have admitted one thing: I knew the parting of the ways was just a matter of time, and I'd known it since the first day we started the paper.

After the generous offer to accept my resignation, I thought about it for a few days and finally decided to resign, not because the chief steward wanted me to but because I needed the time for my own paper. I knew that with the resignation I'd have to stop the publication of my second union paper. By and large, the second paper was dependent on the first, in that I had a cut-rate deal to reuse ads which were already made up.

December had been a good month; my net take from the three papers amounted to approximately twelve hundred dollars. I bought my second auto and was getting ready to move to a suburb, as any successful young man should. Getting out of the union-newspaper business was something of a relief, which I'd not expected. I continued devoting long hours to work on my weekly.

In January 1954 my sins began to catch up with me. The excessive use of a stimulant, followed by the excessive use of a sedative, put me in the hospital, suffering from fatigue and the after-effects of excessive living in general.

Lying in the hospital bed, I reflected on my position. It was to be envied, I decided. I was making good money; I was accepted by the community; I was the youngest newspaper owner in the state; I was happy, I told myself.

My first slip came in February. It was unintentional. On Lincoln's birthday, I ran a front-page feature on him. In it I referred to his death as "unfortunate" and praised him as the personification of the Great American Story. A couple of subscribers took issue with me, saying the death of Lincoln was not "unfortunate," except that it had come years too late. I didn't apologize; but the exception worried me. And to top it off, February was a bad month in volume of business done.

Besides those two things, I grew more unhappy at being a good Kiwanian and being forced to smile, shake hands and in general go against my nature. However, I didn't bother to analyze my feelings; I continued to "joy-boy." And often, in the midst of laughter and good-fellowship, I suffered the deepest loneliness.

When I'd become aware of my state of mind, I would be frightened and snap back with a healthy smile and a hearty handshake. Such is the effect of the sweet smell of money, and I doubt whether anyone loved the smell better than I.

Not only did I feel uncomfortable at the weekly meeting of the Kiwanis Club, but I began having trouble with my temper.

A leading merchant suggested that I attend one of the churches each Sunday. "It would help your business," he told me.

"I appreciate your suggestion," I replied, "but I'm damned if I'll use the church for business purposes."

One word led to another, until I walked out of his store. The week following he did not see fit to run his usual ad in the paper, nor did he run it the second week. Naturally, I considered what a good prostitute would do, and I did it. I apologized to him, making some excuse about having felt bad that day. I never did go to church.

A second blow-up was the result of the same man's effort to get me to move to Petal and buy a house there. I lived in Hattiesburg; owned my home, and my wife put her foot down at the suggestion of moving to Petal. She pointed out that inasmuch as Petal was unincorporated, living there was out of the question. She stressed the lack of fire protection, police protection, the complete absence of garbage disposal, the high cost of water, which was owned by a private company, and she didn't exclude a few other minor items.

The merchant continued his pressure. "So many of the folks here have asked why you don't move to Petal."

I was nice, pleasant, even decent about it for as long as I could be. The subject came up every time we met, and I was getting tired of it. Finally the nice man said, "You know, P.D., your business would be a lot better if you lived in Petal."

"By God," I exploded, "if I have to be subjected to the whim of every bastard with three bucks to buy my paper, I'll quit publishing the damned thing."

Such shouting at an advertiser was not the way to make a fortune. I was upset for days over my sudden explosions. Needless to say, I made another apology to the man—and made no attempt to understand myself. I don't think the merchant understood me either, but he reinserted his advertising and that was the important thing to an operator like me.

I never did move to Petal.

Chapter 20

Probably the most important court decision in the history of this nation was handed down on the seventeenth day of May 1954. As for me, I was unaware of it. Of course, I read the daily newspaper, but not for its news content; rather, I read the display advertising, to see who was advertising in the daily and not advertising in my weekly. So, on May 18th, I didn't read a news story.

I was so busy promoting my own paper that I was unaware of most things going on around me—with one exception. I had acquired over $400 worth of photographic equipment and was taking pictures of everything that came by. I photographed a 100-pound turtle, a P.T.A. supper, children in school, the high-school band, and Kiwanis speakers. On the day of the Supreme Court decision I was photographing an egg which measured ten inches around the long way, eight inches the other, and weighed over a quarter of a pound. I was more concerned with the size of a hen's rump than I was with the basic rights of one man in every ten.

The days moved on. The paper showed a profit; needless to say, I missed the profits from the other two papers, but I didn't regret having got rid of them. I continued with full force my efforts to make money. I tried every promotion in the book on subscription drives, offering prizes of washing machines and television sets. I stopped short of an automobile give-away. In spite of the efforts, subscription sales stayed far short of my goal of five thousand.

Three months after the Supreme Court decision I ran an editorial on my front page, giving credit to the *Christian Science Monitor,* titled "Decision of the Century." Naturally, I saw to it that I was protected, in that next to the *Monitor* editorial I ran one titled "Black Monday," written by Clayton Rand of Gulfport, Mississippi. Again in 1954 I'd have won a Pulitzer for fence-straddling. For the editor's note accompanying the two editorials I wrote:

The important question of segregation is indeed good editorial material, and possibly we should take a stand for or against the recent Supreme Court ruling. We feel that more important than segregation or non-segregation is the right of every individual to decide for himself—on all things. We present herewith two views on the question—it is, in our opinion, a hard-won privilege by man to decide for himself, to seek his own destiny, express his own thoughts, follow his own reasoning. So, Segregation or Non-Segregation—the thing that makes it right or wrong is your opinion.

126

That final sentence did indeed reflect inspired prostitution.

While it wasn't much, I can say with complete honesty the only redeeming factor in my favor was that I never once entertained the thought of coming out against the decision of the Supreme Court. At the same time, I didn't entertain any thought of coming out against the mores of the society in which I had been born and reared. So, as I put it then, segregation or non-segregation, the best thing I could do would be to leave it alone.

Finally, on November 11, 1954, we reached the first anniversary of *The Petal Paper*. I considered holding "Open House," serving Cokes and throwing a sober party. My wife said she didn't think such an orgy would be necessary. Naturally, I was crushed by her lack of enthusiasm over my success as a weekly newspaper publisher and editor.

In the last issue of the first year I carried two news stories which were to be significant. One was a slanted story, aimed at getting people to vote for a proposed amendment to the state constitution. This would allow the legislature to abolish the public-school system in the event of a threat of integration. In the story, former Governor Fielding Wright said ". . . that a vote against the amendment is tantamount to approval of integration."

The second story was also slanted, favoring the opposition to the amendment. While those opposing the amendment were segregationists, they said it was the first step toward destruction of the public-school system. Naturally, I had no thought on the matter at all.

At the end of the first year I was satisfied. God was in His heaven, all was well in Petal, and nothing else mattered to me. I was still a Kiwanian in good standing, and the paper showed a profit. I had two automobiles, a nice white house, a hearty handshake, and a toothy smile for all potential customers.

I was so delighted I couldn't limit myself to writing a simple Thank-you note as my wife suggested. Indeed, I ran a three-column ad on the back page with my picture and copy which read:

Before we organized the paper here we planned for something like a year; we tried to take into consideration every conceivable possibility

127

—and one thing that was then, and has during our first year, been predominant in our efforts was the downright, honest-to-goodness friendliness and helpfulness of those whom we have tried to serve.

From us, to everyone of you who have so graciously given your help and encouragement, we thank you from the bottom of our hearts.

We are looking forward to another year of pleasant associations with each of you.

Chapter 21

The Petal Paper, Volume 2, Number 1, Thursday, November 18, 1954, was, I'd have sworn, in accord with my policy of "Loving Mother and Hating Sin."

The "East Side" column was light and cheerful, filled with names of local citizens, all with a humorous overtone. The paper carried the usual news stories on the P.T.A., V.F.W., American Legion, 4-H Club, football team, church service, and on and on. The issue had thirty-five ads, and nothing offensive to the local folk.

My acts continued in the set pattern—that is, I photographed quarter-pound eggs, visitors to Petal from England, and the dedication ceremonies at the Masonic Temple. I was far from satisfied with something, and I knew not what, except possibly myself.

Naturally, I dismissed that thought from my mind. How could I be dissatisfied with myself? Wasn't the paper showing a profit? Wasn't I accepted as a part of the community? Everyone spoke to me and was friendly—well, almost everyone. What was wrong? Why the necessity to take sedatives to induce sleep? I simply didn't know; I couldn't answer a single question I asked myself. It seemed to me the best thing to do was to stop asking questions. And that I did—as best I could, anyway.

News releases were coming in from both sides on the question of the proposed school amendment. The "pros" said, repeatedly, that a vote against the amendment was a vote for integration; the "cons" said that, while they favored segregation in the schools, there was no point in destroying the public-school system by emotional thinking and acting. I read the releases with care and gave what thought I was capable of to the matter. The more I thought about it, the more I decided that the opposition to the amendment was right. The group which had formed to oppose the measure was headed by a young attorney at Wiggins, Mississippi, Joel Blass, who was also a member of the state legislature.

Blass said he thought the amendment was the work of a small group who feared higher taxes more than integration. As an example, he pointed up the case of Washington County: "Washington County spent $185.14 for education of each white child and $49.82 for each colored child in 1952. To equalize facilities for operation of schools alone would require an increase in the local tax to approximately 51 mills to raise a total of $2,580,-219.59 annually. This is due to the fact that their white schools are far above the level required by the new school laws." Blass pointed out the same situation in other counties in the state.

Joel Blass caused me considerable confusion. For the first time in my life I began to realize the situation around me. Of course, I can't say I didn't know of the existence of "separate but unequal schools," but an awareness of injustice had escaped me. I tried to dismiss the matter, saying, "Leave it to Blass," or someone else, that it wasn't any of my business; my world was secure, why go out and look for trouble? While I dismissed it from my mind, I continued to run news stories released by Joel Blass, and not stories released by the other side. It did not occur to me that I was violating my policy of fence-straddling.

Still I couldn't rest; my mind was in a turmoil over the business. I knew in my heart I had to try to express my views; also, I knew in my pocketbook I had to be careful. I could no more keep myself from writing on the matter than I could control an act of nature. On the Thursday before the election, I ran the following editorial in my paper:

MISSISSIPPI'S BRAIN DEPARTMENT

Mississippi's Brain Department, the State Legislature, and the Governor as well, expects the citizens of this state to go to the polls next

Tuesday, December 21, and give them authority to commit an act that will be a black mark against the state as long as it exists.

As matters now stand, Statesmanship in Mississippi is at an all-time low, and by allowing the proposed school amendment to pass, it is apt to take another dive.

Without wasting words we will say that we are opposed to the amendment because:

We think the Brain Department is handing out pure malarkey by telling the voters that "those who oppose the measure are in favor of integration." From our point of view we oppose the measure, and we know darned well that we do not favor integration. We favor segregation because we think integration would be detrimental to both white and colored races.

We think that behind this mess is considerably more than the voters know about—we don't know where or who or how, but somewhere someone stands to gain personal profit, and in that case, which certainly seems logical to us, we oppose them. And if it isn't true, then why does the Brain Department seek to confuse the issue? . . .

We don't believe in paying bills by handing a signed blank check to someone; we sort of like to fill it in ourselves.

We believe the power of the people must continue to be the ultimate power in a Democracy. When the people's power is lost, all is lost insofar as individual freedom is concerned.

We believe the Brain Department's proposal is a threat to our basic freedoms. And that we fear.

We do not believe in putting big sticks into the hands of anyone —you can never know when they'll be turned on you. We believe if everyone has a little stick, things will remain fairly safe; at any rate we'll all have an equal chance.

We don't believe in contrived confusion . . . and in this matter pending the Department of Pure Brains has tried to confuse us all . . . or we're badly mistaken.

We don't believe that the ruling of the Supreme Court of the United States created an emergency that has to be solved without first doing just a little thinking—and at the present time we fail to determine any thinking on the part of the Department.

We don't believe in placing a man, no matter how strong his character, in a position where temptation can overcome his sense of honor. And the very instant our public schools become private they will have to be in the name of someone, and it would seem logical that the person would be a politician. And in that unfortunate case the first order of the day would be graft and corruption.

We don't believe that taxes we pay, earmarked for public education, should be used for anything else. And whenever we are forced to pay taxes for private education we are just that much closer to a dictatorship.

We don't believe it's sound business to try to swindle the Supreme Court of the United States—especially with them knowing it all the time. We disagree with their decision, true enough—but we respect them as being the highest court in this nation, and we know they're not a group of idiots—and when the time comes that you can't have respect for the greatest power the world has ever known—even though you disagree with them wholeheartedly—then, if the Indians would have it after we've worked things out so beautifully, why, we should give the country back to them.

We don't believe we have a taste for messes—and if this isn't the darndest mess we've ever seen, we are again mistaken.

We think our opinion can be summed up by saying that we oppose the proposed amendment, and that the greatest thing needed in the Mississippi Brain Department is brains.

To be sure, I lied like a dog in the editorial. I didn't know whether I disapproved of the decision of the Supreme Court or not, but I knew what everyone else said, and I was trying to remain a good Kiwanian and live with myself at the same time.

It would be completely dishonest to say I wasn't afraid to print the editorial. I was afraid not of any social pressure but of economic pressure, and with good reason, too. I had the typed pages of the editorial folded in my pocket the day before press time. I was in a store in Petal. The owner was talking with me about the proposed amendment, stating the party line that "a vote against the measure was a vote for integration." As politely as I could, I disagreed. He was straightforward in what he said: "Well, I sure won't advertise in any paper that's against the school amendment. Anybody who wants niggers to go to school with my children, I won't do business with."

I didn't argue with the man. I walked back to my office and suffered the agonies of hell in trying to decide what to do. I ran the editorial, and the merchant was as good as his word. He hasn't advertised with me since.

On the twenty-second of December I learned the amendment had passed by a vote of about two to one. I knew all along the proposal would pass; I also knew it was wrong and reeked of stupidity, but I didn't know the vote would be only two to one.

I was highly pleased to learn that one third of the voters of my state had not been stampeded into an emotional act.

I trembled with commercial fear, although I slept a little better at night, but not much.

With the school amendment passed and Christmas having come and gone, I did what I could toward clearing up my mind on my editorial policy.

In the first place, I wasn't really sure what an editorial was; I thought I knew, but I had a long talk with my printing contractor, Easton King, of *The Chronicle Star,* in Pascagoula. Easton was, and is, in my opinion, the best newspaperman in the entire state, barring none. A simple rule he follows—"By God, be honest"—makes him the man he is. As best he could, Easton explained what an editorial policy was.

After talking with Easton and with myself, I decided that I had to make a decision of some sort, for better or worse. In my utter simplicity, I thought my decision would be acceptable to my subscribers; I thought, honestly and sincerely, that with rare exception a man could say what he wished without fear of reprisal, especially a man with a newspaper who was seeking to expand his commercial and unhappy soul in a direction that was, for a rare change, decent and honest. I had a lot to learn.

Finally, on the thirtieth day of December 1955, I got what amounted to a policy into words, as follows:

AND EVEN THE DEVIL SHOULD HAVE HIS DUE

On a number of occasions we have been asked, "Just what is your editorial policy?" And, we presume, we are expected to answer with one of the words often used to describe editorial policy, like "Democratic," "Republican," "Conservative," or "Liberal." So . . .

We will say that we are "Democratic," so long as we think it's FAIR.

We will say we are "Republican," so long as we think it's FAIR.

We will say that we are "Conservative" or "Liberal," so long as we think it's FAIR.

The editorial policy of this paper is dictated by logic, common sense, and conscience—such a policy, we feel, has to be fair, or else the basis, "Conscience," cannot be upheld. That is, in short, what we think today. Tomorrow, in the light of additional facts, additional reasoning, we may think something else; however, whether it be today, tomorrow, or next month, fairness is still the one thing that is to be satisfied ultimately.

We have supported measures which we knew would be defeated. We supported them because we thought them to be right and fair. And here and now we would like to say that fairness is never defeated—the infection is ever-present, and sooner or later that which is fair, and is defeated, will have to be done over. . . .

As to being safe editorially, we are reminded of the safest of all editorial policies, that of "loving Mother and hating sin."

We think well of Mother, and goodness knows we hate that Sinnin', but anytime a mother sticks a lighted cigarette to her baby, well, we are against that mother. . . .

We do not think that we are right and everyone else is wrong. Some time ago we learned that of all the people in this world who should be tolerant, a newspaperman is foremost. We are aware of the fact that you have an opinion, and we respect it, even though we may disagree with you totally.

And in that respect, we expect just as much as we give.

Chapter 22

I felt much better after summing it up in those words. In a manner of speaking, I had simplified the matter. All I had to do was to decide what was "right and fair" and go ahead without fear of having to live with myself. I slept well at night—but we had to let our maid go.

I decided to use the first few days of January to take stock. I was more than surprised to learn that I had little stock to take. Subscription renewals were not coming in as I had expected them to; advertising was off more than I had anticipated. I got a subscription campaign under way, but it didn't amount to much. I pondered the situation, trying to determine the cause. I decided that, after all, it was January, and most folks were paying bills from Christmas. Having so decided, I stopped worrying about it, thinking ahead to the day they'd all renew. Thus, the first two weeks of January passed without conflict with anyone, including myself for a change.

One subject kept coming to my mind, a matter that I had

133

found ridiculous as far back as I could remember, and that was the business of legalized liquor—or, rather, the lack of it. The state was dry, yet I'd seen more drunks in Mississippi than any other state in which I'd been. It was not only silly, it was downright stupid. I had once discussed the liquor situation with a county official and from him I learned that in the year 1954 over a million dollars' worth of whiskey had been sold in Forrest County, Mississippi, a dry county and state. Not being able to leave well enough alone, I decided to make something of a joke about it, and on the twentieth day of January 1955 I asked, editorially:

WELL, WHY NOT LET'S JUST FORM A CO-OP?

Somewhere in the County of Forrest there is an enormous hole in the ground—to be sure, we don't know its exact location, but the logic of the reasoning that leads us to our conclusion is infallible.

Information from an unimpeachable source has been given to us, stating that in the County of Forrest during the year of 1954, in excess of a million dollars' worth of whiskey was sold.

We dropped by the courthouse and looked at the record on the "County Option" vote, held on August 26, 1952, and learned there were 2396 "wets" and 3460 "drys" in the county at that time.

Therefore, so it seems to us, those 3460 "drys" are helping protect the 2396 "wets" by buying whiskey and pouring it into a hole somewhere—and it certainly would take a big hole to take care of that much booze. . . .

The reaction was minor but immediate. A Petal merchant had a talk with me about my views on certain subjects, the Negro question and the liquor question topping the list. According to the gentleman, I had offended certain persons of influence in the community, and it wasn't good for my business to do so. He told me he'd had several persons come to him and talk about my editorial comment. He was courteous and polite. He was an advertiser, and being of my unfortunate nature, I replied that such talk proved one thing, that the paper was being read, and as long as it was being read, the ads in it would be seen. He wasn't convinced or, at least, didn't share my point of view. Shortly after our conversation he stopped advertising in the paper.

Since the first day of the paper, I'd been calling on a business, owned and operated by a fellow Kiwanian, and he always had an ad for the paper. One morning early in February I called at his store and he was busy, so I waited. Finally, when he'd finished, I approached him, and as I did he turned and walked away. He told a salesman who had arrived after me that he'd see him. I was puzzled but not too upset. This happened twice. I was determined not to become angry. I waited and waited and waited. Finally, over an hour having passed, the merchant walked from his office and, with an indifference that was something to behold, asked of me: "Well, P.D., you waiting for something?"

Inwardly I blew up, but managed to contain myself. For fourteen months I'd called on the man once a week, and he wanted to know if I was waiting for something. In a voice hard to control, but with indifference to match his, I couldn't refrain from replying, "Yes, sir. I was just standing here waiting for the second coming of Jesus. I know damned well his pappy wouldn't let him come to Petal without first checking in with you."

The peace of mind and tranquility I'd experienced such a short time earlier were gone. I was in conflict with myself again, but did not recognize the conflict for what it was. I only knew that something was wrong somewhere. Earlier I had had a difference of opinion with the Kiwanis Club over selling Petal booster tags. Each member was supposed to sell a certain number, and a drive was planned to have members canvass the town. Some were due to take shifts at the intersection of the two main streets and stop passing motorists to sell them a tag, the price of which was one dollar. Others in the club were supposed to divide the town into sections and solicit sales house by house. The project called for a type of glad-hander which I was not and could not be and, finally, refused to be. There were members of the club who failed to understand my hesitancy in the matter. Finally, I bought my quota of booster tags, took them to the river and threw them in.

Another matter caused me a certain loss in peace of mind. The club house needed painting. Again, each member was supposed to give a certain amount of his time with a brush in his hand. I knew the painting job needed to be done, but I refused

135

to paint. My only excuse was that I simply didn't care to paint; anyway, that's what I told myself. My refusal to co-operate was not good for business; I knew that, but at the same time, had anything else been good for my business as far as the club was concerned?

The gross revenue for the month of February was well under the gross for the previous February; it worried me, but I was inclined to dismiss it because it was an unpleasant matter, and I did. For almost a month I didn't write an unpopular editorial or column in the paper. I stuck with local coverage and local features.

On March 3, 1955, I devoted the editorial space to a statement on the upcoming elections. I was trying to walk easy, to be fair and honest. I stated that I was supporting three men, one for governor, one for sheriff of Forrest County, and another for supervisor in the county. Also, I said I'd not support them on the demerits of their opponents but on their own individual merits. And in what I had written, I was as honest as I knew how to be. Anyway, the reaction was such that the week following I felt inclined to comment in my "East Side" column:

I sometimes wonder if honesty is really the best policy after all. Did an editorial last week stating where the paper stood on three candidates, and have since been told that I was trying to run the State with a weekly paper; got one ad cancelled, and one fellow said he had planned to run his announcement in the paper, but had changed his mind since I took the attitude I did. As a result, I was also charged with selling the editorial to those mentioned in it, etc. And the crowning blow came in that I was trying to run the World with a weekly paper. Good Heavens! There are times when I have one hell of a time paying my bills at the end of the month.

In spite of all that, I'm still country enough to believe that by being as straightforward and honest in your convictions as possible, it will pay in the long run.

I was not only honest, but I was also right: I was country!

Chapter 23

While I didn't call it Peace of Mind, I decided to have it anyway—even if by another name. I was determined not to engage in anything where I had to take a stand. I was going to recoup my advertising inches some way or other and let controversial matters be discussed by others. I tucked my tail and watched the coming of a telephone strike. I'd received press releases for several weeks but had paid no attention to them, being engaged in losing advertising. Determined as I was to stay out of anything which might prick my conscience, I decided the best thing I could do would be to present both sides of the question. I printed a statement by the Southern Bell Telephone Company and the Communications Workers of America, Local 3509. I said my natural inclination was to be on the side of the working man; however, I added, management had a side also, and in view of my limited knowledge of the situation, I'd decided to sit it out. Both company and union officials called on me, explaining their positions. I was nice, but noncommittal. I knew I was right in my decision to ignore the strike—but strange, I thought, that I couldn't keep it off my mind. Every day the daily paper reported instances of cables having been cut, of the destruction of other company property. It was not my affair, and I continued to ignore it. What had I to gain? How was I to have peace of mind? It seemed simple enough: turn off that which offended, as if it were a water faucet. And I did, but the water continued to run, much too freely. I had closed my eyes, but I continued to see. Something seemed wrong with my theory.

While I had resolved to disregard all matters which were not profitable, I was surprised to note certain happenings in the Magnolia Jungle. In February of 1955 the Board of Trustees of the Institutions of Higher Learning entered a resolution in the minutes of a meeting. It read:

All speakers invited to the campus of any of the State Institutions of Higher Learning must first be investigated and approved by the head of the institution involved and when invited the names of such speakers must be filed with the Executive Secretary of the Board of Trustees.

137

I saw it; it was unbelievable. Surely, I decided, it would be safe to comment on anything as widely discussed as freedom of thought. The comment I printed, in part, read:

It is rumored that the Board's action will not be enforced, that it is "just for the books," that there are "political pressures behind it."

Even if the ruling is enforced in a nominal way only, the total effect on the faculty and students may still be disastrous. There is fear abroad in the land today, fear of saying the wrong thing, fear of making honest inquiry into certain fields, fear of stating one's views. Courage in seeking the truth has given way to expediency.

There are people who say: "Sit tight and wait. The ruling will not be enforced." We ask these cautious people where to begin objecting? We ask them, shall we not object to the principle? Shall we wait and object to the action? Then it will be too late.

Someone has said that thought control is an indication that we don't really believe in our economic and political systems, that we don't believe they can stand the light of free discussion.

If democracy is what we have been taught to believe, it will be able to stand the onslaught of all the opposition. We believe in democracy and we believe the people will do the right thing when properly informed.

The only way they can be properly informed is to have absolute freedom of thought and discussion.

No one at that time could have foreseen what came to pass in subsequent months. For example, at the University of Mississippi, department heads have told me that when they submitted a list of possible speakers, the list was sent to the American Legion for final clearance. However, in 1955, that was future history.

Another thing I'd not been able to shut out was an incident in Hattiesburg. A group of Negro leaders had been invited by the County School Board to a meeting at the courthouse. They were invited in good faith, and went in good faith. The meeting, designed to discuss mutual school problems, was under way and a candidate for the office of district attorney arose and made a speech. In the speech he said, in effect, that Negroes and whites could not attend the same meeting, that it was a violation of the law of the state of Mississippi. The Negroes walked out. There

138

hasn't been a meeting between Negroes and whites since that time, not in Forrest County, Mississippi.

Though my eyes were closed, I noted with alarm that the legislature of the state passed a voter registration bill, aimed at keeping Negroes from voting. The purpose of the bill was an open secret. Peace of mind, indeed! That's what I wanted, not to see these things as they happened, not to feel concerned with them. But if closed eyes continue to see, if closed ears continue to hear, there doesn't seem much point in having a closed mouth. I hesitated to say anything on the subject. I'd felt a touch of social and economic pressure, and found it unpleasant. My paper was in bad financial shape, and I had to consider that. Yet I couldn't ignore the feelings I had within me. I was disturbed, and to be so disturbed was not logical; it was poor business. I reached a decision: I would sell the paper. Like many of my theories, that was a good one, too. There was one hitch: no one would buy it. I was caught. My money was invested, and I had to protect it; yet, I couldn't sit by and not see and hear much longer, and to speak out would be to court disaster as far as finances were concerned. I'd give no more thought to the bill or to kindred subjects; the matter was resolved. My financial stability was my first obligation.

I closed my eyes and ears tighter. I attended every Kiwanis meeting; I reported each in full. I had succeeded in my desire neither to see nor to hear. But inside my heart and mind something was wrong. My moods of depression were frequent; my outbursts of temper were frequent. I knew neither why nor what. One thing I did know: I had to get it out, whatever it was.

One Sunday morning in late April I was in my office working and I felt that if I didn't say something about what was stuck in my craw I'd explode. Giving no particular thought to it, I wrote an ironic piece in which I compared the progress in my native state to that of the crawfish. It was something of a relief to me. Before exploding, I'd actually laughed! As a matter of fact, my ego got the upper hand and on April 21, 1955, I printed the piece. I know of nothing I've written which gave me the personal satisfaction I got from writing:

Once you have seen a Magnolia, you have seen all Magnolias; once you have smelled a Magnolia, you have smelled them all—every Magnolia looks alike and smells alike.

But with Crawfish, there is a difference—many kinds, numerous shapes, colors, and sizes; however, with rare exception, there is one thing common to them all, and that's the direction of movement.

Once we can get every single crawfish to move in the same direction, we propose to suggest to our Legislature to adopt him as our state symbol, replacing the Magnolia, which, as you can see, could never be truly representative of progress in this state.

Now, at first you may find this a little hard to believe, but the crawfish is synonymous with our progress. Here in the State of Mississippi we are making progress, progress such as no state heretofore has known. Our sagacious leaders are showing us how; they are leading the way. Their aim is to protect us from those crawfish who haven't the intelligence to move backward (as any sane crawfish knows), backward toward the mud from which he came.

Progress is a rare something that deserves reward; it is something that should be recognized, fostered, and nursed. Realizing this (and just as soon as we can rid ourselves of the few crawfish who insist on moving forward), we humbly suggest that the smelly, snow-white Magnolia, present symbol of Mississippi, be replaced by the progressive, intelligent crawfish.

This state is on the threshold of its greatest movement—and, as we have said, there are some who want to travel uphill, straight ahead—and, of course, they must be dealt with before we can hoist the crawfish symbol.

From those crawfish in reverse, we are protected greatly. Indeed, we have our magnificent Legislature; we have our own great leaders going before us, pointing out the true direction in which progress is made—among them such greats as ex-Governor fielding wright, His Excellency, Governor of Mississippi, hugh white; we have that Spark of the citizens council, robert patterson, and of course, that Delta Flower himself, walter sillers.

In Mississippi today there is nothing to fear, not even that small group of misguided crawfish who insist on going in the wrong direction.

For our own protection, here's what we've had the foresight to do: Some six months ago the citizens of this state voted for a Constitutional amendment, and it has now been written into the State Constitution, requiring voters who register to write out the answers to twenty questions on three legal sized sheets of paper. And they're good, protective questions, too; for example, question eighteen: Requires the voter to copy a section of the State Constitution, requiring voters who register to

140

write "A reasonable interpretation of the section." And question twenty is a real whingding: It requires a voter to write his understanding of the "duties and obligations of a citizen under the constitutional form of government."

Now, at first, you may not think those are good, protective questions. We have given them considerable thought, and can assure you they are real peaches. Too, they fit so nicely into the progressive move directed toward hoisting the crawfish as our state symbol.

Well, let's take a look at how it can work to our advantage—here's one way: The sole judge of the "reasonableness of the answers" is the person in each county whose duty it is to register voters. Not only can he keep Blacks, Yellows, Reds, Pinks and Greens from voting, but he can keep anyone from voting who is so foolish as to disagree with our way of thinking. Now, that's real good—it is truly representative of progress.

You can take it one step further and immediately realize other benefits. This state needs a good, strong Huey P. Long type political machine, and someone with the courage of his convictions can, we would say within 5 to 19 years, build such an organization by taking full advantage of this situation. It's relatively simple: If a youngster wants to register to vote, and his family has been so foolish as to have disagreed with our efforts to protect him, naturally, he would have to be disqualified—unable to give us a satisfactory understanding of the "duties and obligations of a citizen under the constitutional form of government."

Can you imagine the foolishness of the cry from some of the unprogressive crawfish, that if they can do it to one, they can do it to all? We answer them with a simple truth: Get on the band wagon, boys— don't be backward and start yelling about freedom and all that sort of thing; it's not best for us.

However, in view of all this, you will find it difficult to understand what happened a few weeks ago. One of those elected officials, whose sacred duty is to keep anyone who disagrees with us from voting, stood on his hind feet (had the curl out of his tail, too) in Jackson and said, "The people are against the amendment. They are sorry they voted for it and never would have if they had understood it. They were told the amendment would solve the segregation problem. They were misled."

That's the crawfish we have been talking about—he's just making a mess of things—see what he's trying to do—go uphill, and in an election year, too. A misguided rabblerouser heading in the wrong direction, that's all.

Our wonderfully gifted leaders have protected us further than most of us realize. They told us to turn over our public schools to the Legislature, and any time anyone, inside or outside our state, tried to differ with our opinion, the public schools would be abolished. That's more progress, truly representative; the kind we need if we're to hoist the Crawfish symbol. And another thing, that will teach those backward, slow-witted, hill-climbing crawfish a thing or two. None of this business of the bull swinging the tail with our leaders; indeed, any time the tail can't swing the bull, why, we'll just simply progress some more toward the mudhole.

An interesting sidelight on this admirable situation is the recent mandate from the Legislature to the Trustees of Institutions of Higher Learning, having to do with screening speakers before they be allowed to address students in the state. Why, indeed, anyone with an idea different from ours should not be allowed to open his mouth—that's how trouble gets started, someone going around putting ideas into the heads of young people. And to think there are those ever-present, backward crawfish who cried out "A backward step for higher learning." We blush to think about them—that is near treason. That someone would question the type of leadership we have is unforgivable.

Poor, sad, mistaken crawfish that they are, who think that uphill, straight ahead, is the best way to progress. Naturally, our splendid leaders will deal with them in a fitting and proper manner. One such misguided unfortunate is Hodding Carter, Demon of the Delta, who would dare put the pursuit of truth ahead of the interest of our leaders. But we sort of figure he has learned his lesson—our sagacious House of Representatives has censured him, eighty-nine nobles of that august body, no less. The noble eighty-nine said that all might hear: Carter sold our Mississippi for 50,000 pieces of silver. And Carter, uninformed ingrate that he is, replied: "Go to hell." A special invitation he offered, mind you.

Now, isn't that just awful?

Among that august group who set Carter straight were nineteen who were not so august—they had the nerve to refuse to vote for the resolution to condemn Carter. Can you possibly imagine that? And one of them, who doesn't know that the silly idea of forward motion is contrary to progress, a youngster from Stone County, Mississippi, Joel Blass, defied our wonderful leaders. "I have been lashed," he said, "by the Citizens Councils. They exist for the avowed purpose of destroying any person who disagrees with them. Economic pressure, chief weapon of the councils, is inhumane and not worthy of white men. Such methods do violence to the principles of justice."

We ask you, just how wrong can anyone get?

Possibly Blass is too young to know the benefits of our movement—but there were eighteen others—something will have to be done with those misguided misfits.

But the Delta Demon, Hodding Carter, should have known better—surely he can realize the fact that our glorious leaders will take the curl

142

out of his tail indeed, may even pinch it off, if he isn't careful and doesn't get in line.

Maybe he thinks the hope of knowing the truth, and trying to understand it, leaves him without the need of a tail, or a curl in it. Well, if our leaders haven't convinced him yet, they will. You know, Carter won the Pulitzer Award once, but, of course, that's of no consequence—it wasn't approved by our sagacious leaders, nor by our glorious, Legislature.

Briefly, there you have it. As a 100% red-blooded Mississippian, we feel the Magnolia should give way to the crawfish—and soon, too. Progress in our state is made that way, and everyone knows that the route is downhill, backward, toward the mud. (This being election year, a lot of good mud is going to be needed.)

Except for a few, anyone can see the glory of our progress—but don't worry about that few, because—

We have Our Glorious Leaders. . . .

May a kind and merciful God help us!

After the paper for that Thursday was out I went home and waited. There wasn't a single call; it was the following night before I heard any comment whatsoever. Two calls came. One of them said to me, "P.D., that's telling them niggers where their place is, by God." I don't think I was any more surprised the time I'd been prayed for in church than I was at that comment. Both men bought subscriptions to the paper. Later, the same two men became charter members of the Citizens Council of Forrest County.

Unfortunately, the lack of reaction gave me a false sense of security; it let me go blindly into a fool's paradise. Reality was to return, and soon. The telephone strike continued in the area. Daily reports revealed the destruction of property from one end of the state to the other. On a Sunday evening a telephone worker, a lady, reported for work and the crowd jeered and called her "scab." To a union person that is an ugly word; personally, I've never cared for it in any way whatsoever. To me, however, an uglier word is "violence." That Sunday night there was violence, in that the lady was beaten by persons in the crowd. Who did it was never decided fully. To me it represented a serious threat; it was an act I could not ignore. Feeling as I did about acts of violence, and having a false sense of security from the crawfish piece, I thought it entirely possible to comment on

143

the matter without incurring too much wrath. And so I did, saying:

LET'S NOT DO LIKE THE BIRDIES DO

Almost every Spring, in newspapers throughout the nation, you can read of an account where a Robin, alighting on the ledge of some building in New York or Chicago, and seeing his image reflected in the window, begins a fight with an imaginary enemy.

Generally, as the stories go, he wears himself down, finally giving up, exhausted and defeated.

The story of the Robin reminds us somewhat of the present dispute between the CWA and Southern Bell Telephone.

Now, let us say that right now: We do not propose to know who is right and who is wrong in the basic dispute over contract negotiations.

Our point here is relatively simple: The Union seems to be fighting something that is not there, and in so doing is weakening itself, a thing we hate to see.

From our very first issue, this paper has supported organized labor; we will continue to support labor, so long as we think it is right. We believe the labor movement as a whole to be right; but the business of violence as has been displayed in the current strike is not right, and in no way will we try to convince anyone that it is.

It is ugly and downright disgusting in every detail.

The sordid act of beating up a woman, as has happened in Hattiesburg, is cowardly and dirty and rotten to the core. The act of beating up a worker, right here in Petal, is a sure sign of Union weakness.

Our contention is that the Union is doing itself permanent harm by such acts of violence. We are convinced that stricter legislation against labor unions will be the result of such acts.

And respect is something any striking Union can use in full measure.

So, instead of doing like the birdies do, why not do like the friends and neighbors, the respected citizens, that they are?

My concern with the violence and the weakening of the union was sincere. On the afternoon following the publication of the editorial two officials of the union called on me at my home. They explained at great length that violence was likely to result when angry crowds gather; they went on to say the destruction of telephone property was not an act of union members. I inquired about a man who had been caught in the act of planting dynamite around a telephone-company installation near Jackson. Those things were unfortunate, I was told. I thought they

144

were, too. One of the officials demanded that I retract what I'd written; it was, purely and simply, a demand, not a request. I declined.

Mentioning they were going to see what their attorney could do about my attitude, they departed. For once in my life I didn't have to look inside to decide if I was right in an attitude.

In the days which followed there were several telephone calls, all from persons unidentified. One I recall with clarity. It was a lady who said she was a telephone employee. "Are you P. D. East?" she asked.

"Yes," I answered. "Who is this?"

"I'm a lady and I work for the phone company."

"Yes?"

"I want to tell you one thing . . ." She paused. "You're a no-good bastard and a stooge for the telephone company."

I did not see any point in arguing about my ancestry; I'd known for years that she might be right on that score.

"You are supposed to be a pro-labor editor. I don't think you're an editor at all—you're a no-good bastard."

"And a phone-company stooge," I injected.

"You're damned right you are. If anybody should be on our side, it ought to be you—you lived off organized labor for years, and now you up and turn tail when the going is rough."

I made an attempt to explain to the lady that I was indeed for labor, but I was opposed to the tactics being employed, no matter who used them. The conversation ended in a stalemate. Neither of us had changed the other's mind. I can't deny that I felt terrible about the whole affair. I felt like a Judas, but I couldn't see violence and destruction no matter what I felt in my mind. To me there was no justification for destruction.

Feeling as I did, torn between mind and heart, I let the strike pass for two weeks.

My tendency toward indecision was brought to an abrupt end by an accident in the town of Laurel, Mississippi. My patience was at an end. I wanted to be on the union side, but at this point I couldn't be. I was more than a little upset when I wrote:

145

Gentlemen:

For over two months now you have been on strike; you have lost your strike. No matter how you figure it, you have lost the strike.

You have said you were against violence and the destruction of private property. But there has been violence and property destroyed. You have said you were not guilty. But members of your union are facing court trials. You have, in short, said much; but you have done little to prove to the public the honor of your intentions.

And last Thursday, in Laurel, a little girl died. . . .

On her way home from school . . . eleven years old . . . they buried her Sunday.

Oh, no, we are not saying you are responsible for her death. It was one of those things . . . like you read about. But it was close to home. And it was another one of those unfortunate things that someone had, on the day of the accident, cut telephone cables, rendering useless some twenty-five hundred telephones.

For forty-five minutes she lay on the side of the road, dying. . . .

You have lost the strike, gentlemen. . . .

And a union member said to us that she would have died anyway. . . . It is no comfort to us to know of mortal omnipotence coming so close to that of God.

She would have died anyway . . . so it has been said to us.

But she died without medical aid . . . and for forty-five minutes she lay dying on the side of a road . . . no one could call for medical aid, for there were no telephones in order.

You have lost the strike . . . and have done permanent harm to all of us who believe in the good of the labor movement in this nation.

The little girl was just eleven . . . they buried her last Sunday.

Once again I was paid a visit by officials of the union. They demanded that I retract every word. I told them to go to hell. I was not making any effort at politeness at that point. One member of the visiting delegation said to me: "That child in Laurel did not die because of telephone lines being out of order. Telephone lines are often out of order."

"I know for a fact that the lines, or cable, were cut. That's why they were out of order."

"Well," he assured me, "limbs break lines; lightning puts them out of order. What's the difference?"

"Goddamnit!" I exploded. "If you are so stupid as not to know the difference between an act of man and an act of God,

146

then you're more hopeless than I thought!" With my temper out of control, I walked out of the room.

Following the editorial, I received a number of telephone calls, all of which were abusive. I've often thought of my attitude toward labor since that strike. I am still pro, but it comes from the mind, not from the heart—not any more—and I often feel bad about it, too.

During the spring and summer of 1955 the Magnolia Jungle was teeming with wild beasts, all politicians seeking elected office.

I had long since noticed two distinguishing traits about myself. First, the more removed from danger, the braver I was; second, the more money I had in my pocket, the more independent I was. Earlier I had stated in my column that I intended to support three men and that I would do it out of conviction. Actually, I had not intended to get involved in the political campaigns, except to say that I thought my choices were good men. On the whole, I was successful in staying out.

However, about midsummer I had a telephone call one day. It was a gentleman seeking the office of sheriff of Forrest County. He said, "East, I've been thinking about running my announcement in your paper. But you're supporting another man. Now, I've thought about it and I've a proposition to make you. If you'll stop supporting the other fellow, I'll see you get a lot of advertising from me."

I couldn't believe my ears. I asked him to repeat what he'd said. He did. I told him to wait until next week's paper to see my answer.

The more I thought about it, the angrier I got. (After all, he'd not said how much money I could expect.) I did a column on the low tactics of some office seekers. I did not call names. Later in the campaign I had another man make a similar proposition to me. Strange, I thought, how a man spends a little money and expects your soul. I held my temper and didn't even preach.

The proposal I enjoyed most was by a candidate who asked me point-blank: "How much would you charge me to come out against me?" Had I not been taking myself so seriously then, I'd have had a wonderful time. As it was, I didn't enjoy it at all; I stayed angry. Finally, in early June, I decided to take a whack at some of those who would purchase support from a newspaper. It wasn't at all clever, and I doubt I got the message across, but I ran a full page, having no advertising anyway, and in the middle of the page I quoted prices on selling out:

(Accusations having reached a new high as to the purchase of the editorials which appear in this paper, we feel obliged to furnish our prices for same. We hope those interested will keep this price list; however, we will be able to furnish additional copies at five cents each. NOTE: All prices are subject to change without notice. There is no tax charged on our editorials. The Legislature hasn't thought of that one yet.)

SELL-OUT PRICES
OF
THE PETAL PAPER

Editorial . . . . Run of the Mill (No Animosity)	$ 9.98	
Editorial . . . . Small Company, Short Editorial	14.95	
Editorial . . . . Small Company, Long Editorial	16.95	
Editorial . . . . Large Company, Short Editorial	24.98	
Editorial . . . . Large Company, Long Editorial	32.49	
Editorial . . . . Small Company (Fightin' Type)	34.98	
Editorial . . . . Large Company (Fightin' Type)	49.95	
Editorial . . . . Small Company (Hell Raisin')	49.95	
Editorial . . . . Large Company (Hell Raisin')	64.98	
Editorial . . . . Individuals (Any Type)	3.95 UP	
Editorial . . . . Politicians (For or Against)	49.98	
Editorial . . . . Completely Honest	No Charge	
East Side Column (Honorable Comment)	4.98	
East Side Column (Dishonorable Comment)	2.98	

* Other type sell-outs quoted on request.
* Engraving and Art Work Extra.

Check, Cash, or Money Order must accompany all orders.

With Best Wishes,
/s/ P. D. EAST
P. D. EAST,
Editor

Out of the campaign came one thing which caused me pain. I had known the man I was supporting for sheriff for a number

148

of years; I liked him and considered him honest in every detail. We had visited for dinner numerous times over the years. I had occasion to call at his home one afternoon to discuss the campaign. I was not invited inside the house. At the time I gave no thought to it. The second time I had occasion to call, the same thing occurred, but it was the third time before it began to dawn on me that perhaps I wasn't welcome inside his home. It disturbed me to the point of depression, for, to be sure, I failed to understand it.

It was a stinging blow.

What with the cooling of my ardor for the candidate for sheriff, and with the same chilling effect on my support for my choice of a candidate for governor because of his stumping the state and shouting "Nigger! Nigger!" my interest in the matter of politics was limited. I'd given up the thought of peace of mind; it mattered little; I gave no thought to anything beyond next Thursday's paper.

On Tuesday, May 31, the Supreme Court handed down its second decision. I did not understand it, not fully, having paid no attention to the matter from a legal point of view. All around me I heard the Jungle echoing with the shout of "Nigger! Nigger!" by the men seeking office, but I was not disturbed. How can one be disturbed by what he doesn't understand? Inside something was uncomfortable, but I didn't know what. I was fed up with my choice for governor shouting the old, old refrain. Out of my distaste for the constant shouting of "Nigger!" and because of things I could not explain to myself, I undertook to write my second ironic piece. For the second time, conscientious soul-searching was not a prerequisite. Stated simply, I enjoyed writing a ... .

NEWS STORY

(Since our only desire is to report, and not inform and reform, nor to preach or beseech, we are presenting herewith the text of a speech made recently by the Honorable Jefferson D. Dixiecrat, president of the Mississippi Chapter of the Professional Southerner's Club. His talk follows.)

I want to apologize to each of you at this time for asking that your Professional Southerner's Club cards be inspected at the door before you were allowed to enter; however, I'm sure you will understand the necessity of keeping out the amateur Southerners, the liberals and the lunkheads.

My talk to you will be short. I want to report on the progress we've made as Professional Southerners as an organized group. We have succeeded in making an issue of a situation wherein our very foundation was threatened. Our way of life, and everything we hold sacred, was in danger of being undermined and pulled from under us. But we have, as Professional Southerners, I am happy to say, thrown stumbling blocks in the paths of the unrighteous and the unholy riff-raff who have not seen our problems our way.

We said they must be stopped, and they were! We have won a resounding victory . . . thrown back the enemy, and saved our Southern way of life. There are problems yet to be solved, however. Our enemies say that our state needs more industry, but I say to you we need no industry where the Nigger can make good wages, buy good clothes, good food, good homes. I say to you we need to return to the days when cotton was a dollar a pound and Nigger labor was a dollar a day. That's what we need here in Mississippi, and it's toward that end we must work.

Our enemies say that segregation is a problem of an economic nature. That if the forty-five per cent of our population that is Nigger were given a chance to earn more money they would become useful citizens and make our state richer for everyone—that's what our enemies are preaching. There's one trouble with that false theory: The Nigger would be richer, too. And to you I say right now, a Nigger is a Nigger and must be kept as such and in his place as a Nigger. As Professional Southerners we have kept him from voting, we have kept him fairly well ignorant and we kept him in debt to us. I say that so far we have been successful in our purpose.

But remember one thing: "Beware of false prophets, which come to you in sheep's clothing, but inwardly they are ravening wolves. You shall know them by their fruits." I caution you here and now to be on guard against anyone who thinks differently from you.

I say to you that we must plant our way of life in the minds of our children right now. We must set the example for them. There is too much liberal thinking getting into our state. And I believe that men such as robert patterson (founder of the citizens councils) are to be the greats of our state tomorrow. He will not allow liberal thought in our educational system. Our legislature now has the power to abolish the public schools and that is another step in our complete victory.

Now, what if the Supreme Court of the United States says that we here in Mississippi are to suffer the same humiliation that other Southern states suffered? Well, let me point out our plan to you on that. We will first have to be sued by the NAC double P or whatever it is, and

150

then we can make various zones, put certain statutes on our books, and in each case the Supreme Court will have to rule on these. Now factual issues can be tied into these little measures and they will require a jury decision here in our state, and you can bet your bottom dollar the juries will be good Mississippians.

Since writing the piece, I have wondered to what extent I tried to hide my true feelings on the matter by the presentation I made. A Petal merchant and a brother Kiwanian said to me, "I'm sure glad you took the stand you did. You know, P.D., a lot of folks have made a fuss about that boy telling them niggers off at the courthouse. But me, I think it's about time the black bastards learned to keep their place."

There were a few canceled subscriptions, but it was difficult to determine the cause. I was still getting an occasional call because of my position in the telephone strike. Also, I had subscriptions canceled because of my support for candidates I'd elected to take a stand on. How many cancellations were due to the pieces on the race situation in Mississippi? There was no way of knowing, not with any degree of accuracy. But I was disturbed, wondering how profitable it was to write about such matters. Further, I was disturbed for even wondering. After all, it was my paper—not much of one, but mine. Also, I was led to a conclusion of sorts by a letter from Mark Ethridge, the distinguished editor and publisher of the *Courier-Journal* in Louisville. Mark Ethridge is a native Mississippian and one man whom I admired greatly. After the editorial, "News Story," Mark wrote a letter:

Dear P. D.:
"News Story" is a fine editorial and I have passed it around to Barry Bingham, Tarleton Collier and Weldon James; they'll give it more circulation, too.
Congratulations! I wish Mississippi had more voices like yours and I hope you stay there.
Sincerely yours,

MARK ETHRIDGE
Publisher

I was delighted to hear from such a man, and my decision to write additional copy on the subject of race was influenced by

151

him. Other factors were involved. My relationship with some of the members of Kiwanis was, to put it mildly, strained. I'd attended meetings and not had a single member speak to me. I wondered if I could be a good Kiwanian and write what I liked at the same time. Since I was concerned with advertising income, not that I got any of it from my brother Kiwanians, I debated long on the matter. Finally, I decided the best thing I could do would be to resign from the club. I bent the ear of Easton King once more. He saw my point and agreed I'd not be free within myself until I'd shaken all bonds. So, while I was about it, I wrote the Methodist church a letter and asked that my name be removed from their rolls. I felt as if a load had been lifted with the resignation from the Kiwanis Club. It did not occur to me to look inward, inside myself—deep down inside. What had I accomplished? Simply this: I was not a member of anything whatsoever; I felt no obligation to anyone or any group. If I felt inclined to criticize I could do so without the yoke of obligation around my neck. I reasoned it was better to be considered an S.O.B. than a traitor, and to belong to a group and criticize it was to be something of a traitor. Perhaps I was justifying my decision; occasionally I have a tendency in that direction. But, thank God, I was free from all obligations. I had neglected to notice one minor detail: I was not free from me. Of course, that was understandable, since I had always found it easier to live without having to think.

The campaign for governor continued in the traditional vein. I took a pot shot or two at Fielding Wright, primarily because of his administration, during which he proposed a state police force to keep unions from striking. Also, it was no secret that Wright was retained by oil interests. The continued shouting in the governor's race concerned me. I had a long talk with my choice and asked him point-blank why it was he berated the Negro citizens in his campaign. With complete candor, he replied: "To get elected." I had more food for thought; I did not argue the point with him. Something was indeed wrong, and not just with me, but throughout the Magnolia Jungle.

About the middle of July my situation began to dawn on me, at least in part. I had a lady working for me, selling advertising.

152

We were promoting something or other and she called on a businessman in Hattiesburg. The next day I found a note on my desk, relating that he'd declined to buy an ad, and his reason for declining. I had not been so angry in many months. I was furious. My first two or three efforts were cruel and mean, and, besides that, libelous. But finally, out of the heat of anger, I was able to salvage my thoughts on the matter in writing:

FREEDOM OF THE PRESS AND THE MIGHTY BUCK

"Congress shall make no laws respecting an establishment of religion, or prohibiting the free exercise thereof; or abridging the freedom of speech or of the press; or the right of the people peaceably to assemble, and to petition the Government for a redress of grievances." So declares the first article of the Bill of Rights, a part of the Constitution of the United States.

We are a Mississippian, born and reared here in the state; but somewhere, somehow in the days while attending the free public schools, we got the notion that the Bill of Rights was about the greatest thing yet conceived by mankind. We believe it to this day. We also believe that Congress cannot nor will not abridge the freedom of speech or of the press, but . . .

There are some of our fellow Mississippians who would, and do, unfortunately. Just last Saturday . . .

"P.D.: Mr. ———— turned it down . . . said he was a Fielding Wright man and that other things in your editorials didn't set well with him."

That was what was written on a note left in our office by a person who works for us. The name of the gentleman has been omitted, for if we named one we would have to name two others, and we see no point in it. The reference to "turned it down" has to do with placing advertising in this paper. Kindly note the reason was not because our rates were too high, or our circulation too limited, but because he disagreed with what we had written.

It seems to us, therefore, that freedom of the press is dependent on idiots who have the mighty dollar bill to spend. And that brings us to one more fine state of affairs!

We confess to being old-fashioned, indeed, even country, but to us the only thing more sacred than freedom of speech and of the press is the right to worship God as we please.

In simple language, what this gentleman said was that he would apply economic pressure. And, to be sure, it's about the only kind of weapon he is familiar with and, we will admit right here, it's a good one . . . but, somehow we haven't the intelligence to submit. And we're

153

glad of it! Had it been our desire to have worked for the gentleman we would have made application for a job.

You may find this difficult to believe, but when injustice is done against any man, be he in Maine or California, or in any part of this nation, and when the truth of the injustice is suppressed by someone, then that injustice stands right at your own front door, and it stands there in the form of disaster. For whom the bell tolls? Every single one of us.

We believe keeping facts or ideas from citizens to be a crime. We believe that any person who calls himself a newspaperman should never permit anyone, for any reason, to keep him from presenting the truth or, at any rate, the truth as he sees it.

So, with the help of God, and to this we swear, as long as we can keep our head above water we will print what we please in this paper, so long as we believe it to be right, fair, or true. And if the time should come that to keep our head above water means to submit to pressure of any kind, then we will go under without hesitation, and at least with a clear conscience.

In the meantime, however, we have only six words to say to those who would attempt to put economic pressure on us; the words are: GO TO HELL IN A BUCKET!

P. D. EAST
Editor

The editorial did little for business, but for my soul—it helped. The reaction was frustrating, yet not without humor. I was told about four businessmen who had voiced protests. I wondered for a brief moment if anyone cared for my paper. I took note of the fact that my circulation in Petal was declining, but, as it did, subscriptions were coming in from a widening area. One fact was pleasing, the other wasn't; however, I did not stop to think about the matter. For the two weeks following my soul-satisfying "go to hell in a bucket" piece, I didn't get involved in anything whatsoever. The political campaign continued, but my enthusiasm was not what it should have been.

I had spent two weeks going into some questions relative to the district attorney's race. The run-off was between the incumbent and a young attorney. I was acquainted with both men, and while I had no desire to get involved, I did have a preference, and it wasn't the district attorney. He was the same man who, uninvited, had made the play to the galleries in the courthouse, resulting in the departure of the Negro leaders who had been invited to a meeting there. To be sure, my tactics were not honorable, but it made little difference at the time. I talked with numerous people who could give me information about the man. With a lead, I'd check it out, almost able to confirm it. In the treatment of the facts I had, I elected to ask questions rather than state facts. By so doing, I could strike harder with less fear of being involved in libel suits.

I did not then, nor do I now, make any accusations against the man about whom I wrote the editorial; however, it was interesting to note the coincidences which followed. The first thing to happen was a shot-gun blast fired over the roof of the home of the parents of his opponent. They were an elderly couple and the man suffered a heart condition. As it happened, he did not get excited about it, not knowing it had happened because he was watching television.

The second thing of interest was that my wife was followed everywhere she went. It was obvious; there was no attempt to conceal the fact that the man, whom we did not know, was following her. I concluded it was a war of nerves. Also, I concluded that my wife was losing it. For the first time in my life I purchased a gun, a .25-caliber Beretta pistol, not for myself but for my wife to carry in her handbag. While she was being shadowed, I was stopped in the Hattiesburg post office one day at noon by a lady.

"Are you P. D. East?" she asked.

"Yes," I replied. "Can I help you?"

"I'm of half a mind to wring your neck," she said.

I did not reply. She continued. "You can stop writing stuff about my husband. He's done nothing to you."

I assured her that was true; her husband, the district attorney, had done nothing to me. There was more conversation.

It was interesting to note that about midafternoon of that day the shadow following my wife disappeared. (She never did get to fire the pistol.)

On August 23 the second primary was held and the D.A. was defeated by a vote of about 5 to 1; also, two men whom I'd supported were defeated. I was glad of the outcome and was especially happy the campaign was over.

With the ending of the campaign a horrible truth struck me: I was about out of advertisers! During the campaign a few subscribers had refused their papers at the post office. I was disturbed by their refusal, but I did nothing to mend fences.

I had an idea for a subscription promotion. I called on a Baptist church and offered them one third of the gross if they'd undertake a subscription campaign. I did not attend the meeting for the discussion, but I was given to understand they wouldn't touch my paper with a Bible in their hands.

I then ran a front-page note to churches in which I offered the same deal. Result? Not one nibble. I should have stopped and reflected on the situation, but I was busy wondering what had happened to my local advertisers and, at the same time, I was negotiating a contract with another print shop. This was a hard decision to make, too.

Easton King and I had become close friends, but with a loss of income I felt that I had no choice but to save wherever I could. I explained to Easton at length why I had to move the printing; he understood, but said, "You'll be sorry." The story of that change is long and unimportant, except that I didn't save a dime in the long run.

Tension between the races had been given great impetus by the politicians, especially since the senatorial race in 1954.

Shortly after the election in 1955, in Holmes County, Mississippi, a matter flared into the open. A co-op farm had been in existence for a number of years. It had been successful and an important part of the community from an economic point of view. The manager of the farm, A. E. Cox, was not an advocate of discrimination in any fashion. His partner, Dr. David R. Minter, was of the same view. No one actually knows what kicked it off, but before anyone knew what was happening, the citizens had a meeting one night and asked Cox and Minter to leave. They had a Negro who testified that the farm had an integrated swimming pool, but from all accounts this was untrue and everyone knew it. In any event, tempers ran high in the County of Holmes in the fall of 1955. I made no effort to

156

find out what was happening, except to read daily news stories. In spite of my lack of knowledge, I eventually got into the act, not so much because of my concern with Holmes County but because of my concern with the apathy on the part of ministers throughout the state.

Subscriptions continued to be canceled; an occasional abusive letter would be received; advertising fell off each month, and I was trying to understand why—not only why the loss of revenue, but the why of other questions beginning to take shape in my mind. They refused to come into sharp focus. I continued to say what I felt necessary to my peace of mind, giving little thought, except vaguely, to other matters. Also, my stringers (the ladies who gathered local news) began to quit; one by one they decided their duties took too much time. I wondered why, knowing they weren't telling the truth; in a manner of speaking, I was glad they quit.

On Thursday, November 10, 1955, my second year came to a close. I thought of the contrast between this and my first anniversary issue, when I had run my picture and that love letter to my readers—when I had contemplated a "Coke Party" for subscribers. In twelve months there had been something of a change. On the editorial page I used an editorial written by Easton King. Easton did not preach, as I did; he dealt in facts, and I thought a factual report on the so-called "Separate but Equal" business was well in order. King's editorial pointed up the realistic situation in the state of Mississippi as it has been since 1890:

EQUAL BUT SEPARATE

The figures cited below were prepared by the state department of education and cover the 1954–55 school term. They are based on actual average daily attendance figures in both white and Negro schools with the per pupil expenditure covering cost of current operating expenses such as teacher pay, transportation, etc. They do not include costs of new buildings or other capital expenditures.

In Holmes County the average daily attendance of white students during the past school term was 1871. The expenditure per pupil for current expenses was $203, which compares well with the national average. But take a look at the other side of the dual educational

157

system in this county. The average daily attendance of Negro students during the same period was 5655. But the expenditure per pupil was $88.

In DeSoto County the ADA for white students was 1747 and the cost per pupil was $219. For Negroes the ADA was 2945 and the cost $51. That figures out to a 4-to-1 ratio under our separate but "Equal" educational system.

These are not isolated examples, but seemingly the general rule in virtually every county containing a heavy concentration of Negroes. Noxubee had 1045 white pupils in ADA last year and 3775 Negro. For the white student they spent $195, for the Negro $68. Sunflower's white ADA was 2203, Negro 3928. Expenditures were $310 and $71. Tunica's was 724 white students and 2749 Negro.

In Jackson County the white ADA was 6666, Negro 1646. Expenditures for the term averaged $165 per white pupil and $134 Negro. In Forrest the white ADA was 5674, Negro 2845. Expenditures were $160 and $120.

On the whole it had been an interesting year. To me the most amazing thing about the year was that my bookkeeper said the paper showed a profit of $3,400. What fascinated me was the fact that I had to borrow $2,000 from a friend to pay my bills.

Chapter 24

The Petal Paper, Volume 3, Number 1, Thursday, November 17, 1955, was four pages and had a total of thirty-five ads, all small, and one legal notice. I was far from sure what it was I was seeing around me. Emmett Till had been murdered. I had not commented on it, my reason being that it was useless; also, I felt there was entirely too much comment. On the other hand, I felt that no matter what, no jury in my native state would find white men guilty of murdering a Negro. To me it was a hopeless matter.

I noted a matter brewing at the University of Mississippi with reference to their annual Religious Emphasis Week. One of the invited speakers was the Reverend Al Kershaw. Since the invitation had been extended, the Reverend Mr. Kershaw had participated in a quiz show on a national television network. When asked what he would do with his winnings, he replied he would give part of it to the NAACP. I found it unbelievable that my fellow citizens would react as they did. They demanded that Kershaw's invitation be withdrawn. The Director of Religious Life at the university, a Baptist minister named Will D. Campbell, refused to withdraw the invitation. I was not acquainted with the Reverend Mr. Campbell, but I began to feel a mounting respect for at least one minister in the state. While I did not want to get myself involved in these matters in the northern part of the state, having quite enough at home to worry me, I felt I had to say something about the foolishness of the situation. The "East Side" column seemed the place for such short comment, and in the first issue of my third year as a weekly newspaper editor I wrote:

Let it be said that Rev. Kershaw made a wrong decision; had he decided to give some of his TV winnings to the Citizens Councils of Mississippi, then he would have been welcomed in our fair State. It's just a simple matter of sin. You know how it is, your sins are much greater than mine.

Except for that observation I kept the column light and fairly humorous, commenting on my daughter Karen's cat and such matters.

During the Christmas holidays that year I was told a joke by a high-school boy and it gave me something to think about. The story was carried in my column.

The giant airliner was loaded to capacity and an emergency landing at sea was inevitable. After exacting care in his calculations, the pilot decided that five passengers must give their lives in order that the others be spared theirs. He asked for five volunteers, explaining the situation. The first to offer his life was an Englishman. He stepped to the open door, and exclaimed, "God save the Queen." With that he jumped. The second one was a Frenchman, who said, "Long live France," and jumped. The third was from Texas. "Remember the Alamo," he shouted, and jumped. The fourth was from Mississippi. He stepped to the open door, exclaimed, "Remember Emmett Till." And with that he pushed out two Negroes.

159

The interesting part about the story was that a restaurant owner in Hattiesburg, a regular advertiser in the paper, pasted it under a glass counter where change was made. It was seen and read by his customers. The man chuckled over it for weeks. He called me on the telephone and related his amusement. I made no comment as to my interpretation of the story. Finally, toward the end of January, I had a letter from the man canceling his advertising. He gave no reason. Later I made a trip into his restaurant to see if the copy was still pasted where everyone could see it. It was not. The man's attitude was slightly less than cordial. I can only guess that someone explained to him the possibility of an interpretation different from his.

Almost every day I received a canceled subscription, generally through the mails. Also, almost every day I received new subscriptions. They were coming in from approximately half the states in the nation. At home the paper was shrinking; away from home it was growing. I had an uneasy feeling about my standing in the community. Some of my old friends who had once stopped by the office to pass the time of day weren't speaking to me on the streets unless forced into it. Of interest to me was the fact that a few persons had asked me point-blank, "What do you believe in?" I presume they were moved to the question by my attitude on religion, liquor and other matters, possibly. Obviously, there were those who felt I believed in nothing in this world. I began to do what I could to focus a few things, to shape them for explanation.

I lay awake many nights wondering why people were so abusive and nasty because someone held an opinion different from theirs. I don't know why it is. I only know it is that way. There was much I didn't understand in January of 1956, and time hasn't improved the situation to any great degree.

One thing I knew but had not admitted—that in the Magnolia Jungle there were no paved streets, no curbs, gutters or sidewalks. Indeed, the Magnolia Jungle did lack certain of the visible signs of civilization at times.

By mid-January 1956 I wasn't sleeping well at all, and not only from wondering why people were often nasty when opposing or different views were expressed. I was beginning to

160

wonder about myself and my motives and my relationship with my environment. For over two years I had moved in a vacuum, giving little thought to the reasons for my views. My reactions had been almost instinctive in everything I did. I was struggling, groping for a certain answer. About those answers I knew one thing: I didn't really care to provide them for anyone in the world, except myself. When I ran the following in the column on January 19, 1955, I was obviously talking to myself.

I've been asked more than once, "What do you believe?"

Honestly, I've been asked that question, just like that. Books have been written by men trying to state what they believe. Personally, I believe very little. Just that simple—very little.

There are, however, a few things in which I believe with all my heart.

First, I believe in God. I hope this will not be confused with organized religion in any way whatsoever. I certainly see the need for organized religion, but I have never felt the need for it personally.

Second, I believe in my family. And of my wife, Billie, and my daughter, Karen, I'm extremely proud, and consider myself unusually fortunate to have them as a wife and daughter. They come first after God with me.

Third, I believe in my country. I hasten to add that I am by no means fanatical on the subject; not to the point of "My Country right or wrong." I certainly prefer that my country be right, but if I think it's wrong, I would never hesitate to say so.

The one thing about this nation that makes it great is the promotion of the ideal of Democracy. I know, of course, such an ideal will never be attained, and I think that's good. It is sort of like the fox hunter, the ideal of this nation, it's not catching the fox, but the joy of the chase. The fox himself is worth very little.

I hold the ten articles of the Bill of Rights to be as important as the Ten Commandments.

I believe the few friends I have are worth more than any amount of money. I admit having but a few friends, and also admit that it's by choice, to a great extent. Those whom I call "friends" are not, to my way of thinking at any rate, average persons. They have, generally speaking, one quality that makes them different, and that is honesty. I hope no one gets the impression that I think all men are dishonest. I don't think that at all. But no man is completely honest unless first he is honest with himself, and that is a rare quality, indeed!

I believe in the dignity of all men, and their individual right to act as they see fit, provided their acts are not aimed at doing harm to their fellowmen. Generally, we have laws which are designed to protect the

161

innocent in such cases, but not always. And with reference to laws, I believe that all men should be viewed in the same light. That is to say, I believe the concept of Justice as being blind is one which is fair to every man. I know, of course, that's an ideal. I know it doesn't work that way, except in rare cases. Justice peeks.

Now, there you have a few of the things I believe.

I have been asked by readers of this paper, "What are some of the things you are against?" I think some expect the answer to that question to be "everything!" That by no means is true.

I know, of course, that it is humanly impossible to overcome ignorance; every single one of us suffers from it in one way or another. But I consider it to be the root of most of our sins, particularly the sins we commit against each other.

Thus, I am wholeheartedly against ignorance. That does not mean I'm opposed to ignorant men. If given a chance most of us can learn. Thus, I am opposed to anyone who would deny the right to another to acquire a degree of education. And here's why: a rare commodity is wisdom. It is, I believe, God-given. But wisdom is not likely to come into its own without education. (Wisdom and education should not be confused; there's a vast difference in the two. A man may well be educated and still be without wisdom.) Anyway, with the first ingredient, wisdom, and then with education a man may acquire virtue. With virtue comes justice. And everything that stands in the way of justice I am very much against.

In my paper I have often opposed certain men, not as individuals, but because they stood for something which I considered wrong. Individuals I am inclined to like, to some degree. But any individual without principle I am always ready to oppose.

In thinking about it, I am more or less inclined to believe that most of the things to which I am opposed result from ignorance. For example, selfishness, conceit, intolerance, bigotry, and injustice.

I am opposed to any man who would force his will on me, or on any other man. I am within my rights to disagree with any person at any time, and by the same token any person at any time is within his rights to disagree with me. Heaven help me if ever I try to force my will on any man.

I have been asked numerous times why my paper has the editorial policy it has. I think if you read the above as it should be read, you will have the answer to that question. Actually, the policy of my paper is summed up in one word: FAIR. It's not a very profitable policy, I'll admit. But I say this most sincerely: I would at any time cut a cake with my brother and give him the first choice of the halves.

Well, to some extent, there you have it. I am sometimes inclined to think that, could I have accepted certain fundamentals, I'd have made one hell of a preacher.

162

January of 1956 was a bad month. I had been forced to examine myself, to inquire into my feelings, and it was difficult and painful.

In the 1956 session of the Mississippi legislature a bill was introduced to tax any church that allowed its congregations to mix. By and large it was taken to be a direct attempt to keep the Roman Catholic Church in the state from allowing Negro members to attend services. I saw the proposed measure as something more; I saw it as an attempt to drive Jesus underground in the Magnolia Jungle. It was not passed.

Also, that my hope of peace of mind be delayed, the state's senior senator, james o. eastland, spoke to a citizens council in Columbia, South Carolina, in late January and told them that the South must educate the United States. "Our position is righteous," said the senator. "The great rank and file of the people of the North believe exactly as we do. The law of nature is on our side."

What was it to me that eastland did or said? He was not my problem, of that I was sure. Day and night I wondered why. It nagged at my mind.

Also, I took note of the fact that persons with whom I'd attended high school and college refused to speak to me when we'd meet on the streets. It stung—it cut deep into me and it hurt. My depression grew deeper and for the first time in years I let the thought of suicide cross my mind. Vicious, nasty, dirty letters did little to help raise my spirits. I cried, Dear God, what the hell am I doing here?

The confusion, frustration and state of depression lasted through the last days in January and into early February. During that time I withdrew; I refused to go to my office. I refused to see anyone, except my poor wife, who had the good sense to leave me alone and to speak to me only when I spoke to her. During those few black days I asked myself hundreds of questions, all of which were important to me, all of which had to do with my relationship to my environment and the other persons in it with whom I had contact.

I had long since known the Magnolia Jungle was without paved streets, but for the first time it began to dawn on me that

163

the jungle was not without its brick walls. I knew there were solid brick walls; I was up against one.

In my desperation I found one place to go, a place I'd not been for a long time, and that was on my knees. I put the matter right up to God, and in the simplest, most straightforward way I could word it. While I still didn't hear a word out of God, I began to understand the value of prayer. It is something like taking a trip with a friend. I know I can drive my car for hundreds of miles and never speak to a friend who may be sitting beside me; however, if I do speak and communicate, the journey is more pleasant. It isn't a matter of begging God to give something for nothing. Rather, it is a simple matter of speaking with a friend when you feel the need to talk. Every day I speak with God numerous times through the course of my working hours. I never get into an automobile but what I say, "Well, God, I've got to go to Pascagoula [or wherever it is I'm going] and if You think You've got any business down there, I'd be pleased to have You ride with me." Now, perhaps that isn't much of a prayer; perhaps God thinks I'm joking. Fact is, I don't know what God thinks, because I'm still not convinced He has ears. That matters little. The important thing is I've someone with whom I can talk. Besides, I have always suspected that God was quite a character, anyway, and that He has an excellent sense of humor. I fail to see how this unknown force or power which we call God could allow man to create something like the Magnolia Jungle and not split His sides from laughter.

There are times in each life when a person cannot talk with anyone, no matter how close the friendship, about certain things on his mind. I'm sure my friend King would have listened, but my state of mind was something I could not bring into sharp enough focus to discuss with him. Thus, I found myself on my knees many times during those dismal days.

Finally, somehow, I survived, but the questions were still unanswered. My depression had run its course by the end of the first week in February. I'd not killed myself. Of course, I knew I wouldn't, if for no other reason than because it took more courage than I had.

Out of that madness came not a single answer, but out of it

164

came another question, first posed by my wife. Sometime earlier she had asked me: "P.D., do you suppose Heaven is segregated?" Slowly I began to speculate on the matter. By the issue of February 9, 1956, I had managed to get on paper some:

Questions About a City Called Heaven . . .

AT THE GATE, ONE KEEPER—TWO GATES?

One of the best means by which a person can acquire an education is to go ahead and do the best he can, and, when wrong, have someone around to correct him. That is education by experience, of a sort.

Our aim here, since we are not too well acquainted with persons who have firsthand knowledge of the situation, is to go ahead and make statements, and, in the event we are incorrect, hope someone will take the trouble to set us straight on the matter.

Since early childhood we have heard from the pulpits of Mississippi the story of a City called Heaven. Our concept, from the sermons we've heard, is that in that fabulous place milk and honey are available in abundance. (They're both fattening, incidentally.)

Well, in view of the ruling of the United States Supreme Court, we have begun to wonder how it will affect that City called Heaven, if at all. We have always sort of thought that Heaven was reserved for white folks, Mississippi Christians, especially. But now we have some doubt about the whole business. At any rate, before doubt takes over our mind completely, we would like to inquire of Mississippi ministers if we are right in our conception of Heaven.

There is a gate; the straw boss in charge is St. Peter. When one approaches the premises seeking entrance he is asked certain questions by the boss. And they're pretty catchy questions, too. He has had considerable experience in catching liars. You pretty well have to tell the truth. Of course, we know most Mississippians have done that.

There are certain requirements, we understand. You must be white, a Christian, of sound mind, and be able to interpret the laws and by-laws of Heaven and Earth to the satisfaction of the gate keeper. And if you can get by the gate, and aren't too fat already, you can gain entrance for eternity.

But what about the Negro? Do they have another Heaven for him? Or possibly just a section of Heaven set aside for the Negro's quarters? Are the streets in the Negro quarters paved with gold, too? Do they give him milk and honey, or does he stay too busy mopping the golden streets that run in front of the white area? Possibly it works like this, and if we're wrong, correct us:

A Negro walks up to the straw boss, St. Peter, and informs him that he's there, seeking entrance.

165

"Well, nigger," asks St. Peter, "what's your name?"

The Negro gives his name.

"Where you from, nigger?"

"Mississippi, boss" is the answer.

"Did you ever try to vote while you lived in Mississippi?" asks the gate keeper.

"No, sir, yo' honor, not me. . . . I know a nigger's place."

"Did you ever talk back to your white boss, or try to own a home as good as a white man, or complain about the difference in the pay scale between you and the white man?"

"Not me, boss. I know a nigger's place."

"What'd you do for a living, nigger?" is the next question.

"Sir, I hoed cotton in Mississippi. I worked from four in the morning till seven at night. And I kept my children out of school so they could hoe cotton, too."

"Pass," said St. Peter. "You're a mighty fine nigger."

Maybe that's how it is—we just don't know. Or maybe it's like this:

"Well, nigger," asks St. Peter, "what's your name?"

"I'm Mrs. Lula Mae Magnolia, St. Peter."

"What do you mean 'Mrs.,' and what do you mean calling me St. Peter?" he asks.

"Well, sir, that's my name, and that's your name, isn't it?"

St. Peter sputters something awful. "My name is Mr. St. Peter to you, nigger, and your name is just Lula Mae Magnolia—you know better than that 'Mrs.' stuff."

"The prefix 'Mrs.' has no social connotation, Mr. St. Peter," said the Negro woman.

"That don't make any difference around this place. Some of you niggers are getting the most outlandish notions here lately. Honest to goodness, I just don't figure it."

St. Peter wipes the sweat from his brow, having been in something of a quandary.

"Well, sir," the Negro woman begins, "the law of the nation in which I lived said that—"

"Don't give me that stuff, nigger," interrupts St. Peter. "I've heard that malarkey before. Anyhow, where you from?"

"I'm from Mississippi, sir," said the woman.

"Well, it's a wonder to me you didn't get up here sooner than you did, considering the way you act."

"I thought you knew I wasn't up here by natural causes, Mr. St. Peter. I tried to vote in Mississippi, and that shortened my span somewhat."

"Well," said St. Peter, "let's get on with the entrance questions. Now, I know your name and I know that you're from Mississippi, and I know you are one of those smart-aleck niggers who tried to vote. What kind of work did you do in Mississippi?"

"I was a schoolteacher, Mr. St. Peter," she answered.

Without another word the keeper of the gate just turned his thumb in a downward direction. "To Hell with you, sister," he said.

We're just asking of those who might know: Is Heaven segregated? Or have they provided two Heavens? Or can a Negro even get to Heaven?

For just a moment let's consider the possibility of the fact that in Heaven there is no Jim Crow law, no segregation, and that one lives on a certain street, in accordance with the size of his halo. What then? Maybe some of us had better begin to get used to the idea—possibly? Still, on the other hand, from what we've seen from time to time there is no use in worrying about it at all. It's likely to be thumbs down just when we tell St. Peter we're from Mississippi.

The first reaction was received the following day in the mail, as follows:

Hattiesburg, Miss.
February 10, 1956

Mr. P. D. East, Editor
Petal Paper
Petal, Mississippi
Dear Mr. East:

Your article on "Questions about a City called Heaven" is the most sacrilegious article I have ever read.

It seems to me you should be more concerned about the welfare of your own soul than as to whether or not Heaven will be segregated.

Furthermore, since you are so down on Mississippi and Mississippians, there are forty-seven other states in the Union, of which I am sure one or two could tolerate you.

Yours very truly,
Miss Elizabeth Williams
Mrs. Gladys Nobles

For the first time in days, I howled.

I went about my business, giving as little thought to the situation as possible. I could not help but note that not a single subscription in the village of Petal had been renewed by the middle of the month. I could not ignore the fact that January 1956 income had been some $300 less than for January 1955. I knew to think through the matter would lead to that ever-present solid brick wall again, and, being human, I had an urge to stay away from it. I had begun to ask myself other questions, like: What is superiority really all about? What is the general situation in my state? Again and again the matter of "social equality" came into my mind. I was by no means sure what I was talking about, but I made an effort to bring into focus for myself some of the general questions. I wasn't sure as to how I should go about presenting such a rambling effort; finally, I decided to use the same form as if I were to write a letter, which I did:

A LETTER TO A FRIEND

And God Said,"Let Us Make Man in Our
Own Image, After Our Likeness." In So
Saying, God Gave All Mankind One Thing
in Common: Brotherhood.

MY DEAR FRIEND:

You have asked of me questions which, were I around a century from now, I could answer with a degree of objectivity which I lack today. The historian of a century hence will then be able to put into place the pieces which I am witnessing today. He will be able to weed out the unrelated parts and events of our time, parts which have no bearing on our immediate problems here in Mississippi.

However, you have asked me questions, and I shall do my best to answer them.

What is our problem here in Mississippi? Where and when did it begin? Our problem here in Mississippi is the same as the problem New Yorkers think they have because of their Jewish population. In Texas a similar problem exists with the Mexicans. In short, our problem should not be a problem at all, and were it not born in man to be superior to other men, we wouldn't have a problem.

. As to the first record of its beginning, it began that fateful day when "it came to pass, as they journeyed from the east, that they found a plain in the land of Shinar; and they dwelt there. And they said one to another, Go to, let us make brick, and burn them thoroughly. And they had brick for stone, and slime had they for mortar. And they said, Go to, let us build a city and a tower, whose top may reach unto heaven; and let us make us a name, lest we be scattered abroad upon the face of the whole earth."

That is the first record of man and his innate vanity in the field of superiority, the building of a Tower of Babel. Many Babels have been built since—and there is no reason to believe that man will ever stop building Babels. But, as to the original Tower built on the plains of Shinar, God saw fit to reduce man to a common denominator. Men

168

have been so reduced numerous times—the Constitution of the United States reduces all citizens of this nation to one common denominator. We are a nation without rank or title that can be passed along from generation to generation.

Mississippi's social problem did not really begin with the formation of the NAACP in 1909, as many have us believe. We got ourselves off to a good start in 1890 with our State Constitution. Impetus was gained by the words and acts of the late and unlamented Senator Bilbo. Bilbo used to great political and personal advantage the Negroes of the state. "Nigger," he cried every single time his sins were about to catch up with him. By yelling "Nigger" the late Senator was able to avert attention from his own shortcomings.

Great impetus was given by the war. Negroes served with honor under the flag of their nation. They were drafted into the Army, as were any other citizens. They fought and died, as did many other citizens. Presently, under the draft laws, every male turning 18 is inducted into the army, unless deferred for educational or other reason. When the white male reaches 21 he can vote; chances of the Negro's ever voting in Mississippi are rare, indeed.

At any rate, along the way, the Negro began to realize that the Constitution of the United States, its laws, applied to every citizen in the nation; he began to take action toward attaining his guaranteed rights as an American citizen. Chances are you have heard a good bit of talk about rights for Negroes being Communist-inspired. Not being on speaking terms with any Communists, I cannot say with certainty one way or another. But one thing I would like to point out is this: It is a well-known fact that from about 1935 until 1950 the Communist Party tried every trick in their bag to make an inroad with the Negro here in the South. It is equally well known that they were unsuccessful in their efforts. But that is something of which we hear little. It is logical to conclude that the Negro, considering every possible reason to turn Communist during the depression years, is a fairly good and loyal American. We don't hear much about that, either.

Were I capable of speaking as a Professional Southerner, I think I would have to say that we here in the South made a mistake; in the beginning our error was letting the Negro learn to read . . . Well, you can see what's happened. If you can keep a person ignorant you can keep him in line fairly well. But it is agreed that a little learning is a dangerous thing. . . .

However, since I am not up to the standards of the Pro Southerner, I must admit that in the history of the world no race has progressed as rapidly as has the Negro race in America. True, the Negro has had help. But he hasn't had the amount that his white masters promised—for example, equal but separate schools. We salved our consciences, but failed to keep our word. Today we have a problem and some of us sit around and wonder what it's all about. And since we won't admit the truth of the situation to ourselves, we place the blame just anywhere we can. Many of us have buried our heads in the sand—that leaves a rather unattractive part of the anatomy exposed. That part is visible for a good long way.

In short, the Negro wants to be treated as a human being. I do not believe for one second the Negro wants integrated schools, at least not in my area of the state. I do not believe for one second the Negro wants to be asked into white homes for an evening of bridge. He is not without his own culture or heritage. Of course, I will admit readily that among the Negro race there will be "niggers" as long as the race exists. We have among our own race "po' white trash," and we will have them as long as our race exists, too.

You have asked about "Social Equality" here in Mississippi. To put it bluntly, my friend, I assure you that no such thing exists, among white or colored persons. Equality is totally non-existent anywhere on the face of this earth. I presume you meant something relative to Negroes' visiting in white homes, and vice versa. And in answer to that, let me say to you that it isn't likely ever to be done, considering the fact that every single one of us is superior to everyone else. Equality? There is no such thing.

But you may be interested in knowing this. I have heard a few whites confess that they knew many Negroes they would prefer to have in their homes in preference to some whites they know. But, assuming they visited, would that make them socially equal? No, it would not. Who would not be honored to have Dr. Ralph Bunche visit him? But, honor or not, Dr. Bunche would never be invited to a white home in Mississippi. Dr. Bunche is unquestionably a great man, a great American, and has done much toward keeping peace in the world—but is he socially equal in Mississippi? No he isn't. Not because of intelligence or accomplishment—but because his skin is darker than ours.

Now, as to what we have done, as a state, about the situation. I would like to point out that we have, in a gigantic way, displayed an unattractive part of our anatomy in a most spectacular way. To be sure, that's putting it rather mildly. Of course we have passed a few laws—all based on a currently magic word in the state: Segregation is the word nowadays. Has magic.

Generally speaking, the Negro can't vote. I know, of course, that our senior Senator has told the nation on a television program that the Negro can vote. I would not be so disrespectful as to indicate that our Senator would tell a fib, but let us presume he is uninformed as to the law passed by the State Legislature last year about voter registration. It is within the power of the person whose business it is to register voters to keep anyone from voting, if he so desires. And the vast majority so desire, considering that they ran on that platform in the elections last August.

Let me give you an example with which I am familiar. Right here in Forrest County there are approximately 12,000 Negroes, all of whom are citizens of the United States. Of that number, and this figure was as of last August, 8 can vote. And with reference to those 8, last month, January, was tax-paying time here. Two of those eight Negroes who are registered to vote went to the Forrest County Court House to pay their property tax, and at the same time to pay their poll tax; they could not find anyone who would accept their poll tax payment. What can they do? Now Forrest County has 6 Negroes who are registered and qualified to vote. Indeed, it's entirely possible that we have none.

So, for the most part in the state of Mississippi, a Negro's asking to register to vote is about like asking Satan for a drink of ice water—just ain't no use in wasting breath.

And, my friend, we have passed other laws. We went to the polls a little over a year ago, and like a bunch of idiots gave the State Legislature the power to abolish the public schools. That, you will understand, was another anti-segregation move. And it might be of interest to you to note that at the present time there is a bill in the legislature to repeal the compulsory school attendance law.

To date this bill has met with little resistance, and that's understandable. ... They say the bill should be passed in order to help maintain our segregated school system. In view of the power the Legislature now has to abolish the public school system, it seems foolish to bother with such a trivial bill.

Indeed, there is more to it than we seem to realize. What the bill amounts to is simple: It will put the stamp of approval on many of Mississippi farmers (this applies mostly to the Delta) to take a Negro child out of school to work on the farm. Either that or they deny him entrance to school at all.

So, friend, the Lord and the Constitution of the United States giveth, and the Legislature of Mississippi taketh away!

Well, one could write a book about it, I'm sure. But one or two other related items and I'll close. Our Legislature is presently considering a bill of pure corn-fed poppycock—it is called "Interposition." Alabama and Virginia, I understand, have already passed such bills. How they got ahead of us is something I can't understand. For we are supposed to have a corner on foolishness. Nonetheless, it is complete and utter nonsense. Virginia has had previous experience with trying to outdo the Federal Government. They leased a state park to an individual and the Federal Court ruled against them. The court would not let them do by indirection what it forbids by direction. And such will be the case from now on.

We can pass bills from now on and nothing will change. We've got a problem of our own making, and now we are afraid to face up to it. The Negro wants his neck from under the economic foot of his master. And some of them are going to get it, too.

But we are making one mistake right behind the other about this situation. We have used everything we have, except our brains—when we get around to that it may well be too late.

Anyway, a century from now the historian will probably finish up by writing this final sentence: "Niggers ain't nothing but human beings, after all." And he'll be right, too.

Sincerely,
/s/P. D. East

I'm still not too sure what it was I was trying to get said, except for one point: Negroes are just human beings, nothing more and most definitely nothing less. I questioned whether or not I was right in my assumption that Negroes didn't want to associate socially with whites; also I questioned whether or not I was right in saying that Negroes didn't want to attend integrated schools. To me it didn't make good sense if they wanted either, but—and I admitted to myself the fact—I was prejudiced, having had the opportunity to do both things. I thought, but did not write or speak it, if Negroes do want to associate with some of the whites I know, my opinion of the Negro was lowered. I was frank to admit my prejudices, as I've said.

The last week in February had all the earmarks of being a repeat of late January and early February. For some time I'd had an odd sort of pain in my stomach, but like most other things I'd elected to ignore it. However, by the end of the month it could no longer be ignored. I hurt, and I hurt constantly and with increasing pain. I called on my good friend and physician, "Deet" Tatum. After an account of my symptoms, he sent me to the hospital immediately for X-rays. As Deet had expected, and as I had not, I had an ulcer. I saw one X-ray of my stomach and was reminded of a map of South America, a nice-sized area, to say the least. I tried hard to disbelieve the fact. "How could I have an ulcer?" I asked Deet. His reply was another question: "How can you *not* have one?" A diet was prescribed, along with medication. For a full week my fare was milk, nothing to eat or drink except milk.

During that week of milk, I sank into a state of depression. I was upset over my health, my business, or lack of it, and the old, old questions returned to haunt my mind and heart. What did it all really matter? Who was I to worry about whether some Negro, whom I did not know and would never know, could vote, or whether his children would have a school to attend? Indeed, what was it that I worried about? Was I concerned with the unknown Negro? Or was I concerned with something else? If so, what?

I spoke often to God; He continued to keep His counsel. Surely God must not have ears. Either that or His reception from the Magnolia Jungle isn't what it should be. I decided to stop bothering with Him. Anyway, to Deet Tatum I confided: "Well, thank God, here in this damned jungle we've got ulcer pills." Deet seemed to think it would be better if we could say, "Thank God, here in this jungle we don't have ulcers."

I kept on taking the Probanthine, kept to my diet, and began preparing an application for a Nieman Fellowship.

The Nieman Fellowships were established at Harvard in 1938 by a bequest of the late Mrs. Agnes Wahl Nieman, in memory of her husband, Lucius W. Nieman, founder of the Milwaukee *Journal*. It is strictly a newspaper fellowship; the aim, as stated by the foundation, "is to provide a chance for studies to add background for newspaper work." I knew of no one who could use "studies" to add to his background more than I. Realizing how poorly prepared I was to do anything, I decided to see if I could get a Nieman. If so, I'd have a chance to get out of the jungle for a while and try to gain a little perspective, which, if I had ever had, I'd lost. I had spoken with Mark Ethridge about it. He seemed to think it was a good idea and said he'd write a letter of recommendation to the curator.

The chances seemed fair that spring. I worked for weeks on my application, making sure I answered all questions completely and honestly. In the application I had written: "I am most interested in human relations, especially relations of one race to another. It is my belief that in human relations lies the history of the world, and in race relations lies the future of it."

I sent my application to Mark Ethridge to see what he

thought; he said it looked satisfactory to him. I was delighted but apprehensive. On the twenty-second day of May I received a telegram from Louis Lyons asking if I could meet with the selecting committee in Chicago the following Sunday. I went to Chicago. There was no doubt in my mind as to my getting a fellowship. I was quite confident about the whole thing. In addition to Louis Lyons, the selecting committee was composed of Dr. Merle Fainsod, Government Department, Harvard University; William M. Pinkerton, News Office, Harvard; C. A. McKnight, editor, the *Charlotte Observer*, Charlotte, North Carolina; and Milburn P. Akers, editor, Chicago *Sun-Times*.

On May 29 I learned the decision of the committee. Confident though I had been, I was not surprised when Lyons wrote saying their decision had to be an unfavorable one. Trying not to weep over my failure to secure a fellowship, I made a feeble effort at being unconcerned, but, I admit frankly, I was crushed.

I asked to apply again in 1958, and with my request I submitted the name of a friend as a reference. I don't know whenever I've enjoyed anything more than the letter written by Louis Lyons to my reference.

Harvard University

NIEMAN FOUNDATION

For Journalism

April 10, 1958

Office of the Curator
44 Holyoke House
Cambridge, 38, Massachusetts
Dear Mr. ———:

P. D. East, editor of *The Petal Paper* in Mississippi, is reapplying for a Nieman Fellowship and asks us to write you about him.

I am sure all the Selecting Committee will welcome your judgment about him.

I should tell you that when he applied two years ago, we were all very favorably impressed by what he was doing in *The Petal Paper* and had supporting letters from editors whom we much respected, who knew him also through his paper.

We brought him up from Mississippi to Chicago for an interview and all the Committee members threw up their hands after the encounter. It turned out that none of the editors who had written us about him had ever met him.

His personality made us all extremely dubious about investing in a year of study for him, which would have meant excluding one of the other top dozen applicants.

If you have ever talked with him, your impression would interest us very much. He baffled us.

Aside from that, we could not satisfy ourselves on such questions as:

Whether he has any chance of doing anything there but being a martyr;

Whether his great urge to come to Harvard is partly to get away from an impossible situation;

Whether he would resume his crusade after such a year;

Whether he would get anything important out of such a year, for his own purposes, to compare with what some of the younger men in more normal journalistic circumstances would get that they can use.

This is not the kind of letter I would ordinarily write to a reference. But we are evidently in for another baffling experience. It cost a good deal to bring a candidate up from Mississippi and there is no other way to get a real impression of P. D. East. I should add that among the candidates, as among this year's Fellows, are several who are doing a good job against the climate of the segregation belt and who want earnestly through studies to strengthen their own understanding to cope with this vital issue in their own communities. The question really is between one of the ablest of these and East.

But these are special reasons why the Selecting Committee will look for any help you can give us.

Sincerely yours,
Louis M. Lyons

My hopes for a Nieman Fellowship faded. Finally, in the fall of 1958, I did get to see Harvard University, from a bus, en route to Boston from Wellesley. No one will ever know how I wanted that fellowship, not so much in 1958 as in 1956. Had I not wanted it for the honest reason of education, I'd have appreciated it because of what happened before I went to Chicago.

What had happened was this: About the first of March I had heard of the possible formation of a Citizens Council in Forrest County. My opposition to the formation was based on the belief that such an organization would do harm to the existing relations, which, to be sure, weren't much, but we'd had no trouble with anyone, colored or white. Actually, I opposed the

175

Suh,

Here's Sweet MUSIC!

Yes, YOU too, can be

SUPERIOR

Join The Glorious Citizens Clan

Next Thursday Night!

What? Worried about being socially acceptable?

Learning to play the piano by ear? Taking dancing lessons? Using the right toothpaste?

Possibly taking a course in public speaking? Want to be the life of the party? No need to worry

anymore! The grand opportunity now awaits you!

Join The CITIZENS CLAN and BE SAFE From SOCIAL WORRIES

(Absolutely No Coupons Are Needed)

176

BE SUPER-SUPERIOR

Compare These 10 Freedoms with other Old Fashioned Offers

- Freedom to interpret the Constitution of the United States to your own personal advantage!
- Freedom to hunt "Blackbirds" with no bag limit, and without fear of prosecution! (To date no member of the Clan has been convicted for killing a nigger)
- Freedom to sit on a jury in behalf of your fellow members!
- Freedom from worry and fear if you happen to sit before a jury!
- Freedom to exercise a great Southern privilege: TO EXERT ECONOMIC PRESSURE!
- Freedom from fear of having economic pressure exerted against you!
- Freedom to yell "Nigger" as much as you please without your conscience bothering you!
- Freedom to wonder who is pocketing the five dollars you pay to join!
- Freedom to take a profitable part in the South's fastest growing business: Bigtory!
- FREEDOM TO BE SUPERIOR WITHOUT BRAIN, CHARACTER, OR PRINCIPLE!

(Many Other Freedoms, Too . . . Only A Few Listed Above)

- - This Wonderful Offer Open To White Folk Only - -

Other Items To Keep In Mind

Remember: No Niggers allowed! (Not even "good" Niggers can join this SUPERIOR Clan.)

Remember: You, too, can be SUPER SUPERIOR!

Remember: For only five dollars, GUARANTEED SUPERIORITY!

Remember: Not to join could mean you're a Nigger Lover!

Remember: The Time: 7:30 P. M., Thursday, March 22nd

Remember: The Clan needs YOU—But most of all, YOU may need the Clan!

This Page in Behalf of Liberalism, Fairness and Progress Donated By:...

The Petal Paper

Councils for many reasons, most of which I could not quite get into words, but in thinking back on the eternal question of "Why?" I recalled having said once with reference to the affair in Holmes County that "if they can do it to them, they can do it to me." From all accounts the Councils were pretty good at doing "it" to anyone whose opinions were different from theirs. For days I pondered the matter. I wrote sermon after sermon; finally, knowing full well I was preaching, I threw all the copy out. The news was released that the Forrest County Council would be formed at the courthouse on the twenty-third of March. My deadline was fast approaching if I was to have any effect. I had to get my comment in print in the issue of March 15, the last paper before the formation of the Council.

At the last possible second, I decided to do an ironic ad in behalf of the Citizens Councils. I did, and ran it as a full eight-column page in my paper.

In addition to the back page of my paper, and the comments in the ad there, I devoted the "East Side" column to the Citizens Councils. Excerpts from that column, all short thoughts I'd jotted down from time to time, are as follows:

Like prostitution, bigotry and intolerance must be a high-profit business—else there wouldn't be so much of it.

I am curious to know which minister is going to bless the organizational meeting of the Citizens Clan next Thursday night.

It wouldn't be at all surprising if after the Negroes came the Jews and then the Catholics. The Clans in Alabama have already split over the question of Jews. . . . Perhaps Mississippi is more progressive by letting them join the holy clan.

Instead of turning toward God or Mecca for our morning prayers, beginning Friday, March 23rd, perhaps we'd do well to turn toward the office of Mr. Dudley Conner (one of the founders of the local councils).

The Clans of today are the result of fear. Fear has its roots in many things, the most notable of which is ignorance. Thus—well, you can figure it out. . . .

Were it within my power to do so, I would not deny the right of organization to the Citizens Clan. They are within their rights to form . . . but they are not within their rights to use economic pressure

178

as a force against those who disagree with them. They are not within their rights to interpret the laws of the United States, or to inject their own views in religion.

I admit readily to a great prejudice . . . but, by the grace of God, I'm prejudiced toward the practical application and interpretation of the Bill of Rights.

That which we are witnessing today in the South is nothing more or less than mass insanity. Mobs. And mobs have never done any good. Indeed, were the Councils truly interested in doing anything worthwhile, they would be out to see that the Negro got an even break; they would be out to see that the Negro got equal facilities, fair wages, a fair chance to live and enjoy the privileges afforded by the Bill of Rights. True, I'm prejudiced. And it's going to take some doing to convince me that there is any good in the Citizens Councils.

But, indeed, fear is such a force that anyone suggesting fairness to a Negro, or anyone else whom a mob is against, is likely to incur the wrath of the mob. Fear breeds fear, and when it's holding sway, reason and common sense and decency are things forgotten. But who among us is without fear of one sort or another? We all have fears. But some of us fear the loss of human rights, decency, freedom as an American citizen. The loss of those things strikes a greater fear in me than the fear of a Negro child attending a white school.

Actually, if I were a Jew or a Catholic in Mississippi today I'd be scared stiff. And if I were a Negro I'd already have been gone.

These times try more than just the souls of men . . . integrity, intelligence, humility, compassion, virtue, principle, and wisdom are being tried. Yes, in one sense even God is on trial at the present time.

Since its publication in March 1956, the "Jack Ass" page has, to my own knowledge, gone into all fifty states, Canada, Japan, England, Ireland, Australia, France, Italy and Germany (West Germany, that is). Additionally, the page was printed in *The Reporter* Magazine in March 1957 and *Harper's* Magazine in January 1959. It would be sheer unadulterated egotism to say it was a page heard 'round the world. However, to say it was heard 'round the Forrest County courthouse on Thursday night, March 23, 1956, would be to state a simple fact. Being a nervous wreck, and a natural-born coward, I did not attend the organizational meeting of the Citizens Council in the county. Besides that, I wasn't invited. I did ask a friend to at-

179

tend and give me a report. From what he told me about the meeting, I wrote for the column the following week:

In Hattiesburg Thursday night, the Ku Klux Council organized a local chapter. Principal address of the evening was made by the most Right Honorable Earle Wingo, who, I am told (having not been invited, I did not attend the meeting), held up a copy of *The Petal Paper* dated March 15th, and told his audience of approximately 100 persons that he was going to cancel his subscription that night. At home I waited patiently for a call, but none came. Friday morning I checked on the subscription of Honorable Earle and found that for non-payment his subscription had automatically been canceled on June 22, 1955. Wonder whose paper he was using? Of possible interest, too, is the fact that Mr. Wingo is the author of a book titled *The Illegal Trial of Jesus*, which, as I understand, has been termed by his pastor as being a masterpiece. Mr. Wingo is also a Sunday-school teacher, or was at the time he wrote the book. Personally, I think it's a fine thing that Christ rose from the grave, because had He not, by now Heaven only knows how many times He'd have turned over in it because of the crimes committed in His name.

Immediately following the issue of March 15, my telephone rang a few times, and I was greeted by unidentified persons, one or two seeing fit to let me know they considered me a "nigger-loving, Jew-loving, Communist son-of-a-bitch." One lady left word with my wife for me, saying that I'd better not show my head out of the house or her husband would knock it off. Such calls did little for my ulcer. My reaction was as it had been before and was to be many times in days to come. I was depressed to the point that I went into my room at home, sat on the side of my bed and wept like a child. Why I should react in such a manner is beyond me. I was not so naïve as to think I could print what I had and not get by without a certain amount of abuse. That time I didn't bother to ask myself those countless questions over and over. I let the tears flows as if I'd been hurt physically. Perhaps that's as it should have been, for, to be sure, I had been hurt.

In addition to being called "nigger lover, Jew lover, Communist," there were isolated incidents which concerned me. Some of them were amusing, others definitely weren't. Shortly after the "Jack Ass" page appeared, Easton King called me from

180

Pascagoula to inquire what the situation was. While his interest and concern were sincere, the call worried me. King is a newspaperman who has been through many trials and tribulations himself, and because of his obvious concern I wondered if I had underestimated the situation. I stayed away from everyone for weeks. Occasionally I would have to go to my office or downtown in Hattiesburg. On these excursions my apprehension would cause my stomach to draw into a knot which was not too unlike a cannonball in shape and weight. I was not too afraid of physical violence; I was apprehensive about the snubs I would receive on the streets. I never knew whether my best friends would speak or not. Many of them didn't.

On one trip through Hattiesburg, en route to my office in Petal, I stopped for a traffic light. A gentleman whom I did not know, nor have I learned his name since, walked from the curb to my left and asked of me, "Aren't you P. D. East?" I nodded in the affirmative. "Well," he said, "if you'll get out of that goddamned car I'll mop up the street with you." My first impulse was to get out and see if he could do it. Then I remembered that I was a natural-born coward, and for the first time in my life I thought of an answer then and there, instead of a day or two later. "Well, now," I said, taking note that the traffic light was about to change, "you don't offer a man much inducement, do you?" With that I drove off, leaving him standing in the street.

While it had been humorous to me, it wasn't a thing I was laughing about. I was thinking of those people from whom I'd not heard a word. These were the ones who worried me. I've never considered a person a threat who calls anonymously. Such a person, basically, is a coward. The man who will crack your skull is the man who doesn't tell you he's about to do it. You turn a corner some night and the next thing you know you wake up in the hospital, or dead. Whether or not that theory is true I don't know, but I accepted it as one on which to operate. I still hold with it.

As the weeks passed my apprehension grew. I had no idea what to expect next. While I have never held with firearms (even as a child I didn't go hunting), I felt it would be wise to have

181

a pistol within my reach. For the second time in my life I purchased a weapon, a .38 mm. Lüger, which I put into the glove compartment of my car. In my few sane moments I knew full well it was a waste of money; I knew I could no more fire at a man than I could call God through the telephone company.

During that period a memory kept going through my mind, and for it there was no possible explanation. When I'd been a child at the sawmill camp at Carnes I had seen a mother feeding her infant child, and the thing on my mind about that particular feeding was the fact that she had given an infant butterbeans, the large, dried kind. I recalled my horror at the incident, even though I knew nothing about infant care. Somehow, though, I had the distinct feeling that large, dried butterbeans were not for babies. Why I should recall that isolated incident at that particular time is something I've never been able to explain. Perhaps it had to do with the Magnolia Jungle in some remote way.

Slowly I returned to a more normal state. Telephone calls were less frequent, though an occasional unsigned letter arrived. I cannot say I've ever become accustomed to abuse, but the mind and heart are much like other parts of the anatomy in that nature protects them by forming a cyst around the sensitive part. A cyst may be nature's protective measure, but it is not desirable.

During the "Jack Ass" era subscriptions were canceled in large numbers; advertising fell off to an alarming degree. Within a month after the issue, my circulation in Petal was less than twenty-five. In Petal I had three advertisers who continued to use the paper, and for taking their money, circulation considered, I felt like a thief. For every loss of a Petal subscriber I would get about three from out of state, mostly from New York City and Los Angeles.

In spite of having become an ulcerated, pistol-packing editor, I was unable to keep from engaging in my hobby, the pursuit of self-destruction, at least financially. By the nineteenth of April, barely over a month after the "Jack Ass" page, I was at it again. In addition to the unanswerable questions which plagued me, I had begun to wonder about other things in the jungle. One of

182

those things was the question of why the ministers weren't doing anything to bring about an understanding between the races in Mississippi, especially in my county of Forrest. I wondered what could be done toward re-establishing communications between colored and white citizens. With that in mind, I aimed an editorial at the Forrest County Ministerial Association, all members of which were white. In essence, what I said was: as men of God, ministers had the responsibility to lead their flocks, instead of follow, as I'd seen so many doing.

It went over like the proverbial lead balloon. I saw to it that most white ministers got a copy of the paper. I knew of nothing else I could do, in view of the brick wall in the Magnolia Jungle. One thing I decided: I sure as hell wasn't going to pray for the local preachers.

Notwithstanding the facts related up to now, relative to telephone calls, letters, loss of revenue and days of depression, the spring and summer of 1956 held moments of pleasure. Among those moments was a weekend in the early spring in Holly Springs, Mississippi, where I'd gone to visit Mark Ethridge, who had come down from Louisville. Mark and I spoke of many things during that visit, not the least of which was our respective opinions of my state's senior senator, james o. eastland. I confessed to Mark that I'd supported eastland, for whatever it was worth; he confessed that the *Courier-Journal*, of which he was publisher and editor, did not support the senator. From him I learned of some editorials the *Courier-Journal* had printed on the subject of our senior senator. I requested that he send me copies; I was keeping a file on the activity of eastland, his statements and actions, and his views on the matter of civil rights.

It was my opinion that to state facts straight about the wild beasts of the Magnolia Jungle was a complete waste of time. I held, and still do, that to poke fun at stupidity was more effective than hell-fire and brimstone preaching. A feather is more effective than an elephant gun, unless you're hunting elephants. While I treated the subject of our senior senator lightly, I was horror-stricken at some of the statements he'd made, especially the words he spoke at Senatobia, Mississippi, on August 2,

1955, as quoted in the editorial I ran on my front page on May 31, 1956, entitled:

"Our Gem," He's Real Gone, Man, Real Gone—

NOW, AIN'T HE A REAL COOL CAT, MAN!

Having grown up in Mississippi (born and ruined), and having attended the public schools of the state, we recall having been taught two things which, with the help of the real gone Magnolia, we shall not forget. First, which has no bearing here, was the fact that a history instructor once told us that the reason our forefathers injected the two-dollar poll-tax clause into the Constitution of Mississippi in 1890 was to keep the Negroes from voting. Upon passing that delightful bit of unbiased information, our instructor smiled serenely. We students responded with a knowing giggle.

Second, which does have some bearing here, was the fact that an English instructor once told us that even in poor writing a statement should be made rarely, if ever. Preference, he said, should be given to "showing," not "telling."

Since this is more of a character study than a sermon, we hope to be able to "show" you that the Most Right Honorable james oliver eastland, our senior United States Senator, is one more Alligator, man! Of course, all the cool cats hereabouts know he is just that, but what do they know of all his other sterling qualities?

(Incidentally, the Most Right Honorable james oliver eastland shall be referred to hereinafter as "Our Jungle Gem," the reference being made for the simple reason that we have such regard, admiration and·respect for him.)

As we all know very well, our cool Magnolia State has numerous enemies outside its boundaries, especially north of the Mason-Dixon line, all being Yankee squares, of course. "Our Jungle Gem" has fought these radicals, these liberals, these carpetbaggers, with the vigor and daring of a real cool lion, man. He has, on numerous occasions, shown his ability as a statesman of the first magnitude, a diplomat of imagination and character, a true Southern Gentleman of the old school, in his encounters with those who would dare call us anything but what we are—100% Red Blooded Mississippians, with a slight sprinkle of real cool blue, that is.

On one occasion, in a Senate hearing, "Our Jungle Gem" called a witness a "Goddamned son-of-a-bitch." On a number of occasions he has called a "nigger" just what he is—a "nigger." On the floor of the United States Senate one day, in his eternal fight for our real gone Magnolia rights, "Our Jungle Gem" called an elderly colleague a "liar." Man, ain't he real gone!

184

At any rate we feel you will agree with us that "Our Jungle Gem" is a polished gentleman of unquestionable—indeed, unbelievable—intelligence.

Well, it just proves that "Our Jungle Gem" fights square enemies on their own ground . . . and wins hands down for the solid Magnolia.

What is considered by a large group of squares to be a great newspaper in a border state (and right here and now let us set you straight on that matter. There is no such thing as a "Border State." Either they're fer us or agin us.) had this to say about "Our Gem": "Senator Eastland's contributions to our wartime harmony were to proclaim that Negro troops 'would neither work nor fight' and to disclose a 'mass rape' of German women in a Stuttgart subway by Senegalese soldiers with French occupation forces. Undersecretary of War Robert Patterson refuted the first charge; General Devers denied the second after correspondents pointed out (a) that Stuttgart has no subway and (b) that there were no Senegalese with the French occupation forces."

Well! Did you ever! You understand, of course, that Patterson and Devers are Yankee squares and are not to be trusted out of sight. That's real plain to see.

Now, what about the editor of the sheet that deals in such "yellow journalism"? Well, Jackson, we took it on ourselves to call that editor on the telephone and remind him that "Our Jungle Gem" just might decide to get some skin, Mississippi style, so there! You know what he said? Get this: "Well, good!" Naturally, we hung up the telephone. Well, wouldn't you have done the same thing? He was disrespectful—subversive, too.

We don't know how it got that way, but the fact is this nation is just full of squares, folks who have gone off their trolley, that is. Example: The Protestant Episcopal diocese of New York (a Yankee state, square, you must remember) has accused "Our Jungle Gem" of subversion just as real and, because it comes from a U.S. Senator, far more dangerous than any perpetrated by the Communist Party. ("Our Jungle Gem" just may get a gunny sack full of skin, limb from limb, man, there.) Seriously, Jackson, wouldn't that just make John Calhoun and Jeff Davis turn somersaults in their tombs—yes, and "The Man" Bilbo, too? Subversive? Maybe the bunch had better look up the word—we Mississippians know who the subversives are. . . . Well, anyway, Jackson, "Our Jungle Gem" took it in his stride and investigated the New York *Times* from top to bottom. And that, we figure, ought to show 'em a thing or two.

As 100%, red-blooded, tolerant Southerners we must overlook those square Yankee Christians. Naturally, everyone knows that Christianity varies from place to place, and the thing which caused the bigoted outburst by the Episcopal diocese was the fact that "Our Jungle Gem" had fought those nine old squares in Washington who

185

would destroy our way of life. They just simply cannot stand a good, clean, intelligent, high-class fighter like "Our Jungle Gem."

And with reference to fighting for our way of life, "Our Jungle Gem" has stood up, a lion among rats, a real cool cat among squares, mind you, in his fight for all of us who are endowed with God-given Southern Rights. (We Southerners must keep in mind at all times that our rights differ from those of other people. We must be alert to anyone who seems even to want to change just one single hair on our Southern heads.) At any rate, "Our Jungle Gem" has not given a single inch in his stand to protect us from those outsiders.

In addition to his character, his integrity, his principles, "Our Jungle Gem" is not only intelligent in the usual manner, but he's sharp as a tack in other ways, Jackson. Example: At Doddsville, Mississippi, he has a small cotton patch, composed of something like 5,020 acres. And in the United States Senate, who has been the strongest fighter for the cotton farmer? Of course, our very own cool cat. . . . And down on the Gulf Coast a few years ago there came up the question of expanding industry in Mississippi, and "Our Jungle Gem" told an acquaintance of ours that Mississippi needed industry like a man needed a hole in his head. (And get the coolness of what follows.) How, he asked, can you keep labor on the farm at a dollar a day with industry moving in and offering them a dollar an hour?

There are some stupid squares, all out of state, of course, who have asked the question of how could "Our Jungle Gem" take the oath of office as a United States Senator, and after having taken the oath make statements like:

"On May 17, the Constitution of the United States was destroyed because the Supreme Court disregarded the law and decided integration was right . . . you are not required to obey any court which passes out such a ruling. In fact, you are obligated to defy it." This was spoken by "Our Jungle Gem" at Senatobia, Mississippi, on August 2, 1955. And he has also said: "The country has entered an era of judicial tyranny. . . . The Court has responded to a racial, pro-Communist political movement. . . . Public opinion is the law, for no law is of any force which does not have the force of public opinion behind it." Thus spoke "Our Jungle Gem" on January 26, 1956, at Columbia, South Carolina.

Well, if you hear any of that left-wing, radical, liberal talk about the majority ruling in this country, and that the majority opinion is opposed to "Our Jungle Gem," you can mark them down for super squares. We would even suggest you call it to the attention of our cool cat; he just might want to get some skin.

Anyone thinking that because a man of sterling character, golden principles, honor, intelligence and integrity such as those possessed by "Our Jungle Gem" would let a thing like an oath stop him from protecting our way of life is not just a square, but he's downright stupid. . . .

Really, now, folks, don't you agree?

Ain't "Our Jungle Gem" a real gone, a real cool cat!

I cannot deny that my duly elected representative in the United States Senate was of concern to me; nor can I deny that the unidentified caller who said to me "You're a disloyal, ungrateful bastard for writing that filth about Senator Eastland" was of concern also. For the life of me, I knew of nothing I could do about either man.

One other item which was of concern to me at the end of May 1956 was the fact that my income from advertising and subscriptions was approximately $200 less than it had been for the same month the year before. By the end of May the circulation of the paper in Petal was less than twenty; the total circulation had dropped to less than one thousand. All in all, I found little to heal my ulcerated stomach and even less to give me peace of mind. God and I continued our one-way conversations, but I fear His receiving set was still not tuned to the Magnolia Jungle. He never did subscribe, not that I asked Him to.

I was tired, disgusted, depressed and worried. Not only did I have the unidentified callers and letter writers, but those old, old questions continued to demand an answer. By the middle of June my Petal advertisers had been reduced to one; the subscription list in Petal had dropped to fifteen. I seldom went to my office, and when I did it was usually late at night to answer letters, and always with my pants sagging from the weight of a pistol in my pocket. The Magnolia Jungle was closing in. The wild beasts were fertilizing the thorns, and everywhere I turned I snagged my britches.

Tired? Yes, I was exhausted. Depressed? Indeed, I was wallowing in self-pity. Worried? It came natural with me. One thing I wondered about at that time, and even this moment, was the question of whether or not I was bitter. I wasn't sure; I'm not sure.

For a few weeks preceding the issue of June 7, I had been calling on Negro families, checking stories I'd heard. On the twenty-eighth day of May a Negro friend of mine, a businessman, called and asked me to meet him. He said he had something he wanted me to see. I went to his store in the early evening, picked him up and followed his directions. We drove to a dilapidated, unpainted two-room shack in one of the Negro sections of Hattiesburg. We went in and I found what I saw hard to believe, not the house, for I was accustomed to seeing such living conditions, but what I saw in the faces of three human beings. A mother, father and their seventeen-year-old boy were as frightened as any people I'd ever seen in my entire life. It took some few minutes for my friend to explain I was a friend and was interested in seeing what had happened to their son. I asked the boy to move under the light so I could see him. He had been hovering near the back door of the shack, but when I spoke to him he moved so that I could get a good, thorough look at his face and head. Whether or not his nose was broken, I don't know; however, I know it was swollen and puffed out of proportion. The eyes were a deep, dark blue, bruises showing on the surface. The boy's eyes were bloodshot; his forehead was cut, and a huge bump was visible from several feet away. His entire body was bruised and sore; he had difficulty in walking and moving. There was nothing I could say, except to suggest I get a doctor. He had been treated but not hospitalized. The parents had relaxed somewhat by the time my friend and I left. As soon as possible, I dropped my friend at his place of business —I didn't want him to see me weep. When out of his sight I stopped my car and let the tears flow. "God," I cried, "why do You let things like this happen?" What had that seventeen-year-old boy done, except to have been born colored?

It was a day or two before I could control my emotions enough to write without pounding holes in the paper. Finally, after several attempts, I managed to get a part of the situation on paper; in the June 7 issue, on the front page, I asked:

A New Organization in Business—

THE BIGGER AND BETTER BIGOTS BUREAU?

Whether or not they have actually organized as a chartered group, as their guardian angels, the Klan and Council, have, we don't know, but this we do know: There are a few young men in Hattiesburg who could easily qualify for the Board of Directors of such an organization as The Bigger and Better Bigots Bureau.

We have been informed, of course, of the riot on a New York ferry boat last week. We know of the riots in Chicago, Detroit and St. Louis. And in the interest of passing along information, we would like to call the following to your attention. These occurrences were not in New York, Illinois, Michigan, or Missouri. They happened in Hattiesburg, Mississippi, and we assure you these incidents have been confirmed. For reasons which are obvious we are not using names of the persons involved.

The latter part of April, directly in front of the Owl Drug Store, located on the corner of Main and Front Streets, three Negro boys were standing talking to a fourth Negro boy who worked for the store. The three boys were on their way to a show. The time was about 7:30 P.M. One of the boys, aged 16, felt a blow against the side of his head; turning around, he saw three white boys whose age he guessed to be 19, 20 or 21. The Negro boys were stunned, for they had not spoken one single word to any white person whatsoever, and they hesitated for a few seconds before doing anything. While the Negroes were standing there, trying to decide what to do, the white boys pulled out switchblade knives. The Negro boys started to run down Main Street, but they saw two other white boys standing beside the drugstore, and not knowing if they were a part of the group who had attacked them, they decided to run down Front Street, toward the police station. They did, in fact, go directly to the police station, and the boy who had been struck stammered out his story. He was told by the officer on duty that the incident would be investigated. However, no information whatsoever, such as name and address, was asked for by the officer on duty. Charges, of course, cannot be made without identification, and identification cannot be made without knowing whom to contact and where to contact them. Thus, to date, the Negro boys have not been called in to identify their assailants.

The second significant incident to occur in Hattiesburg happened on the corner of Main and Pine Streets at 10:15 P.M., May 1st. Two Negro women, a mother and her twenty-year-old daughter, were walking home from a motion-picture theatre. There was no one on the streets, except a few cars passing. One car passed and the older Negro felt a sharp blow on her right leg, near the ankle. She was startled for a few minutes, but realized she had been hit by an egg from a passing car. Looking up the street, she saw the car. She stated that as best she could judge there were four or five white boys in the car, one with his head stuck out the window yelling something to the Negro woman. The car had gone too far for her to read the tag number, or to deter-

189

mine what make of car it was. Unfortunately, there are too many autos the same color for that information to be of any help.

Item three, a minor incident admittedly, happened the following afternoon on South Main Street. A Negro man stopped his car to wait for a parked car to pull out into the line of traffic. Naturally, cars behind him had to stop, too. But one potential member of the Bigger and Better Bigots Bureau, driving an old-model Hudson, pulled alongside the Negro man and yelled to him: "Get that G—— d—— thing out of the way, you black s.o.b."

On Sunday evening, May 27th, at 7:30, a Negro boy, aged 17, was walking home to get dressed for church. He was about a half block off Walnut Street, going toward Manning Avenue. The street was dark, without adequate lighting. He noticed a car drive by two or three times, but paid no attention to it. Without warning, the car stopped, and as best he could remember, four, possibly five, white boys jumped out and beat him into a state of unconsciousness before he realized what was happening. They were gone when he regained consciousness. He managed to get home, blood dripping from him, his clothes soaked with it. He guessed the ages of the white boys to be 18 to 21, but couldn't be sure, because of the split second in which he had seen them. We saw the Negro boy four days after the beating, and saw with our own eyes the effect of the beating he took. His lip was cut through, swollen unbelievably. His face was swollen completely out of proportion to its normal shape. There were bandages covering his right cheek; the skin had been burst from the blows he received. He was having some difficulty in moving around due to the fact that his body was badly bruised.

Frankly, we admit that these four incidents are indicative of something which we have not yet been able to define—but, nonetheless, they are exceptionally significant. This is not an accusation, for we have no proof and do not make charges without evidence, but it is interesting to note that prior to the organization of the Citizens Council here there were no such incidents reported. Each of the four incidents has happened since the organization of the Council. We do not believe that Council members were in any way involved, but we believe that with the organization of such an outfit, certain unintelligent, bigoted, inferior whites feel something resembling guardian-angel protection in their existence. Thus, they take out their feeling of being inferior (which, indeed, they are—they don't just feel inferior) on Negroes, who, by all standards and concepts, are creatures of a lower order.

A number of possibilities occur to us as a possible result of this kind of action on the part of the whites. First, aside from the humiliation suffered by Negroes in the incidents mentioned (which they must also view with fear) is the fact that one of these nights some member of the Bigger and Better Bigots Bureau is going to run into a Negro who isn't a woman or child, and when he does he is likely to get carved up

190

like a turkey at Thanksgiving. Any Negro attacked would most certainly be within his rights in fighting back, but—well, just recall our record in the state for justice to a Negro.

Another possibility is that, in view of these whites operating on the assumption that they are superior by virtue of their being white, Protestant and native-born, they will not limit their brutal and humiliating attacks to Negroes. Of course a Catholic, a Jew and the miscellaneous are harder to identify than the Negro, but those thoroughly bent on being superior would determine a person's race or religion, and act according to their limited intelligence.

Of course, if the Bigger and Better Bigots Bureau does decide to organize, get a state charter and collect dues, they could promote an advertising campaign directing all who are not white, Protestant and native-born to wear a sign around their neck reading: I AM A CATHOLIC or I AM A JEW or I WAS BORN IN EUROPE—or whatever distinction is theirs.

Oh, yes, if they do decide to organize, we'd be glad to suggest an attorney to draw up their papers for them. There seem to be two or three around these parts who would probably do the work free, seizing it as an opportunity to strike a blow for the sweet magnolia.

I had reached a decision about the situation in Petal. I saw no point in keeping an office, paying rent and other expenses connected with maintaining it. My wife and I decided to buy a larger house, one in which I could have a work room. We worked out a transaction whereby we could make the down payment on a three-bedroom home with the equity we had in our two-bedroom house, and the additional cost of payments would still be less than office rent in Petal. We made the move in July 1956.

As stated already, there were pleasant moments in spite of the ever-advancing jungle. One of those pleasant memories grew out of a letter I'd had from a professor at the University of Mississippi, in Oxford. Dr. Josh Brass had written me saying that since he subscribed to a labor paper and other radical publications, he supposed he could stand *The Petal Paper*. In his letter he also said he and William Faulkner had discussed the possibility of forming some sort of moderate group in the state. My response to the idea was immediate; it was something I'd given thought to ever since my realization of the need for communication. In subsequent correspondence we arranged a meeting for the purpose of further discussion. Dr. Brass invited me to Oxford to meet with him and Faulkner. There was some hesitation when I thought of a meeting with William Faulkner, but the idea of a moderate group was more important than my apprehension over Faulkner. It was true that I wanted to meet Faulkner, but when I thought of the tales I'd heard about him, I had no idea what to expect; as usual, I went with a blank mind. Josh Brass filled me in on minor points: don't discuss Faulkner's work with him; don't try to force a conversation; leave him alone; he'd speak when he wanted to and not before. To follow Josh's advice was easy enough for me, since I'd not read Faulkner's works, except for his short stories. Nor was I given to forcing conversations with anyone, even though there were times when I'd wanted to do so.

I drove to Oxford on a Friday in June. The following morning Brass and I discussed conditions in the Magnolia Jungle, as well as William Faulkner. Immediately after lunch we were to pick up Faulkner at his home. I'd seen a number of Junes in Mississippi, but none had been hotter than the one in 1956. I was suffering from the heat, barely able to breathe, when we turned into the Faulkner driveway. Faulkner's home sits off a dead-end street, not visible from any approach. However, it seemed that entirely too many curious persons had found it anyway. Driving in, I felt the bottom of my car scrape the road; it was extremely rough, the ruts deep and filled with holes. "Good God," I said to Josh, "you'd think a Nobel Prize winner could afford to care for his driveway!" Josh said he thought Faulkner left it that way in order to discourage visitors. "As a matter of fact," he continued, "I wouldn't be surprised if he dug the holes in it himself."

What I expected in Faulkner I don't know. Perhaps I thought he might look a little like God, or perhaps one of the better-known archangels. I suppose it would have mattered little how he appeared, I'd still have been surprised. We parked behind Faulkner's Plymouth station wagon, about a 1950 model. Faulkner walked from around back of the house. I stood there with my mouth open. He was a small man, short, slightly inclined to be chubby, not fat. He was dressed in a sailor cap, the kind

192

you can buy for a dollar at any variety store. A pipe was sticking in his mouth. He wore a faded, thin blue shirt and a pair of khaki pants torn off just above the knees. They'd not been cut, not those pants; they'd been torn. I can't recall his shoes, but he wasn't wearing socks. Josh introduced us. We shook hands; he was polite, courteous, and his voice was soft, but strong and clear. It was a pleasant, delightful voice. He was brown as an Indian, having spent much of the summer on his sailboat. His mustache was trimmed neatly. His eyes were dark brown, almost black, in color. His facial features were clear-cut; it was a strong, calm face. The presence of Faulkner, with his soft-spoken, quiet voice, his strong face, had the effect of making me want to keep my own voice at a moderate pitch. I felt at ease with him; his presence had an over-all tranquilizing effect on me. After I'd closed my mouth and taken note of the man, I was keenly aware of a great liking for him as a person. I couldn't help but wonder how those wild tales of Faulkner had come into being; but, of course, I realized I was always prejudiced in favor of any person I liked.

After hoisting sail, we moved out in the Sardis Reservoir, a large body of water about ten miles west of Oxford. From the time we were introduced at one o'clock, until around three— after the trip out to the reservoir, the setting of sails and a tour around the water area—Faulkner said not one word to me. Nor had I spoken to him. For the better part of two hours the two of us sat in the stern of the boat, our knees touching, and not a sound was made. I watched him closely, observing the great patience he seemed to have, and anyone sailing a boat in June on the Sardis Reservoir, with the wind as still as death, has to have patience. After about an hour, my rump hurt. The seat was a six-inch board, and what with my standing six feet two inches high and weighing two hundred and twenty-five pounds, a six-inch board was hardly conducive to a comfortable rump.

Finally, after that long silence, Faulkner said to me: "Well, East, anybody put any dead cats on your porch lately?" The silence had been broken, and he'd broken it. I was most cautious in my conversation with Faulkner; I wasn't sure of anything about the man. Finally, I felt free to speak as I pleased, which

I did, and he responded as I'd hoped. I was glad to know Bill Faulkner was human; indeed, I was happy to know he wasn't really God. After that slow, hot sail, we were preparing to return to Oxford. The car was parked near a little store, and Faulkner asked, "You want a Coke, East?" I said yes; the Cokes were opened and Faulkner didn't have any money with him. I paid. Upon returning home, he asked if I'd be his guest while I was in Oxford. As it was, I'd already checked into the Alumni House at the university, so I declined. Later I was to learn from Josh that I'd been honored by the invitation, that Faulkner hardly ever asked anyone to stay at his home as a guest.

At dinner that evening, and again the next day, we discussed at length the possibility of forming a "Mississippi Moderates" group. It was decided, finally, that it was impossible. Faulkner felt that we'd spend all our time fending off attacks rather than getting anything worth while accomplished. After deciding on the impossibility of the moderate-group formation, we turned to the question of what we could do to bring about some hope in what we viewed as a hopeless situation. Someone recalled that a group of students at the university had done a series of papers on the general situation. They had called them "The Nigble Papers" and had lampooned the Scotch-Irish, of whom the vast majority of Mississippians will tell you they are descendants. Copies were gathered; we considered what we could do along that line. It was finally decided that if we could let other moderates in the state know of our attempt at moderation, that in itself would be worth while; also, we saw the possibility of getting college students whose minds had not yet been closed to laugh at the stupidity around them. The publication of a paper was decided on. Faulkner suggested to me that if it were known the two of us had anything to do with it, the effectiveness would be lost. I felt inclined to agree with him again. Our plan was to print a paper about twice a year, pointing up with humor the prevailing situation in our state. I volunteered to edit and publish the first paper. What's more, I even said I'd pay for it.

And so it was that *The Southern Reposure* came into existence, having been born in Bill Faulkner's living room. I returned home, loaded with "Nigble Papers" to edit, rewrite and shape

194

into something to appeal to college students throughout the state. Almost from the inception of the idea, I ran into trouble. After days at editing, rewriting and trying to write a suitable introduction to the paper, after checking with Faulkner on it, my printers refused to print the paper for me. One of the vice-presidents, of whom they had many, called me and said they'd decided that if it were known they did the printing it might offend someone, especially the Boy Scouts of America. I was surprised but not angry at their decision. I failed to understand it, in view of the fact that they were on the verge of bankruptcy and it was a cash printing job. There was only one thing to do about *The Southern Reposure,* and that was to get Easton King to print it for me. I went to see him. Not only would he print it, he said, but he'd help me edit the copy if I wanted him to do so. I was pleased to have his help. The project was under way.

In the meantime another minor problem arose. My paper was due out on July 5; what with the fourth being a holiday, I had agreed to go to press on the sixth. On the afternoon of July 5 the telephone rang. It was the shop in Gulfport. The vice-president who didn't want to offend the Boy Scouts said they had decided to close down the business. I was not a Boy Scout, but I was offended. Indeed, I was angry. Great God from Gulfport, I exploded, it seemed to me any business about to go broke would know it more than eighteen hours ahead of time. It was from experience that I spoke; I'd been going broke over two and one half years. I had occasion to visit Easton King once again. There was no hesitancy about his taking back my printing, and he didn't bother to complain about the short notice. The turn of events delayed the printing of *The Southern Reposure.*

When *The Southern Reposure* was printed, it was a tabloid, five columns in width, sixteen inches in depth, and we printed about 10,000 of them, 2,000 of which were mailed to individuals in the state. The additional copies were sent to most of the colleges, to moderates on campus whom we knew, for distribution. No one knew the source of the paper, nor did anyone know who was responsible for its appearance on campuses throughout the state. From all reports the effort was worth while. One of the most interesting sidelights on the Scotch-Irish effort was re-

195

ported to me from a Baptist college located in the state. The college was a segregation stronghold, its president having justified segregation through the Scriptures and more than one faculty member having made the speaking rounds for the Citizens Councils. Our moderate contact distributed papers in two buildings; the students began to read them and to laugh. One faculty member ordered all "that trash be gathered and burned." The result was the same as such efforts have had through history: those who had had no interest in reading the paper at once made efforts to get a copy. I was told copies were selling for one dollar each on the campus. I sat back and hoped such would be the case all over the state.

Shortly after the papers were distributed I had occasion to visit with Faulkner again. "East," he said, "you did a damned good job with that paper. I've sent copies to New York." It wasn't much of a compliment, true; but coming from Bill Faulkner, and knowing he wasn't given to gab, I was most grateful for his having said it. While Faulkner never put the question to me directly, he seemed interested to know how I happened to hold my views. There it was again. That old, old question, and still I was without an answer that made sense. I had given much thought to it, and I thought about it again in the hope of giving an understandable and satisfactory answer to Faulkner.

"Bill," I answered, "I think for the simple reason that I believe in God." That's all I came up with; he made no effort to pursue the subject further, and I was glad about that.

As to *The Southern Reposure*, it amounted to a *tour de force* and nothing more. We were never able to come up with another idea. However, on the whole, I feel *The Southern Reposure* served a worth-while purpose. It is true that certain persons were offended. I was told one minister was upset because of a quote from the Bible. I inserted the quote and deliberately misquoted it in text and reference. Somehow to my mind it seemed to fit under the name across the top of the front page. It was "Know Ye the Truth and Be Ye Then Free, John 3:16." I still think it fits, especially when I consider the ever-present, teeming jungle.

In view of our desire to be anonymous, and in view of my

196

accepting the job of getting the paper together and circulated, I decided it would be fitting to have a highly proper person as editor, publisher and crusader. That person was Nathan Bedford Cooclose, whose masthead read: "*The Southern Reposure* is published quarterly by the Solvent Publishing Company, Blue Ribbon, Mississippi, and is edited by Nathan Bedford Cooclose." With the co-operation of Faulkner and Easton King, I wrote copy for Nathan Bedford, his

PUBLISHER'S INTRODUCTION

It was late spring that my son, Ernest Chris, returned to our plantation, "The Southern Manor," and brought the worst, certainly the most disturbing, news of my entire life.

I was stretched out on my hammock in the front yard, relaxing with a cool mint julep before dinner. Ernest Chris had returned from a college near Jackson, Mississippi, which he had attended during the year. I attended the same college; so did my father and so did his father.

Never have I been so upset by any news as by that brought home by my son, Ernest Chris.

He had been a member of the U.S.D.S. (United Sons and Daughters for Segregation) at our college. My son informed me, and I confirmed it, to be sure, that the Scotch-Irish among us were a real threat, indeed, a terrible menace to our way of life.

Here are some facts which I have confirmed about the Scotch-Irish in Mississippi today.

SMELL: The average Scotch-Irish smells like smoke. This is most unpleasant, and is caused by drinking a concoction known as "Uisgebeatha." This drinking causes bad breath, naturally. It is only natural that if the Scotch-Irish wanted to act civilized, as you and I, he would flavor his drink with mint. No, my friend, mint and smoke do not mix!

HABITS: The average Scotch-Irish is a repulsive and obnoxious creature who is apt, if the notion strikes him, to pull a highland fling on the main street of any one of our towns in Mississippi. They are a group who, except for the women, carry long-bladed knives to church with them. This, I assure you, is a heathen practice. In addition, they have come to expect to be served oatmeal in our finest restaurants simply because they have the required fifteen cents. Anyone with good breeding knows that oatmeal is horse food! And to top off the whole business, they eat popcorn in the movie houses. Which, of course, is not very couth, and, besides, it's damned annoying.

SPEECH: We Southerners have tried for years to keep the "r" sound out of our language, and have tried to teach the same basic good taste to the Scottrish among us. But, lo and behold, they insist on pronounc-

197

ing the "r" and, what's more, they do it with a roll. They are, no matter how hard we try, still barbaric.

MORALS: You should know the low morals of the Scottrish among us! Why, indeed, they breed like turtles! Their divorce rate is outrageous! They even like the smell that is their own; therefore they don't take baths every day as you and I do. To put it mildly, the Scottrish is a trifle lax in writing checks around the first of each month. They cannot and will not accept business responsibility, no matter how hard we try. You know this to be true as well as I. In addition to their poor breeding, they are vulgar to an unbearable point. How many times have you heard one exclaim "Hoot mon" or "Begorrrrah!" How disgusting!

In view of all the above information, I have taken the only means of which I know to bring certain news and views to you; I have undertaken the publication of this little paper, *The Southern Reposure*.

I have asked myself, as surely you must have, "Do I want my young daughter to marry a windbag, highland-flinging, kilt-wearing creature whose ancestry is questionable?"

Like your answer, mine is the same: *No!*

Knowing, of course, that the best thing that could be done would be to send them back to the bogs from which they came, I offer it to you for speculation. If that fails, then, we must stick together in an all-out effort to make it clear to the Scottrish that we will treat them kind, but they *must* stay in their place.

In short, this paper proposes to maintain segregation of the Scotch-Irish, no matter what the cost!

It is a known fact that smoke and mint don't mix.

So, why try it at our expense?

Sincerely,
NATHAN BEDFORD COOCLOSE

Following his introduction, Mr. Cooclose decided to run a five-column streamer at the top of the front page, above the name plate, in which he sought to catch the eye and interest of anyone seeing his paper. The two-line streamer, actually written by Faulkner, declared: EASTLAND ELECTED BY NAACP AS OUTSTANDING MAN OF THE YEAR. He did not follow up with a news story. However, there were a number of news stories, each having to do with a phase of the Magnolia Mess. Mr. Cooclose declared his paper was a member of the Confederate Press Association; also across the bottom of the two inside pages his war cry was sounded: THE SOUTH WAS BUILT IN THE SOUTH FOR SOUTHERNERS. As to news stories, Nathan Bedford gave an impartial account of reports reaching his desk. Examples:

ADDIT TRIAL REACHES CLIMAX

Addit, Mississippi (CPA)—The trial of sixteen-year-old Alexander Graham Tell, young Scotch-Irish boy hauled into court for insulting pretty Mrs. Ruby Jean Hollofield, 23, reached its climax yesterday when A. J. Elliss, prosecuting attorney, announced, "This trial may very well cast the die—either for keeping our blood pure or for mongrelizing with the Scotch-Irish. If Tell is set free, the bars are down, and the undefiled heritage of our ancestors is at an end."

Mrs. Hollofield, wife of blond young farmer Lonnie Hollofield, told the court that as she passed Tell on the street, he turned to a companion and whispered, "What a wee bonnie lassie!" She immediately reported the offense to her husband, who had Tell arrested. The boy did not deny saying this, but said he meant it merely as a compliment.

Attorney Elliss asked that the boy be given a severe prison sentence for his offense. "Such audacity and lewdness," he said, "are the norm of behavior for a people whose history includes such notorious figures as Mary, Queen of Scots and Macbeth. There can be no compromise with them."

Red-haired young Tell, wearing the plaids of his clan, is being kept under heavy guard at the county jail for fear that the citizens of Addit, among whom feeling over the incident is running very high, will throw him into the river with a horse collar around his neck.

GREEN MOUNTAIN COLLEGE IS TO GET $128.60 FOR BLACKBOARDS

Green Mountain College, Miss. (CPA)—In a new measure to facilitate equalization of facilities, the State Legislature is reported to have passed a bill appropriating $128.60 for the express purpose of buying real blackboards and four pieces of chalk for Green Mountain College, pending approval by the Governor.

The stipulation has been made by the Legislature that these blackboards and this chalk may be used for any purpose other than the teaching of American history. Stanislaus Bodinsky said to reporters, "History is the cause of our present malady."

BOYS WILL SOMETIMES BE SCOUTS

Minnowsville, Miss. (CPA)—Last night a happy, jovial Irish wake was disturbed when a troup of mischievous Boy Scouts descended upon it like Philistines on Assyrians, casting acid about irrespectively.

Cries of "Hoot mon!" and "Begorrah" were heard in the night, and the wake was postponed indefinitely.

There are rumors to the effect that one Scotch-Irish national was

199

painted with luminous paint and set afire, but there are neither witnesses nor ashes to substantiate this unofficial report.

It is honestly believed that the Scotch-Irish are indignant over the affair. J. P. McSweeney, who shouted in the middle of the fray, "I wish you wouldn't do that any more," is in critical condition in Minnowsville County Hospital.

S.E.M. RALLY HUGE SUCCESS

Crawdad, Miss. (CPA)—A splendid attendance was reported for the first session in this year's Segregation Emphasis Month. A large crowd gathered to hear guest speaker Elsie Dinsmore discuss the topic "The Botch Made by the Scotch."

This was followed by a two-hour period of quiet in which those present medi-hated and comtemplated earnestly the many-faceted inferiority of the Scotch-Irish race.

After this fruitful interlude of hate, Dr. Praetorius P. Prudhomme closed by pronouncing the malediction.

DR. KERSHEE ADVISED "IT WOULD BE TACTLESS OF YOU TO COME!"

Corn Pone, Miss. (CPA)—Dr. Boswell J. Kershee, D.D., pastor of the Second Baptist Church of Spring Falls, Nebraska, and noted writer of inspirational books, was told Monday that his proposed address to the congregation of the Eighth Baptist Church here would have to be canceled. The decision was reached, after due consideration, by a committee of prominent laymen. "Because of Dr. Kershee's background, we think it would prove to be tactless and bothersome of him to come," said Elmer P. Frisbey, spokesman for the committee.

The action was taken after it was disclosed that Dr. Kershee had recently contributed $30 to the Salvation Army and $50 to the March of Dimes. When questioned, Dr. Kershee did not deny this charge. "Yes, I have to both organizations given," he admitted. "I passed a Salvation Army lady ringing her bell on the street corner just before Christmas time and she looked so pitiful that I made a contribution. I do not regret my action."

Dr. Kershee was to have spoken on "Medieval Ascetism: Its Kinship with Symbolist Existentialism in the 20th Century." Mr. Frisbey said that a replacement has not yet been found.

As an editorial, Mr. Cooclose promoted:

THE CONSERVATIVE CLUB

Since we first conceived in Mississippi the notion of building a conservative club, a great many questions have been raised by interested

200

citizens as to what we are all about. What are the aims of the club? Is it true that we will fight for segregation? When do we meet? What in the ever-lovin' blue-eyed world do we do? And one of the more interesting of the raised questions—how does one join? We shall try to quell these questions as quickly as possible. It is rather difficult to answer these questions comprehensively, as we formed the club before considering many of these things. There are answers, though, to be sure.

Our primary aim, we suppose, is to ponder, promulgate and propagate the true Southern principles, culture, traditions, and as many of the dear old Southern customs as the law allows. We trust this is perfectly self-explanatory. And we shall meet as often as one of the above-mentioned elements of civilization is being threatened. Now it must be granted that we are interested in segregation but only insofar as it is a treasured and revered side of our Southern way of life. Of course, we are racists. But we will not see our society walked upon by Northerners and other unfortunate phenomena.

We don't want to take sides. But obviously segregation is here to stay. Everyone wants it. And we won't be talked out of it. As for what we do otherwise we don't know.

Time will tell! Mostly, we shall just sit around and discuss two sides to all our problems and make sure no one changes our mind about anything important. That's perfectly clear, in its way.

How does one join? Well, now we ask you to trust us on this one. Trust us. Don't worry about this question. If you are a conscientious Mississippian, an honest, clean-cut, level-headed, well-informed, tight-lipped, large-eyed, able-spirited and determinedly interested person, don't worry about a thing. We will get to you one way or another.

Being a reasonable and practical man, the publisher and editor felt his paper should have a few "Letters to the Editor." He called on several friends to state their views on the menace of the Scotch-Irish to the Southern way of life. There were others, but two of his friends expressed their views and concern by writing:

DEAR SIRS:

For a long time I have suspected that my little son Ignatz was being influenced by insidious propaganda. But imagine my horror when I realized the full extent of his mental pollution. Today I found, securely hidden under his mattress, a copy of *Emerson's Essays*. God alone knows what strange ideas are seething now in my child's head. The reading of Emerson can only lead to questioning, thinking and, ultimately—yes, though I shudder to say it—to an open mind. Mothers, I implore you—sooner kill your own flesh and blood than see it come to this. If your child is hiding books by Emerson, Paine, Whitman or Walt Kelly in his dresser drawers, destroy them as the un-American trash that they are.

Respectfully,
MRS. WIENER WALD, JR.

DEAR SIR:

I do not believe God wants us to mix with the Scotch-Irish, else why did he put them off on a little island by themselves? They do not want integration any more than we do. I love the Scotch-Irish, but only if they stay in the place God appointed for them. A careful reading of the Holy Bible will show you God's stand on segregation. John 22:19 and Mark 17:14 tell us what the Master said on the subject.

The Scotch-Irish have only been in this country two hundred years. Before that they lived in the highlands of Scotland, totally without washing machines, electric lights, automobiles, and all the other basic elements of civilization, and dressed only in the rudest sort of kilts. Furthermore, I maintain that after two hundred years they are still Scotch-Irish, and no amount of civilization will change the fact. I think I need not point out to you the basic immorality of their characters. There is hardly a one of them that does not get divorced, and eat meat on Fridays. Their music, as typified by such dances as the jig or the highland fling, is characteristically lewd and shows the primitive rhythms of the highlands from whence they came.

I have a little daughter, a sweet, cherubic little girl, and sooner would I take up arms as my grandfather did in '61 and pour out my life's blood before I would see her go to school with Scotch-Irish children. The tragic results of such a contact—perhaps someday red-haired, freckle-faced children with such names as Patrick or Andrew—would be too much for me. May the Lord take me before such a day arrives.

I am willing to grant that the Scotch-Irish have given us great men—like Andrew Carnegie or Robert Burns, for instance—but for the most part they have shamefully wasted the opportunities that our great land has given them.

Again, let me repeat: let the rabble-rousers do what they may, the Scotch-Irish were meant to till the soil: God has appointed it. (Genesis 52:2.) We are kind to them, let them keep their place.

Respectfully,
STANISLAUS WOCKINSKY

Being a man of taste and culture, Mr. Cooclose felt a column devoted to book reviews would be in order. Space being at a premium, he requested his reviewer to keep his comments short;

nevertheless, he had a sincere desire to bring to public attention the best book buys of 1956. Excerpts follow from the column given to:

BOOK REVIEWS

Best-Selling Books in Our Dixieland

Green Tuesday—Nester Breedy tells the story of heroic people who built this country out of the wilderness before the advent of immigrants. Delightful for its Technicolor pictures of genes and chromosomes.

Orange Wednesday—Otto Krazi. An account of a blow-by-blow description of a battle between the hardy pioneers and filthy immigrants.

Whitey—Tandalia Schwartzkoff. Illuminating biography of a Scotch-Irish immigrant who, because of her lack of freckles, tried to pass as a red-blooded American. It is a heart-rending story which should be required reading for all children.

How Green Was O'Malley? An anthology of top humor, in colorful dialect, all at the expense of the Scotch-Irish. It's great fun. It may seem to some acutely sensitive American mind that the humor is crude and somewhat blunt, but there is a certain natural charm to be found.

Twenty-Seven Wagonloads of Shamrocks—Mississippi Ethredge. Searching analysis of the primitive and barbaric rhythms and crude harmonies of the savage Scotch-Irish. Mr. Ethredge is obviously the foremost authority on this subject. He has seen the elephants dance. Some of you may remember *Coming of Age in Cork*.

Democracy and the Southern Way of Life—Dr. Osgood Norblotch. A stunning, poignant essay on the difference between the two.

Where Are We Going?—Ridgely Darblanski. The author wants to know.

Inside Dixie—J. B. Gunnysack. Endless account of important facts concerning our Beloved Southland, including best places to eat, interesting motels and bootleggers.

Nathan Bedford Cooclose was a satisfied man; he felt he'd done a service to his native state. He returned to his comfortable hammock, with a cool mint julep to enjoy before each meal, including breakfast. The fate of P. D. East was not the same.

I had spent well over three hundred dollars on the venture, not one cent of which I could afford. I had gotten my friend

203

Easton to share the expense, in that he printed it at cost, possibly below. It had been fun. I'd laughed until my ulcer hemorrhaged. While confined with milk and pablum I wondered how silly, childish and immature the whole venture had been. I wondered if the cost and effort had been a complete waste. I can say frankly and honestly that I felt much better about the entire matter when contributions began to come in from various parts of the nation. Obviously we had a blabbermouth in our midst, but he'd blabbered where it helped. Not only did I feel better about the matter with the contributions arriving, but I was delighted and happy when a check from one of the great educators in the country arrived. Dr. Arthur M. Schlesinger of Harvard sent a check to help pay for *The Southern Reposure*. And Bill Faulkner? Hell, he didn't even buy the Cokes. But it was good to know he was on the same side as I.

While engaged in the Scotch-Irish venture it was my good fortune to make the acquaintance of the Reverend Will D. Campbell, Director of Religious Activities at the University of Mississippi. Will was the man who had refused to "uninvite" Al Kershaw. The situation of Preacher Campbell was not a desirable one. Yet, in spite of the possibility of losing his job, Will Campbell helped in every way with *The Southern Reposure*. He's not a person given to wild talk or subjective thinking, but over the years I've known him I have been able to learn that Will was born and reared on a farm near the town of Liberty, Mississippi, and was brought up in the Baptist Church. After the war he returned to college at Wake Forest, where he received his bachelor's degree; later, at Yale, he took his B.D. After that he accepted a pastorate in a small town in north Louisiana; it was a typical Southern sawmill town, owned by a select few, and those few were opposed to organized labor. Will was aware of that fact, yet he was asked to pray at a town meeting one night during a strike in the area, and he requested that God be on the side of the union men. After that, he went to Ole Miss. His days at the University of Mississippi were numbered, too. He was caught playing ping-pong with a Negro minister from Oxford in the "Y" on the campus. The chancellor requested the presence of the Reverend Will D. Campbell to dis-

204

cuss the matter. In his naturally soft, Southern voice Will told the chancellor: "Sir, I assure you the ping-pong paddles were separate but equal." And after his resignation at the university at the end of September, I wrote in the "East Side" column:

WILL D. CAMPBELL

That's a name you may want to remember. I doubt that Will can change the course of history or anything so dramatic as that, but if ever I've seen a man whom I call one of God's Noblemen, it's Will Campbell. He has been for the past two years the Director of Religious Life at the University of Mississippi. He resigned at the end of last month to accept a post with the National Council of Churches, having to do with racial and cultural relations. Mississippi has lost not just a good man, but a true, honest, sincere man of God. At any rate, that's my opinion.

Any way you look at him, Will is a paradox. His physical appearance is far from being that of one of the prophets of old. He's just an ordinary guy to the eye. And for quite a long time I confess that I figured him for just another preacher, possibly a little better educated, even a little more moderate in his views than the average. But from a few more contacts with Will, I had no choice but to revalue the man. There is no pretense in his makeup. It seems to me honesty is just a natural thing with him, sincerity is a part of his nature. Well, let's do it this way: I have the greatest respect and admiration for Will Campbell. And from me that's about the highest compliment I can pay any man.

Indeed, the university, as well as the state, has lost a man whom they cannot replace. Personally, I hate to see him go, but he will have a larger field in which to work in his new job. Oh, yes, I might add the fact that everyone doesn't think the same thing of Will as I do. There have been one or two who disagreed with him in past times. But I repeat, if God has any noblemen walking the face of this earth today, Will is surely one of them.

It was far short of capturing the personality of Will, but perhaps an incident which was to occur later will give some insight into Will. The two of us were having lunch one day. We'd spoken of many things; finally, Will got his pipe going, looked me straight in the eye and said, "P.D., you're stupid."

"The hell you say, Brother!" I exclaimed, more than a little surprised.

"Yep," he said softly, "you say you're not a Christian. Hell, you don't even know the Gospel of Jesus Christ."

205

"Will, you Baptist bigot," I said, joking, "suppose you tell me about it."

"Be glad to," he said, lighting his pipe again. "The gospel of Jesus is quite simple. It is simply this, boiled down: all men are bastards—but God loves them just the same."

It made sense to me, but I didn't rejoin the church. There aren't enough Wills around to suit me.

In looking back from this point in time, I'm sure it was some sort of freakish accident that I had two full weeks of reasonable tranquility. It was not peace of mind, but at least my spirits were higher than they'd been in months.

Following the issue of October 11, I caused no trouble for the balance of that unhappy fiscal year, which ended on November 8. Of course, I took pot shots at the Citizens Councils and bigot boys in general, but nothing to provoke indignant wrath. Also, I was working on a booklet I planned to publish early in 1957. Over the months requests had come in for many of the editorials in the paper, and, being unable to furnish them, I had to return money, and that wasn't the way to cure an ulcer, not for me. I had spoken with Mark Ethridge about the idea of the booklet; he had spoken with Joseph Barnes, a senior editor of Simon and Schuster, in New York. Nothing came of it, Barnes explaining that such copy was difficult to handle and probably even more difficult to sell. Anyway, I planned my own venture, Easton King helping me as printer.

And so on the eighth day of November 1956 my third year closed as owner, publisher and editor of *The Petal Paper*. When the audit was finished for that year's work, I'd cleared the sum total of $113.95. My God! I thought. Jesse Wild paid me that much, and I didn't get an ulcer.

Chapter 25

The Petal Paper, Volume 4, Number 1, was dated Thursday, November 15, 1956. It was four pages long and carried a total of twenty ads, not one of which was from the village of Petal.

While my Petal advertisers were gone, the local circulation was holding its own at nine. I was concerned with the paper, but my major interest was in getting the booklet of editorial reprints under way. I had made contact with a half dozen organizations of the "do-good" variety and two thousand sales were made. From that amount I would have the cost of the venture, so I planned to print twenty-five hundred. The selection of copy was based on requests for back copies of the paper; and those editorials for which I'd had the most requests were the ones I was going to use in the booklet. There was the damnable job of writing some kind of prefatory remarks to each editorial, explaining as briefly as possible what led to the writing of the piece and what followed by way of reaction. It was about a day's work for any normal person, but I managed to drag it out for three months.

At the beginning of the fourth year of the paper, the circulation was steady at about one thousand. For months the local subscriptions had declined, but from every state in the nation subscriptions had trickled in from week to week. I had reached the point where I flinched when an advertiser, or a potential advertiser, would ask about my circulation. The conflict was simple: I refused to lie to him outright, yet to tell the truth was to lose the account. I told the truth and lost the business.

Other things did nothing to give me peace of mind. On two occasions when I'd called on accounts in Hattiesburg and asked to see the person on whom I'd called many times before, I was told he wasn't in. In both instances I'd seen him in the office less than five minutes after I'd walked out. Perhaps I was wrong in my judgment, I told myself, but later I tried again and the occurrence repeated itself. It was an upsetting business to me. Frankly, I resented it to the point of near explosion, but I kept my mouth shut and said nothing. I stopped calling on them, which, I'm quite sure, is what they wanted. Such action has a tendency to make a person of my nature wonder if he has mental B.O., or something equally offensive. Slowly, I was withdrawing more and more from the competitive scene week after week, although I managed to ward off a fit of depression at that time. I had the booklet to get ready and I looked forward to December 1, for at that time I would begin to sell Christmas-greeting ads. I'd always been successful at that, because not too many people will refuse to buy an ad sold in the name of the Lord. Besides, many people get mellow around Christmas.

With the coming of the issue of November 22 I was confronted with a problem which I did not know how to handle. I simply didn't have enough advertising for my usual four pages. Actually, I didn't have enough for three pages. Finally, I decided to take a shot at the Citizens Councils on the page I couldn't sell. I wrote copy and ran it at the extreme top of the page and said it was:

In Appreciation Of—

THE GOOD OF THE CITIZENS COUNCILS
OF MISSISSIPPI

(We present below our views on the good that has been and is being done by the Citizens Councils of Mississippi since they went into business. The appreciation of the councils, as presented here, is not likely to be subject to change.)

It was my exact opinion of the good done by the Citizens Councils, too. Because that was all I ran on the full page; the balance of the page was blank.

One of the possible reasons why it took three months to do a day's work on the forthcoming booklet was that I stayed away as much as possible. It was not that I cared for conversation with people, but at times I most definitely cared to get away from a place where people wouldn't converse with me. In 1956 I drove something like 25,000 miles in the state of Mississippi. It was, possibly, an attempt to escape, but I made some use of the effort by stopping and talking with people, at service stations, restaurants, grocery stores, and wherever it was convenient. While it was a great strain at times not to argue, I kept my opinions to myself and asked leading questions whenever I could. On those weekend trips, and on such trips in the months which lay ahead, I discovered some wild beasts in the jungle about which I'd had no idea. Also, I discovered some beasts which were kind, gentle and concerned with the problem of remaining one nation, with equality under the law.

Even though I was busy selling Christmas greetings, I stopped long enough to take a poke at a situation I'd found disgusting in the months past. At Clinton, Mississippi, a Baptist school, Mississippi College, is located. The president was Dr. D. M. Nelson, an elderly gentleman. Dr. Nelson quoted Scripture from hell to breakfast proving that God intended the white man to be superior, that segregation was the will of God. In past issues of my paper I'd printed certain of Dr. Nelson's letters, in an exchange with a former student who didn't agree with Nelson's point of view. In December of 1956 he was retiring. On the front page I ran a

CLASSIFIED

WANTED: One man for presidency of old-line, firmly established institution of higher learning.

PRIMARY QUALIFICATIONS: Must be Baptist preacher, have Ph.D. union card. Must arrange for time for various speaking engagements for the Ku Klux Councils of Mississippi, Inc. Must be a Southerner with Southern principles and views.

SECONDARY QUALIFICATIONS: Botanical knowledge not a necessity, but applicant must be able to determine difference between white magnolia and black orchid.

If you have the necessary qualifications, address your application to Clinton, Mississippi.

None others need apply.

What good is accomplished by such foolishness? Absolutely none, I'm sure, except that if I hadn't laughed at something every now and then, no matter how silly, I'd have gone stark, raving mad.

Except for that brief "Classified" I kept at the Christmas issue and at work on the booklet copy. It was shaping up fairly well, but not rapidly. I'd been promoting sales in the paper and the response was encouraging; orders were coming in from throughout the nation. One thing that wasn't coming in as it had in the past was the Christmas-greeting ads. I was actually so dense as to wonder why. Finally, after beating the bushes day and night, I got together a fourteen-page paper for Christmas, and of all the greeting ads it carried, only three were from Petal people. God, I couldn't even sell them in the name of the Lord! But, in all modesty, I'll say this: it was one fine Christmas paper. I had been given permission by the estate of H. L. Mencken to use his short "Christmas Story," which I ran, starting on the front page. There were some in the community who took exception to both Mencken and East because of that delightful bit of fiction.

One lady called on the telephone and said to me, "You're certainly no Christian, running that kind of story on the day of the birth of our Lord."

"Well," I replied, "I'm sorry if it offended you, honestly. But, you see, I've not professed to be a Christian, not in many years now." I was as polite as I knew how to be.

"I knew good and well you weren't. Anybody who'd print a story like that ain't a Christian. They're nothing but a heathen."

Remembering what Mencken used to write in reply to irate readers, I said to the lady, "Madam, you may be right."

"I know damned well I'm right, you heathen fool!" she said and slammed down the telephone.

In 1956 Christmas fell on Tuesday. Though dated the Thursday before, the paper was actually in the mails a full week before Christmas Day. While I had plenty to do, what with getting the booklet edited and proofread, I indulged myself in what seemed to be one of my favorite recreations—self-pity. It came about as something of a cumulative thing. The fact that I'd been called a "Heathen fool" by a Christian lady was only one link in the chain of events. From the middle of November through the middle of December I'd lost through cancellation approximately fifty per cent of my standing ads. They were those small, standing ads which are the backbone of any weekly newspaper. Since I was far from having a sufficiency for support in the first place, the cancellation of about fifty per cent was a blow that hurt. In three or four cases I'd asked the advertiser point-blank why he'd canceled, and the reasons ranged from "business being off" to "other media more effective." The first reason I had no idea about, and the second I couldn't argue with, considering that the town of Hattiesburg had a large daily paper, three radio stations and a television station.

210

It was to be several months before I learned what had happened. And what had happened was related to me by a merchant in Hattiesburg. He told me members of the Citizens Councils had made the rounds (at any rate, they called on him) and suggested that advertising with P. D. East's paper was an economic liability. In addition to the abrupt decline of my standing ads, the Christmas greetings had not sold so well as they had before. Additionally, I felt the sting of social isolation. Of course, I tried to convince myself that I cared little whether or not I was invited to the home of anyone, but notwithstanding my constant reminders of how tough I was, the lack of an occasional invitation stung. It was inevitable that in driving in town I would pass the homes of erstwhile friends, and I was not a big enough man to ignore the fact that many times there was a party going on to which I'd not been invited. The sting would become a bruise. It hurt; it cut deep into my ego. As a result of those things, and my own emotional immaturity and insecurity, by Christmas Day I was in a state of depression again.

Through contacts made by Will Campbell, I decided it would be a wise investment to make a trip to New York to promote booklet sales. Before leaving in the latter part of January, I managed to take a couple of pokes at my pet peeves. On January 10, I agreed that

Really, Mississippi Is—

THE MOST LIED-ABOUT STATE IN THE NATION

A growing number of autos in the State of Mississippi are sporting tags which read: Mississippi, the Most Lied-About State in the Nation.
We agree with the tags.
Unfortunately, the lies are not necessarily being told by persons out of the state.

A little later, and with a number of things in mind, I carried a news story on the front page in which a political announcement was made. I've often wondered how much bitterness there was in that bit of fun-poking when I announced the possibility of Cornpone P. Neanderthal's seeking a seat in the U.S. Senate.
Anyway, the story read:

211

NEANDERTHAL TO SEEK SEAT IN U.S. SENATE

Cornpone P. Neanderthal, an outstanding Mississippian, has announced that in 1960 he will be a candidate for the seat in the United States Senate now held by james oh eastland.

Cornpone and his complete platform will follow at a later date. "In the meantime," he said, "I would like to point out that I got as much sense as the present choice of the people of Mississippi."

Cornpone is a seasoned politician, having served several terms as a Justice of the Peace. He is a graduate of Mississippi College, and has never played basketball against anyone except his own kind.

Mr. Neanderthal is a charter member of the Ku Klux Councils of Mississippi, Inc., and is an ardent supporter of our way of life. Also, he has been quite successful in his chosen profession—coon hunting. He has the beaver badge.

Indicative of his adroitness, Cornpone stated for publication: "We got to keep those which aren't like us in their place."

Political circles in the state expect Cornpone to give eastland a run for his money, considering that he is more typical of the Mississippi politician than anyone else. Also, said informed sources, if Mr. Neanderthal is given the post as president of Mississippi College, he will withdraw from the Senate race.

On January 30, 1957, I left for New York, my first trip in over seven years. I stopped off in Atlanta for a day, one purpose being to meet with Harold Fleming of the Southern Regional Council. While there I managed to sell 2,000 booklets. In New York I sold another 1,500. I increased the printing order to 7,000, all of which were finally sold.

The trip to New York resulted in a number of things of interest to me. In New York, a friend, Edwin J. Lukas, Chief Counsel for the American Jewish Committee, called a meeting of several organizations to discuss a subscription promotion campaign for my paper. The representatives included Negroes, whites, Jews, Christians, Democrats and Republicans. It was decided they would take a certain number of copies of a promotional issue, pay for them at cost and mail them to persons throughout the country. As a result of Ed's interest and effort, I printed 15,000 copies for the purpose. Also, I was asked by a friend, Albert Vorspan, to call on him. Al was working on a feature article about the paper for *The Reporter*. (Ultimately, as a result of Al's piece, which ran on March 21, 1957, and the promotional copies, I picked up over 400 new subscribers.)

My aim in New York was to sell booklets, which I had done. While there I met two persons whom I'd wanted to meet for some time. One of them was Roy Wilkins, NAACP national secretary. I was curious to know if Roy really had horns, as so many Southern newspapers seemed to indicate. Upon being introduced to him, I extended my hand, shaking his. I withdrew my hand and with great deliberation inspected it. Roy stood looking at me with a puzzled expression. Slowly, I finished my inspection, looked Roy straight in the eye and said, "Well, I'll be damned. It really didn't rub off on me!"

The sale of the 36-page booklet had a soothing effect on my ulcer. As reported previously, the final distribution was 7,000. A breakdown of that figure is interesting. In the village of Petal, where I hung my masthead, total sales amounted to 0. In Hattiesburg, in a two-year period, total sales amounted to 30 copies. Elsewhere, literally throughout the world, the sales amounted to 6,970.

In Atlanta, in February 1957, I had first learned of the existence of Koinonia Farm at Americus, Georgia, and of Dr. Clarence Jordan and the attacks and violence from which both had suffered. A Georgia editor had said to me, "Well, hell, P.D., you know as well as I that they're a bunch of screwballs." My reaction was almost instinctive. I won another friend by replying, "Well, good God, there are no laws to stop any man from being a screwball. Even if they are a bunch of screwballs, they have the same rights under the law as you or I. Besides that, I wonder why either of us thinks we're so damned sane, anyway?"

Reports of the situation at Koinonia Farm in Georgia concerned me. I sought more information on it from friends in New York. What I learned was scanty, but it began to take shape in my mind as to what Koinonia Farm was and why. After I returned from New York, Will Campbell visited me and I learned additional facts about the farm and about Clarence Jordan. Will had visited the farm shortly before. The facts stated by him were nothing short of frightening. One of my basic ideas, which I'd printed and spoken many times, was simply: if they can do it to them, they can do it to me. Since I accepted this as a premise which was sound, I felt so long as any man was in danger, no matter who, where or when, I, too, was in danger. I made no pretense about it; I've always been vitally interested in me.

I was not acquainted with Clarence Jordan and was not to meet him until June of 1957 in New York; however, from what Will told me, and from a news letter written by Dr. Jordan, I devoted my column of February 21, 1957, to the farm. In the "East Side" column I wrote:

By way of background, and a smattering of other information, Koinonia Farm was started about fourteen years ago. The name given it, "Koinonia," means, as I've been told, "Community." The farm has been highly successful, and presently living on it are twelve or fifteen families, consisting of about seventy persons. Dr. Jordan, who has a doctorate in New Testament and Greek, has been asked to withdraw his membership from a Baptist church to which he belonged. The reason given him by the powers which ran the church was that his views of the Bible were not in accordance with those of the church. (Frankly, that's not a hard crime to commit, I know.) Such were the words spoken, but the real reason, it seems, is because Jordan is blind. He cannot see the superiority of his own race. Being an authority on the Bible is not too profitable in Georgia, I'd say.

Just after Jordan recommended a Negro to attend the University of Georgia last year a boycott began against his group. It has grown worse.

On Monday, January 28, after a National Guard meeting, one house on the farm was sprayed by .45-caliber machine-gun bullets, complete with tracers. The bullets missed two persons by inches.

Actually, the Koinonia Farm is composed of a group of pacifists who, as I understand it, are practicing to the letter the teachings of Christianity. It seems they may finish up about like the founder of the religion did.

Aside from, and in addition to, the amazing fact that Jordan shows no anger toward his fellow citizens is the unbelievable lack of concern of those charged with enforcing the laws of the land, and I mean that from Federal enforcement on down the line. Every guarantee given by the Constitution of the United States—well, almost all of them—is being violated. Koinonia Farm is basically a religious ideal, as I understand it. The Bill of Rights states plainly the fact that a man's religious belief is his own business and will be guaranteed. Yet when the F.B.I. was asked to intercede in the case, they could find no grounds on which to concern themselves. It's simply amazing, as I've said.

That I should concern myself so with a man in Georgia seems a little foolish perhaps. Right here in Mississippi, Holmes County, to be exact,

214

we came close to the same thing last year in the case of Mr. Cox and Dr. Minter. I think the only reason we didn't have the shooting and allied violence was because the two men moved. Had they chosen to stay, I feel sure we'd have led Georgia in the business under discussion.

There are so many facets of the case that it's impossible to go into them all. But how in the name of common decency, which appears to be quite a rare thing, can people act worse than their ancestors hanging by their tails in the jungle? It seems to me so obvious that to deny the rights of Dr. Jordan, or any single citizen of the nation, is to eventually deny these same rights to oneself.

Please pardon me for waving the flag, but these things for which it stands are of the utmost importance to me—and, I think, to any person in his right mind.

Upon my return to the Magnolia Jungle from New York in February of 1957, I made a feeble effort at being funny by reporting on two things in my column; in that effort I wrote:

The government (Northern government, that is, not Southern—there's a difference, you know) should be investigated! And there's a good reason.

Last week in my mail I received a letter from a man in the American Embassy in Bangkok, Thailand. The letter had a clipping from the Bangkok *Post* which told of the Negro churches in Alabama that had been slightly shaken by dynamite blasts. The gentleman wrote as follows: "Ask some of your readers how to answer this question out here." Of course, the thing that stunned me was the fact that he had the nerve to sign as "An American."

Because of the gross ignorance of this person I suggest that the government be investigated. Why should we of the South continue to support a government that hires a person so ignorant that he fails to answer a simple question which might arise from a trivial incident like a blown-up church? As we of the South know, the answer is simple. The churches were blown up to let the Negroes know who is boss. It's that simple. Some of the colored folk here of late have been getting some uppity notions, and that presents a threat to our God-given right as masters by virtue of our white skin. And as any red-blooded, 100% Southerner knows we'll not sit by and be threatened by the second-class citizens. As a matter of fact, I think everyone north of the Mason and Dixon line should be investigated! . . .

And while on the subject of that which is North, I will report briefly on a trip from which I returned last Friday. (My aim is not to convey to you the fact that to undertake such a trip was the epitome of bravery, which, of course, it was, but to record for other Southerners a few facts which I hope will prove helpful.)

215

Well, as it came to pass, the boll weevil was under control last year and the cotton crop was good, and mine having been ginned, and subsidized, I found myself with nothing to do. I decided, as a matter of self-education, to go to New York, having heard quite a bit about it and having seen integrated TV shows from there. Well, I hid my horses from them Damnyankees, packed my suitcase and got on a Southern airplane and arrived there Monday morning of last week.

I am pleased to report that only one Negro was on the same plane with me—but it was okay because he sat in the back. However, he got on in Atlanta, and I do suggest that Governor Griffin and Senator Hermmmmmm look into the matter.

After getting settled, my first stop was to visit Roy Wilkins. I thought it fitting that I tell him a thing or two about the way his outfit was getting a bunch of our happy and satisfied darkies into trouble here in the Southland. Knowing full well that I was doing him a favor, I suggested that his firm pay my expenses. I must say, and with sorrow, that some folks are so ungrateful! As matters now stand I will submit my expenses to the wcc's of Mississippi, Inc., because I have considerable information that would be useful to them.

Just one example, I was at Columbia University and actually saw a Negro man and a white girl sitting at a soda fountain together comparing notes on an examination they seemed to be preparing for. It was obvious that they were actually in the same class! My heart bled for that girl—and if I had possessed any knowledge of Northern history I'd have offered my help to her. It was a sad sight.

But I have so much information which will help any Southerners who are brave, or foolish, enough to go up North. I am unable to impress on you the tragedy of the way of life I saw those people living—and right under our very noses. No wonder that they are called by those of us in the South "Damnyankees," and rightly so, too. I wish it were possible for our Southern states to make funds available to rescue them before it's too late. My heart bleeds.

Oh, the frightful things I saw are too many to relate in this one piece. I departed with a feeling of doom, resulting from the things I saw those Northern people doing while I was up there.

I'll never forget the return to Jackson. The plane landed and I walked into the terminal, and out front I heard a radio playing and I approached it with great pleasure—Elvis was singing "Hound Dog." I knew I was home—back to the land of Baby Doll.

216

Chapter 26

From the many incidents and experiences related up to now in this narrative, I set out in March of 1957 in a deliberate manner to ask myself questions which I'd been unable to answer to my satisfaction. First, I concluded, I'd have to approach the matter in a manner as completely objective as if I were a machine of some kind. Second, I concluded, I was incapable of such objectivity; therefore, I would have no choice but to approach the questions with as much objectivity as a subjective person could, and how much that was remained to be seen. I was pleased to have realized my limitations with reference to subjectivity and objectivity. I was not in a state of depression or anger or emotional instability at the time I began to ponder the matters I wanted to resolve. It was an effort to be honest with myself, and, frankly, I wondered why I wanted to do that. But from within myself something compelled me to seek the answers, to make the effort toward self-honesty. Being human, and therefore an egotist, I asked of myself: *Who are you? What are you? Why are you? What has value to you?* And one such question opened the way for countless others in the days which followed, and especially did the question of *What do you Want?* keep recurring and demanding an answer.

Answers to such questions are not come by with ease—at least, not for me. Indeed, not even the effort was easy. It was painful; to search oneself demanding the truth is harsh treatment, and not many of us would inflict it even on our enemies. I know I wouldn't. I wanted a satisfactory answer to *Who are you?* To begin with, I didn't know, and I didn't know where to start the search for an answer. I wanted to ask someone—anyone. Had I done so, I'd have had his opinion, but it would not have lent itself to the soul-searching self-answer I felt necessary. I knew my name; why not start there? Yes, my name was P. D. East, the adopted child of James C. and Birdie East. But wait! No, that was only as I was known to others; actually, I didn't know my name, not when you got down to it. I was the child of Laura Battle, true; and I wondered if my uncle Larson had told me the truth about my father. There was, and is, considerable doubt in my mind. Not that I think Larson was a liar, but I knew he was human and was capable of trying to reduce his pain about his sister. Well, so what? Perhaps I'm the bastard child of Laura Battle. That was not a pleasant thought, but it opened another question. Was it the fault of any person if he should be of illegitimate birth? Certainly not. I realized one thing, and that was the fact that I'd had nothing to do with my conception. Who was I? That question remains to be answered. As near as I could come to a conclusion was to say to myself: You, P. D. East, are only another child of God. And that beats nothing.

What are you? was the next question to be answered. Well, maybe a bastard, I admitted: certainly, others had said so, and many times. That was hardly an answer. Well, let's see. What am I? A male, six feet two inches tall, of average intelligence, so tests had said, but I've never been convinced, considering the kind of questions I asked myself. An honest person? I didn't know—still don't know. A kind person? At times, but at other times most definitely not. Did I despise anyone? Even those whom I knew to despise me? I could not bring myself to admit I despised any man. I was, and am, sure I felt compassion and considered it a sign of weakness. Compassion is not a sign of weakness, except to the ignorant and stupid. How could I despise any man without despising myself? And who and what am I? Until something more satisfactory presents itself I have to accept as a working theory that I, P. D. East, am a child of God, and as such I'm involved with mankind.

Why are you? The answer to that was quite simple. I didn't know, but, then, all the answers, old and new, lapped over into the range and field of other questions. I doubt whether any question can be answered with a simple, matter-of-fact statement. Inasmuch as my effort was being made as objectively as possible, in a subjective manner, I would have to say I, P. D. East, am a child of God and as such I'm involved with mankind and I am indebted to my Father. I don't propose that my answers make much sense. I accepted them for the want of something better.

What has value to you? Many things, countless things, but

218

nothing is more valuable to me than human life. Inasmuch as I think human life is the highest value we know as mortals, and inasmuch as I am involved with mankind, and inasmuch as I'm a child of God, I feel a pressing obligation to pay for the gift called life. I don't know why I should feel such an obligation. If I were honest with myself, and I tried to be, then I found no way to pay God for life, except through His other children. Their rights were my concern; also, I never forgot that my own rights were involved with theirs. So to protect them I must protect myself; conversely, the same is true.

How honest was all this? I wish I knew; if I knew I'd be much happier, I'm sure. Perhaps I was selling myself a bill of goods, goods without value. Again, I wish I knew. I tried as best I could to take into account my personal relation to my environment. I was not a person whom everybody liked; indeed, it was quite rarely that anyone liked me. Was this the manifestation of a persecution complex? What about the Kiwanis members and my opinion of, and relation to, them? Were they really "joy boys," as I'd told myself? Some were, surely, and some weren't. Some were honest in their interest and efforts to have a better community in which to live. Good and bad, sour and sweet, black and white, *per se*, they seldom existed. They were relative and they were mixed. But, boiled down, I think my basic trouble stems from the simple fact that I, as a child and man, failed to realize there were rules other than mine. I could not say with any degree of honesty that I think my rules are better than those of any other person on this earth, but I can say with some honesty that I'm more comfortable playing by my rules, even if they do lend themselves to the moments of discomfort, despair, depression and loneliness which I've come to accept as my fate.

Anyway, in mid-1957 those answers served a purpose, for I'd often said, "I'm not concerned with integration and I'm not concerned with segregation. The rights of all men are my business." And that's what I believe.

From any point of view, I'm certain I'm my own greatest pain.

Having a desire to share that pain with others, particularly those whom I opposed, I commented in my column in the promotional issue of the paper, dated March 14, 1957, on the Citizens Councils' "Manual for Southerners." The column is self-explanatory:

DEAR MAMA:

I reckon no one knows better than you that I spent twenty-one years in the public schools of Mississippi, having entered at the age of four and having stopped at the age of twenty-five.

But I was took—and I'm unhappy about it. I was the victim of "progressive education," a theory which has caused me great unrest, and is now causing me no end of unhappiness.

Well, at last the great light is shining, and I'm beginning to clear my thinking a bit. Praise God for the Citizens Councils, and especially for their paper of February 1957, in which they point the way to true happiness for a Southern boy!

Their paper, Mama, carries a "Manual for Southerners," and I have long since been an advocate of such a publication. You remember last year when I got caught in that airplane with them Negroes? And I didn't know what to do, so upon returning home I suggested that the Council of Citizens put out a manual for fouled-up Southerners such as me, you recall?

Well, it's here, and I'm so happy. Salvation at last! They said that "for too long Southern children have been 'progressively educated' to scorn their origins and the reasons for our bi-racial society." And, Mama, the manual is to correct this blight from which we children of a dark age suffer. Praise the Lord!

The portion which appeared in the February 1957 issue of the paper is for grades three and four. But, Mama, every adult *should be made to read it!* And especially them Damnyankees ought to be made to read and understand it.

For your enlightenment I will quote a few excerpts from the "Manual." Too, I will point out how much in error my "progressive" teachers were. I think the whole educational system should be investigated, and anyone disagreeing with the views stated in the "Manual" should be fired. They are dangerous to formative minds. I know, as do all Southerners, that there is but *one* way . . . there is but *one* truth . . . there is but *one* way of life worthwhile—and that is ours!

From the "Manual," Mama, from the "Manual":

GOD MADE FOUR RACES

God made all of the people in the world. He made some of them white. He made some of them black. He made some of them yellow. And He made some of them red."

220

But, Mama, do you know what I was taught? I heard it in school and also in Sunday school. They told me that the first chapter of Genesis, verse twenty-six, read: "And God said, Let us make man in our image, after our likeness." Now, what with this having been taught me in those early, formative years, and now with the *real* truth facing me, I have a mental picture of God as something like tutti-frutti. He's a mess of colors! Of course, I've always suspected that, in truth, God really came from the Southern side of infinity.

GOD PUT EACH RACE BY ITSELF

God put the white people off by themselves. He put the yellow, red and black people by themselves. God wanted the white people to live alone. And He wanted the colored people to live alone. That is why He put them off by themselves.

WHITE MEN BUILT AMERICA

Some white people came to America. America is where you live. It is your country. The white men built America for you. They want you to have a free country that you can grow up in.

Now, Mama, don't you see what is causing my confusion, which, in turn, is causing my wholesale unhappiness? Here the truth is, finally, that God put this tutti-frutti bunch off by themselves, and I was taught that the white man actually brought over the Negro from Africa to hoe his cotton. I was taught in error, out of pure ignorance by teachers. According to my instruction, the white men took the Negro man out of the place where God had put him and intended him to stay and began selling him like a sack of potatoes. And, Mama, about this business of some white people coming to America; I was taught the same thing, but I understood that the red man was here and that the white man took the land from the red man. Since God put the red man here, could it be that God really didn't intend him to be here? But, and Heaven forgive me, I didn't mean to question the *truth* of the "Manual." I'm sorry. But it was my teacher's fault.

AMERICA HAS FOUR PARTS

The United States of America has four parts. There is the part in the North. There is the part in the East. There is the part in the West. And there is the part in the South. Our country is very big. And white men built it all.

221

YOU LIVE IN THE SOUTH

Do you know what part of our country you live in? You live in the South. You know you live in Mississippi. Mississippi is a state in the South. The South is a big part of our country.

YOU ARE A SOUTHERNER

Do you know what Mississippi people are called? We are called Southerners. Southerners are people who live in the South. You are a Southerner. You live in the South.

Mama, is Mississippi bigger than the world?

You know, Mama, that part about "do you know what Mississippi people are called?" is to me, in view of my progressive education, misleading. Of course, I know what some Mississippi people are called—and it ain't Southerners, not altogether.

GEORGE WASHINGTON HELPED BUILD AMERICA

Have you heard about George Washington? He was a brave and honest white man. George Washington built our country. Can you guess what part of the country he came from? Let me tell you.

WHITE MEN BUILT AMERICA

White men built our country. It was hard work. It is not easy to build a new country. The white men cut away big forests. They did not have big homes like yours. The little boys and girls did not have nice schools. Wild animals lived everywhere. It was not safe outside.

Well, like I've always said, it's a hard job to get one of the black people to do a day's work. I reckon grandpa did have a hard time building this country. And as to the wild animals outside, Mama, they still are!

AMERICA WAS MADE STRONG

The red man is the Indian. You know what an Indian is. The red man fought the white man. But the white man won. He worked and worked. He wanted you to have a strong, free country. It was not easy to build.

You know what, Mama? Stealing gets harder all the time, too! From my erroneous learning I suspect that it was harder to steal than it was to build . . . with slave labor.

222

WHITES AND NEGROES LIVE APART

The black man is the Negro. You have seen Negroes all of your life. The Negro came to our country after the white man did. The white man has always been kind to the Negro. But white and black people do not live together in the South.

I am inclined to suspect of the Negro the very worst. How he managed to sneak into the place God allowed the white man to live in is beyond me. But, like the "Manual" says, the white man has been good to the black man. Why, Mama, I've known of certain cases where the black man could borrow from the white man two bucks against next month's work. How kind can we white men expect to be? Anyway, Mama, white and black people don't live together in the South because it's God's will . . . and nobody knows the mind of God like us Southerners.

We get an inside track, and anyone who questions it is disobeying the will of God, I'd say, and since I'm a Southerner, I have the right to say.

Well, Mama, this note to you is to let you know that I recognize my "progressive education" as being a failure and to state that I am in process of *un*-learning those fallacies which were taught to me in my childhood.

I will write again and let you know of the progress I'm making and of the new light that is being shed on me, a misguided Southerner.

In the meantime, would you give my regards to Uncle Remus?

Your renegade son, now reformed,
P. D.

There have been moments in my life when I've doubted whether or not I'm a good sport.

Since its beginning in 1953, *The Petal Paper* had been an eight-column page, twenty-one inches deep, which is near standard throughout the United States. My decision to reduce the page size to tabloid (five columns wide, sixteen inches deep) was not a sudden one. To be quite accurate about it, the advertisers reduced the size of the page for me, what with wholesale cancellations having started in November of 1956. I had made jokes about the financial strain of keeping the paper going, but by the middle of January 1957 it was not a joking matter by any means. When I laughed about it, I had only one purpose: to keep from breaking down and weeping like a bankrupt publisher. I regretted changing the format and size of the paper, but I had brought it on myself by the cancellation of advertising.

223

I knew the rules by which my fellow citizens played, but I was not capable of playing by them; therefore, I had succeeded in having my way, playing by my own rules, but I was so close to being out of the game that it made me wonder about my I.Q. I gave thought to several possibilities as to what I should do. I could contradict myself editorially and regain advertising. I dismissed that thought without hesitancy, the reason being that I didn't believe I was wrong in what I thought about the racial situation. I considered closing the paper and going to work to make an honest living, preferably on the West Coast, or as far away from the Magnolia Jungle as I could get. I paused to ponder that possibility. It seemed to me such a move would be a waste of time, in view of the fact that no matter where I was I seemed to carry my own jungle, of one sort or another, with me. And the first person I'd have to face, should I attempt to escape, would be me. I saw no possible way out of the jungle, and I wondered if indeed the jungle were of my own making. Somehow it mattered little; I knew I could not escape me, no matter what my location or set of circumstances. Finally, I knew I had but one choice, which was to reduce the size of the paper, thereby cutting costs, and hope for the best. I cut, and I still hope.

Notwithstanding the booklet sales and the subscriptions coming in from throughout the nation, I was still hurting financially. One thing that made it bad at that moment was the fact that I couldn't put the blame on anyone but myself. Heaven knows how nice it is to pass the buck. My paper served no purpose, not in the accepted sense of the word. I had stopped carrying local news of Petal, primarily because all my stringers had stopped gathering it for me. I wasn't interested in news anyway. I had succeeded fairly well in withdrawing, insofar as Petal and Hattiesburg were concerned. I seldom saw anyone, except in passing on the street, and more often than not they would refuse to speak to me, which was slight inducement to pound the pavements. It is an unpleasant thing to realize one is so obnoxious that old friends cease to speak, but, I suppose, such was the case.

I went to Petal once a day to pick up my mail; seldom did anyone speak to me, nor I to them. Slowly I began to realize something which had somehow escaped me. I had been carrying a pistol with me for many months, if not in my pocket, then in my car. I realized how stupid it was. If someone wished to do me harm, he'd have already done it; too, simply beating hell out of me wouldn't change my mind. I knew full well that I could do nothing but what I was doing. Whatever there was within me dictated that, and I knew it and accepted it as best I could. So why carry a gun like a fool? I locked it in a filing cabinet at home, where it has remained.

To get the tabloid off to a good, healthy, wholesome start, I ran a classified on the front page:

FOR SALE

Have quantity of used lumber desirable for making crosses. 2 x 4s well seasoned in 5-foot lengths. Kerosene furnished with orders of half dozen or more. Save on your cross burnings! Write Box 678, Petal, Miss., for full details. "How to Build Your Own Cross Kit" free with all orders. Act today . . . or tonight!

If a lamb, en route to slaughter, why not make silly jokes, if it eases the pain?

Certainly not the most misunderstood editorial ever to appear in my paper, but it ranked high, was a bit of foolishness I did in April of 1957. The first time I'd met Will Campbell he'd made some remark about changing a verse in the Bible from the reference to the Common Chalice to Dixie Cups, separate but equal. Over the months which followed, I thought of one or two more such items and a young Methodist minister at Mississippi Southern College, Sam Barefield, also presented me with a couple of items. With my two sources of supply, I did an editorial, the aim of which was to point up certain blind spots we all seemed to have in the Magnolia Jungle. While it had nothing, absolutely nothing, to do with religion, it was not so accepted by some. Actually, what it amounted to was:

A Scholarly Bible Study

FROM KING JAMES TO DIXIECRAT

Dear Bible Belt Brethren:

Since our earliest recollection it has been our burning desire to make some small contribution to the society in which we live. At long last

225

we have begun, and in a more valuable way . . . well, there isn't one.

From our scholarly studies we have learned of the Scotch-Irish influence on the King James translation of the Holy Bible. Thus, many of the words appearing therein are those of man, not of God.

Our aim is to right this wrong. That, we feel, is our sacred duty.

Exodus, the second Book of the Bible, clearly states that Moses, during the big chase, crossed the RED sea! That, you must agree, is not good. We have decided, therefore, to exclude the entire number of Books which compose that part of the Holy Word known as the Old Testament. That fellow Moses may well have been a subversive of some sort, and it is not good that the young minds of our land be exposed to any person having crossed the RED sea. Had it been some other sea, that might have been all right, but not THAT sea.

Rather than to be misled in our translation of the New Testament we decided to work on it in part, or on excerpts from various Books, instead of beginning with Matthew 1:1.

"In the beginning was the Word, and the Word was with God, and the Word was God." John 1:1.

Into Dixiecrat, clearly that should read:

"In the beginning was the Word, and the Word was spake by 'Our Gem,' and having spake, there bloomed forth the Cotton and Magnolia over Dixieland." (Let there be no question as to who did the speaking.)

"But Jesus called them unto him, and said, Suffer little children to come unto me . . ." Luke 18:16.

"But Jesus called them unto him, and said, Suffer little WHITE children to come unto me . . ." Dixiecrat Luke 18:16.

"And he took the cup, and gave thanks, and said, Take this, and divide it among yourselves." Luke 22:17.

"And he took the DIXIE CUPS, and gave thanks that they were SEPARATE BUT EQUAL, and said, Take this MINT JULEP and divide it among yourselves." Dixiecrat Luke 22:17.

"For God so loved the world, that he gave his only begotten Son . . ." John 3:16.

"For God so loved Mississippi that He gave it 'Our Gem' . . ." Dixiecrat John 3:16.

"And he arose and went: and behold, a man of Ethiopia, and eunuch of great authority under Candace queen of the Ethiopians, who had the charge of all her treasure, and had come to Jerusalem for to worship, was returning, and sitting in his chariot read Esaias the prophet. Then the Spirit said unto Phillip, Go near, And join thyself to this chariot . . . And as they went on their way, they came unto a certain water: and the eunuch said, See, here is water: what doth hinder me to be baptized? . . . And he commanded the chariot to stand still: and they went down both into the water . . ." Acts 8:27, 28, 29, 36, 38.

"And he arose and went: and, behold, a man of color, who worked

226

for Candace queen of the Ethiopians, was driving her chariot down the road. And the Spirit said unto Phillip; Go near, sit in the *back seat* of this chariot . . . As they went on their way, they came unto a certain water: and the colored man said, See, here is water; what doth hinder me to be baptized? . . . And he commanded the chariot to stand still: and they segregated the swimming pool with a *chain* across it and they both went down into the water . . . separate but equal."

The above, clearly, was one of the most difficult passages to translate. Here, according to the King James translation, was integrated riding and swimming, so naturally the original translation had to be corrected, but good!

The name of the Lord (and just who He is has never been quite clear) is difficult to work with in the Bible Belt. Of course, I knew that already, but I thought surely no one could misunderstand what I was getting at by the Dixiecrat translation. I fear it was misunderstood. I had telephone calls and letters about the translation. It more or less boiled down to a simple statement of fact: that I, P. D. East, was a damned heathen.

In the hope of changing the subject, in the issue which followed I ran a front-page ad:

FOR SALE

Don't suffer from the summer heat by using your regular uniform of a muslin bed sheet! Be modern! Inquire about our complete stock of cotton Eyelet Embroidery, designed especially for summer wear. Klanettes may enlarge the holes for arms, but your heads will fit nicely through the eyelets as they are. Keep cool this summer on your rides of mercy. (This special offer open only to Klukers in good standing. Pay your dues and save money and be comfortable!) Address orders to Big Brother.

Slowly, and in spite of my determined effort to avoid it, I was beginning to be caught up again in a fit of depression. My circulation in Petal at that time stood at six; advertisers in Hattiesburg continued to cancel and my reception in certain business places was slightly less than cordial. The ever-nagging financial strain was more than nagging: it was jerking and slapping at me at every turn. It was during this time that I received a letter which, to me, seemed unusual. It was nasty, also un-

227

signed. Postmarked in Hattiesburg, the letter wanted to know from me: "You seem like an intelligent man, why do you want to destroy things?"

I paused to ponder that question, along with several others. Why did I want to destroy things? Indeed! God help me, that was the last thing in the world I wanted to do; why was it so difficult to explain? Of course, in fits of anger I'd destroyed things by throwing them. But over the years I'd stopped, because after such a fit of temper I'd always feel shame and guilt for having destroyed whatever it had been. Destroy? Never in my life had I desired to destroy anything whatsoever. While it was certainly true that I had a desire to dispose of or dispense with certain things—intolerance, bigotry, violence, for instance —and any single thing which hampered or bound the mind of man, I had no desire to destroy, because I felt that even those things with which I'd dispense were I capable were of value in the negative sense. They were not to be practiced or put into effect, only studied.

Once in my life I had destroyed willfully. It had been as a child at the Carnes logging camp. I had been backed into a corner by a dare and had reacted like the child I was. In a rage of anger I'd killed a cat by striking it with a baseball bat. After having done so, I had been sick as I saw the battered body of the cat lying before me. Not only had I been sick, but once out of sight of my playmates I'd sobbed like an infant. The image of that dead cat had never left my mind; I could see it anytime I thought about it; as I write these words at this moment, I can see the murdered animal before my eyes. I'd never been able to determine why it should be so, and never had I been able to evaluate my feelings about having killed a cat. But as others had often wondered, I also wondered why I never went hunting. Some of my associates in days past thought me odd because I had no desire to kill animals, and they thought me crazier than I was because I refused to kill even a snake in the woods.

I had no desire to destroy anything. How could I make that understood? I had an overpowering desire to create. How to make it understood? Somehow it all had to do with my respect, indeed, my reverence for life, no matter what its form. That

228

which lived, that which we call life, is a part of the power, force, or whatever it is we call God, and somehow it seems to matter little that it be in one form, shape or another—all life is a spark of the same source. Somehow, in my mind, creations of and by those who are sparks of the great force are manifestations of that force; therefore, to destroy willfully, without cause or reason, involves that which we call God. To destroy? Never! To build, to create? By all means, yes!

I'd often thought of an analogy having to do with life. It was as if this living and breathing and thinking and hoping called life was the passage across a bridge, a journey from one side to the other. It was not a toll bridge, except on a volunteer basis. For having crossed, a person was at liberty to pay what he wished and could afford. And in spite of fits of depression and despair, I was glad to be making the trip, and for the opportunity and privilege I owed something to the owner of that bridge, who, in the case of life, was God. Now, I did not see God standing at the end of the bridge with His hand out. No one was watching for the purpose of doing you harm if you didn't leave something. To me, to create, to leave more on this earth than I'd found when I got here, was, indeed, an obligation, an expression of thanks, a means of paying respect. To take more than I gave would be to shirk an obligation. For the passage over that bridge I felt, and feel, I owe something to someone. Inasmuch as I do not believe in a life after death—that is, that God isn't standing at the end of the bridge with His hand stuck out—I can only hope to pay my fare by creating, by giving to those of my kind who are, as I am, a spark of that which is Divine. By leaving something for my brother, though yet unborn, I'm paying my Father. I think of it in those terms. Of course, the thought has occurred to me that perhaps I'm worked up over nothing—maybe the whole thing is one gigantic joke, designed to fool idiots like me.

In May of 1957 I worried over how to make it known that I would build and create were it within my power; that, no matter what, I'd never destroy. I've never been able to get it across. When speaking of the idea, the analogy, I'm apt to be stared at as if I were just short of some kind of frenzied rage. It is difficult to explain.

Meanwhile, my friend in Pascagoula, Easton King, was having certain troubles. Shortly after the publication of my booklets, a Citizens Council representative inquired if the *Chronicle Star*'s shop had printed them. The man got a true and honest answer to his question. King is too honest for his own good at times, and that time was one of them. Shortly after the question by the Citizens Council man, a cross about six feet tall was burned in front of the shop. The exact connection has never been quite clear. King is regarded by some as an integrationist, a liberal, a Commie, and the usual like of name-calling. Easton was not exactly happy about the incident; however, he said he considered the cross well constructed, a good piece of carpenter work. I had a long talk with him about printing my paper, asking him if he'd care to stop.

"Hell," he exclaimed, "no red-neck son-of-a-bitch is going to dictate to me what we print for you or anyone else!"

We've not discussed the matter since. I pointed out to him it was much better to get a cross burned by proxy, and a hundred miles away, than in my front yard. Really, it *was* a well-made cross.

In the spring of 1956 I did a column about Easton for my paper. Being stupid, I made the mistake of letting his wife, Irene, see it. Easton, ever nosey, saw the proofs lying on a table at home and called me and asked as a personal favor that I kill the copy. At the time I wrote the column I didn't know Easton nearly so well as I do now, but perhaps it'll give you some insight into a dear and wonderful friend.

I've known Easton for about two and one half years now. He doesn't know it, but for some time we didn't get along worth a darn. Maybe he did, but I didn't—but, as I said, he doesn't know it. On my part it stemmed from having had dealings with print shops whereby I had to keep a pencil in each hand to keep up. In short, I distrusted any and everyone who operated a shop. I don't mind saying it, because I have never made any bones about the importance of the dollar bill, but for months after I started printing in Easton's shop I checked and double checked every invoice and statement. As it happened I missed an item one month amounting to something like twenty dollars, and they didn't know about it for something like sixty days. Even then I didn't catch it; Easton found it on his books and called it to my attention.

It was after that incident that I took a second look at this man called Easton King. I watched closer than ever. Another such incident happened, and I decided finally that maybe the guy was honest, in spite of the fact that I couldn't figure anyone's being a full hundred-per-cent honest. But after two and one half years now, I can say, as a matter of fact take an oath on it, Easton King is the most completely honest man I've ever known. I do not have reference to just matters of business, but refer also to a much rarer thing, and that is being honest with one's self.

Well, let's put it like this: Easton is one of three persons I have known in my entire life whom I would trust with anything I had, no questions asked.

But of all things about him I can't figure, the most notable is his complete disinterest in himself. For example, not once but many, many times he has been asked to send copies of his editorials to *Mast Head,* a magazine containing outstanding editorials each month from the entire nation, and he has chosen always to ignore the request. Possibly that isn't too bad, but try this one: Easton was nominated a few years ago for a Pulitzer Prize, and upon receipt of a letter from the committee requesting copies of his editorials, Easton ignored that request, too.

How do I figure that facet of his character? Well, I know for a fact that he does not suffer from a defeatist attitude, and I know he is unafraid of competition. It is my sincere belief that Easton just doesn't care for attention to himself, preferring that a job be done.

With reference to editorials, I think Easton has taught me more about editorial writing than any other person. Many times he has stopped a busy work day for half an hour or so to answer questions I've asked of him.

In England, after the turn of the nineteenth century, there lived and wrote a poet named Leigh Hunt. He wrote a poem which seems to fit well the man called Easton King.

In his poem, titled "Abou Ben Adhem," Leigh Hunt wrote, "May his tribe increase!" As a man and as an editor, I would say of Easton King, "May his tribe increase!"

It is impossible for me to convey the intensity of my desire to get away from the jungle, to leave and not bother to look back. I'd been through that line of thought so many, many times. I knew it was impossible. I could leave the jungle I grew up in—but the jungle which was within me? From it there was no escape. All I could do was to keep hacking. That I knew full well,

231

but to laugh at the work of hacking was important, and laugh I could not. Absolutely nothing was amusing; the absurd was painful to me, not funny.

Unable to work up a good chuckle, I sat down in late August and speculated on a sermon. I wondered what sort of candidate I'd be should I run for the office of governor. God knows I had no intention to do so, but the speculation helped relieve the pain within me. I wrote:

Can't say about Diogenes—

BUT WE'D TURNED THE LIGHT DOWN LOW

The 20th state admitted to the union was Mississippi, in 1817, on December 10th.

The 2nd state to withdraw from the union was Mississippi, in 1861, on January 2nd.

In the 140 years we've been a state we've had good years and we've had lean years. (The leanest of all being from 1861 to 1869.) We've had good and bad; however, we've always had a shortage of two items: cash and honest politicians.

It is our opinion that we would have the cash, provided we ever got an honest politician, the possibility of which seems remote at the moment. (By honest we mean a man who would be willing to tell the citizens of the state the truth, as he sees it, instead of telling them what they want to hear, which at times seems to be anything but the truth, however relative.)

In less than two years from this writing there will be a bunch of tailless (and brainless) anthropoids roaming the state seeking the office of Governor. At this moment they are preparing themselves for that great day; some are already yelling "Nigger," some are harping that old, old song about States' Rights, while others are trying to put the blame on Maine, Boy!

It seems to us these potentials have the idea that the citizens of Mississippi want to hear this rot. And many might well want to, we wouldn't deny that possibility. But there are thousands and thousands of decent, honest, fairly logical people who would like to face reality for a change. We believe the number to be great . . . silent though they be.

What about a platform for these people? An honest office seeker? A realist with a conscience, social and political? What would happen if such a man appeared on the scene?

Well, frankly, we don't propose to have the answer to these and other questions. We can only hope that such a person will make his

232

appearance on the political scene here in the state. We can only hope that sanity and reason will one day rule.

How could a man such as we have in mind make a campaign for the office of Governor? What could he say in an effort to be honest with the people whose votes he hopes to win? How could he convince them, or could he? How could he translate political idealism into political reality?

We think it can be done, possibly, in one way, and that is by being honest to the point that it hurts, or seems to hurt; such honesty, based on fairness, will, we believe, be received first with shock, followed by rapt attention, and finally by a conviction to try to do what we know by reason to be decent.

You don't think so? Well, perhaps not.

Were such a hoped-for and idealistic man to appear on the Mississippi scene seeking the office of Governor we would like to hear him say, in effect:

He wanted to be Governor of Mississippi because he was concerned over a state of affairs which had caused him an amount of worry, the energy of which could have been used to produce, to have created in his lifetime something of value for people yet unborn, not even to mention his fellow citizens of his day.

His platform would be based on one word: Fairness. Fairness to him would mean several things, among them Justice, Honesty, Virtue, and Conscience. Perhaps Webster doesn't define "fairness" in such a manner, but he would, and he has to live with himself, not Webster.

He would hold that the Constitution of these United States is as fair in its scope as man has yet been able to devise. He would hold it to be good, realizing, of course, that good is a relative term. He would hold that the laws of this Nation must be obeyed, for, after all, the law is based on the Constitution. He would not mean to say or to imply that he thinks all the decisions made by the United States Supreme Court relative to an interpretation of laws are good; however, he would still hold that the law must be obeyed and he would so hold because if any single person is allowed to break a law without consequence, then his family is not safe, nor is he, nor are you.

He would not hold with the decision of school integration. He would think he understood why such a decision was made; he would believe we brought it on ourselves by our refusal to face up to our obligation. He would ask you to keep in mind that we had something like sixty-four years to comply not just with the Federal law, but with our own commitment stated in our State Constitution which we adopted in 1890. He would favor a segregated school system, yes. But he would have asked himself many times, "What price will I be willing to pay for it?" And he would ask of you the same question. "Are we willing to destroy a system of government and education which has time and time again proved its worth just to have two school buildings? What price are you willing to pay?"

And that he would have to leave to you and your conscience. But as for him, he would refuse to destroy that which is rightfully his children's and their children's just to satisfy his own ambitions.

He would hold that men are equal under the law and any infringement thereof is a direct threat to him personally, as surely you must realize it to be a threat to you. He would hold with equality—equality by virtue, not by vice. This is to be distinguished from matters social. Equality has nothing whatsoever to do with whom he would spend an evening. However, equality does have to do with who can vote; it does have to do with who can serve on a jury; it does have to do with who can seek a public office; it does have to do with his right to associate with whom he pleases, and since it has to do with his right, surely it must have to do with your right also. Conversely, the same is the case— he would have the same right not to associate with whom he pleases.

He would hold with complete and total individual freedom in every respect—up to a point. He would hold that any man who so chooses has the unquestionable right and freedom to be a Jack Ass. He would give his life, if the need arose, that any one of you might bray. He would hold that any man has the right to bray. He would hold that the same man does not have the right to kick over the traces and smash the teeth of any other man—there he would draw the line on the limitation of individual freedom. Bray, brother, but don't kick, he would say.

He would hold that justice, with regard to law, and, indeed, anything else, must be blindfolded. Justice must not peek. She may have prejudices which would make a decision unfair. And if his lot is to suffer unfairness, then you and your children are in some danger of so suffering. He would hold that justice to him is but justice to you. Can any one of us afford not to be just?

He would hold that punitive laws are unpleasant, but are at times a necessity. How he would get it passed is something he wouldn't know, but he would like to see any member of the State Legislature unable to accept a retainer from any business source whatsoever over which the state has any authority. In short, he would like to see men serving in offices throughout this state who would willingly put the public interest before their own personal interest. Such, he would know full well, is impossible. But in that connection, he would veto any bill which reeked of business sticking its finger into the affairs of the state; the state, after all is you—him. Since he would not allow the state to stick its finger into the affairs of business, unless the public good was concerned, he would most certainly not allow business to meddle with affairs of state. As the Church and State are separate, so should State and Business be separate, except as mentioned previously.

234

He would hold that any and all persons, race, creed or color notwithstanding, are citizens of this state, provided they have met the requirements which entitle them to citizenship. He would hold, therefore, that any member of a minority group has the same rights and liberties as he has, certainly no more, nor will they be less. He would be saying once again that the law of the land must be obeyed, not that he likes all the laws so much, but he would be interested in his own rights and in order to keep them he must be interested in the rights of any other single person, no matter who. His own interests would be in direct proportion to the interests of all citizens of this nation and this state. He would respect theirs—if for no other reason than because he would want them to respect his—and yours, too.

He would hold that if we—as Human Beings first, American citizens second and Mississippians next—would but give ourselves a chance we could lead the way to industrial progress and come close to having the social progress keep pace with it. We have kept a large segment of our population down for years. Whether you agree or not, he would hold that in so doing we have kept ourselves down. You've heard it before a thousand times, but he would repeat: You can't keep anyone down without staying down with him. Personally, he couldn't afford to stay down—perhaps he could, but he wouldn't want to. If his grandfather or his father had wanted to, that was their doing—doings of which he wouldn't approve, because had they not been so shortsighted his plight today would have been better—but as for him, he would hold that his child should be better off than he; therefore, he would hold back no man—because the possibility exists that if any man moves an inch forward, he might move a fraction forward himself.

Were that time-wasting old Greek, Diogenes, around we don't know if he'd put out his lantern. We can't be positive that we would; but, for once, we'd turn the light down low.

The jungle around me continued to close in; there was no possible way to clear the dense brush of stupidity, ignorance, intolerance and bigotry. In spite of what some persons seemed to think, I had no illusions about being God. Any mortal could see the stupidity of an incident which occurred in the little town of Forest, Mississippi, in September of 1957. A simple decision was handed down at the high school there. In effect, it said they would no longer play the "Star-Spangled Banner" at football games; instead, they had decided to play "Dixie." The jungle closed in day by day, hour by hour, and I could do nothing about it. In spite of the absurdity of the Forest High School matter, I could not laugh; it simply was not funny, nor had anything else

235

been for a long, long time. I decided I was sick; also, I decided that I was not alone in my illness.

The end of Volume 4 was on the seventh day of November 1957. I either had a hemorrhage of my existing ulcer or had developed an additional one; I did not know, and I could not bring myself to spend money on a series of X rays, having gone in debt in excess of $4,000 during the year of 1957.

Chapter 27

The most pressing question with which I was confronted was whether or not to continue the publication of the paper. I wanted to do so, even if I didn't know why; however, I felt the views of friends away from the Magnolia Jungle could be of help from an objective point of view. To seek the views of friends was one of three things in my mind when I went to New York in late 1957. In addition, I was to see about a lecture tour and I wanted to sell group subscriptions to whatever groups I could. On the plane en route to New York, fragments from Ecclesiastes kept coming to mind. Many years ago I'd read the book with great interest. The Preacher had always left me with a feeling of futility, of a sadness of sorts. I was not in need of additional frustrations at the time; however, futility and frustration breed on themselves. What was it the Preacher had said?

> Vanity of vanities, says the Preacher,
> Vanity of vanities! All is vanity.
> What does man gain by all the toil
>   at which he toils under the sun?
> What has been is what will be,
>   and what has been done is what will be done;
>   and there is nothing new under the sun.
> For in much wisdom is much vexation,
>   and he who increases knowledge increases sorrow.
> Moreover I saw under the sun that in the place
>   of justice, even there was wickedness
> and in the place of righteousness, even there
>   was wickedness.

236

Better is a handful of quietness than two hands
full of toil and a striving after wind.

The injustice and futility of life, as stated by the Preacher, depressed me, and the futility of things as I saw and knew them was almost more than I could take. What for? Just simply what for? Why keep hacking at the jungle? It grew faster than I. It was without hope; I was without hope of clearing a single poisoned leaf from the entire jungle which I called home. Yet, someone had to hack away; someone had to try. Why me? Was it not better to be a good Kiwanian, minding my own business, than to be a confused, frustrated, depressed screwball whom few persons could tolerate? Of course, it was better to be a conforming Kiwanian; but even in that state of mind I knew such a fate would be worse for me than the one from which I suffered.

Two questions often asked of me by others I asked of myself: Why are you the way you are? What is it you want? For so long I'd wondered about answers to the questions, realizing, of course, that no man could answer them with any degree of intelligence and probably with even a lesser degree of honesty. However unintelligent and dishonest I might be, I had no choice but to try.

To myself I said:

You are ignorant and uninformed. Perhaps because of this you would like to see every human being wise and learned.

You are greedy and selfish. Perhaps because of this you would like to see every person generous and unselfish in his mind and heart.

You are bigoted and prejudiced. Because of it perhaps you would like to see all mankind openminded and tolerant.

You are arrogant and egotistical. Perhaps you would like to see all of humanity humble and broad-minded.

You are a liar, especially to yourself. As a result you would probably like to see every person be true to himself.

You are the essence of foolishness. Perhaps you want to see every soul and mind and heart possess wisdom.

You are narrow-minded and spiteful. You want to see a day

237

and a time produce persons who are broad-minded and benevolent.

You are a creature of poverty. And the result is that you want every man to have wealth.

You are without faith. Possibly you want everybody to have an abundance of faith in his God and in himself.

You are drab and dingy and stupid and dull. Because of it you would have every human being alert and keen-witted and sharp and bright.

You are dishonest and a hypocrite. You would have it that all persons be honest and sincere.

You are proud and conceited and confused and frustrated. You would will it that all men be humble and walk in humility and have peace of mind.

You are but a human being, made of this earth and that of which it is made. It would be your wish and hope that every person realize that in him there is a spark of that which men call God.

You are nothing more than a slave to all things. As a result you would wish, hope, even fight that all mankind be free.

Needless to say, the thought occurred to me that I had a relatively low opinion of myself. The thought also occurred to me that I might think I was God; but, fortunately, that would be an easy matter to disprove. Others knew it already.

But how honest with myself was I? That I did not know. One thing I did know, however, and that was the fact that such an opinion of myself as I'd stated did nothing to shake the turmoil in my soul.

In the days of old, God had seen fit to give mortal men signs from heaven. Moses saw a burning bush that didn't burn; the Wise Men saw a star in the East, but at the time the plane landed that November day in Newark, East had not seen a sign from anywhere, least of all heaven. But, then, I wasn't expecting to see a sign. My nature being what it is, had I seen a sign, I'd not have believed it; instead, I'd have rushed to the nearest doctor. I got a sign the next day in New York. It was the first of three to come my way during my six-day stay. Those three signs, however, weren't from heaven.

For many months I'd struggled daily with the problem of insufficient funds. While I had every desire to escape the situation in which I had placed myself, I could not ignore the hard facts of reality. First, what had once been a business operation was now a personal hobby. If *The Petal Paper* wasn't a hobby, then I don't know what else it was. At the close of my fourth year the number of subscribers in Petal was two; the amount of business I received from the village annually amounted to zero. True, the circulation grew outside the immediate area, but that income was far short of what was necessary. With those basic facts in mind, I had decided that one way to have money for my hobby was to make a lecture tour. It was one thing I didn't want to do, but it was a means to an end, even though I could not define the end to my own satisfaction. In the hope of arranging for a tour I called on an esteemed Southern editor and asked how to go about it. He had been kind and considerate, pointing out the good and bad of such tours. Of his own free will he said he'd write his agent in New York and see if he'd help line up a series of lectures. This had been about six weeks before I left for New York.

On the day before I left I called the gentleman and inquired if he'd heard from his agent. He had not, he said, but he had written, and any day there should be a reply. I failed to mention to him that I was leaving the next day and intended to see the agent. I checked with the agent immediately upon my arrival. Had the editor written to him about me? No, was the answer. The agent had not heard from the esteemed Southern editor in about two years, not since he'd broken his contract with the agent. To me it was a hard blow. I could not understand it; in fact, until this day I fail to understand.

In March of 1957 Albert Vorspan did a feature for *The Reporter* under the title "The Iconoclast of Petal, Miss." As a result of Al's story the head of a certain "do good" organization had made contact with the magazine and expressed a desire to be of help to me. He did not mention what he had in mind, and at the time I couldn't think of anything to suggest. Now, in my near desperate struggle to keep alive, I called him and suggested the possibility of his helping me line up speaking engagements. He indicated he'd do what he could. An appointment was made with him; meanwhile, he suggested I talk with the editor of a national magazine in New York. I made an appointment with the editor, explaining the situation as best I could by telephone. Once in New York I confirmed both appointments. When I arrived at the editor's office for my appointment, his secretary said he couldn't see me. To date I've not checked back to see when he could see me. The next day the "do good" man was so tied up that he wouldn't have a chance to see me. That was the last time I've called his office.

There was nothing to do but continue on my course. In the following days I talked with friends whom I respected and put the question to them as to whether or not the paper should be kept going and, if so, why it should be. Among those to whom I talked were Albert Vorspan, Joseph Rauh, Jr., Irving Jay Fain, Edwin J. Lukas, Harry Fleishman, Roy Wilkins, John Morsell, J. Oscar Lee, and Rabbi Eugene Lipman. Many times I'd discussed the matter with Easton King and Will Campbell. I knew their opinions, and while I trusted and respected them, I wondered how objective they could be about the matter. The opinions of those with whom I spoke in New York, Washington and Providence were almost, to the man, the same as Easton and Will had expressed. Easton had once summed it up by saying, *"The Petal Paper* is lousy, P.D., but it's a beacon of hope in an otherwise dark area. If you can take the stand for the moderation you have and survive, others will take hope eventually and may speak out in behalf of sanity. If you fail, if you are forced out of business, the bigots will take full credit for it and then other voices will not be heard for a long, long time. If for no other reason, *The Petal Paper* is important as a symbol."

Will had said virtually the same thing, adding this remark: "Even the Yankees think there is some hope for us as long as your paper keeps going." I wondered, and still do, which Yankees Will had in mind.

In spite of the disappointments over my lecture tour, the trip was not entirely wasted. I managed to sell 300 subscriptions to groups, and discovered other possibilities for group subscriptions. On the way home, the stewardess on the plane, who was a philosophical young lady, sat down beside me and began a conversation. After a while, and out of a clear blue sky, she asked of me, "Do you believe in free love?" Rising to the occasion, I replied, "Well, yes, I suppose I do. Anyway, at least a couple of times a year."

Perhaps it wasn't much of a joke, but I thanked God in all humility that I could still laugh.

And so, back in my favorite jungle, I began the fifth year—then the sixth . . .

Chapter 28

The answers to the questions which have plagued me day and night are still unanswered. Perhaps to answer them is an impossibility. Perhaps to give an absolute answer would be to bind myself and restrict myself from possible growth. Perhaps the search is the thing, not the finding. The question once asked me by Joseph Barnes is still of interest to me. "Tell me, P.D.," Joe had asked, "how the hell did you get that way?"

Can it be answered? I don't know that it can. I wonder what factors and forces go into the making of any man. Perhaps I'm the way I am because two million years ago some ancestor of mine fell from his tree and hit his head on a rock. Perhaps I'm the confused and frustrated soul that I am because of a man whose name I don't remember, a man "who's just not our kind of people," who sold fruit and vegetables at a sawmill camp. It could be that a dingy pair of yellow shoes enters into the picture; perhaps a drab tent revival meeting had a bearing. It could be one factor is my inability to appreciate an outdoor privy. Or maybe because I shudder at the thought of seeing an infant fed large dried beans. It could be I've seen too many dingy shacks in which dingy people live their drab gray lives. Perhaps it could be—God only knows what all the factors are which it could be. One thing I know: it not only could be, it is, the fact that I want a better place in which to live. What I have and what I know are not good enough for me; they are far short of being good enough for my daughter and for her children and theirs.

And what is it I want most of all? Perhaps it's quite simple. I've seen so much that is drab, gray and dingy that I want enough bleach to remove the tattletale gray from the Magnolia Jungle.

Chapter 29

Tomorrow? And what about tomorrow? I can't get too excited about where it it is I'm going, not when I consider the fact that I don't know where it is I've been.

Eventually the day will come when I, P. D. East, will cease to be a living, breathing, confused, frustrated, hoping mortal. And when that time arrives, and when I'm forced into a necktie and put on display and the crowd gathers around for the festive occasion, I have two wishes—hopes, perhaps they are hopes. First, I hope no one allows a preacher to have a field day over me. All my life I've preached and I grow weary of it. Surely, in death, I should be free of preaching. Second, I hope, and most sincerely, that one of my friends—Easton, Will, Clarence —some one of them will feel inclined to say, and can say in truth and complete honesty, a few words, first to God, then to man. Let them begin by saying, 'Well, Lord, here's P. D. He wasn't much, Lord, but he was all he had."

Then to man: "These are the remains of P. D. East. He had a heart and he had a hatchet. They were both the same size. One could hardly determine the difference between the two. He lived and died confused and frustrated. He did not know where he came from, nor did he know why. And for years he worried about it. Finally, one day he stopped worrying about it. He realized that where he came from and who he was mattered little. He realized that what he was and where he was going did

242

matter. And that was all he knew. It was about all he cared to know. His beloved Magnolia Jungle needed a path. It needed clearing so that all of us could look up and see the light of the sky—the face of God. Let it be said of P. D. East: With his heart and his hatchet he hacked like hell!"